FLYING GUNS

WWI

FLYING GUNS

World War I
and its
Aftermath
1914–32

Anthony G. Williams

and

Dr Emmanuel Gustin

Airlife

First published in 2003 by
Airlife Publishing, an imprint of
The Crowood Press Ltd
Ramsbury, Wiltshire SN8 2HR

www.crowood.com

British Library Cataloguing-in-Publication Data
A catalogue record for this book is available from the British Library.

ISBN 1 84037 396 2

Photograph previous page: The business end: a Lewis MG. (Courtesy Philip Jarrett)

Typeset by Celtic, Wrexham

Printed and bound in Great Britain by The Bath Press

Contents

Acknowledgements

THIS BOOK WOULD NOT HAVE BEEN POSSIBLE WITHOUT THE generous co-operation and assistance of the late Herbert Woodend, the Curator, and the staff of the Ministry of Defence Pattern Room, whose unique library and weapon collection was extensively consulted.

Particular thanks are also due to several people who have provided invaluable comments on various drafts of this book series: Dr Jean-François Legendre, who contributed to the sections on French, Swiss and Russian developments as well as producing cartridge drawings, Ted Bradstreet, who provided much information about German – and especially Japanese – aircraft armament, Alexander Diehl, for painstakingly translating Russian texts, the late Peter Labbett who also offered his collection of ammunition illustrations, John D. Salt, for commenting on armour penetration performance, Tom Cooper, who provided information on post-Second World War air combat, Michael Rausch and Hans-Christian Vortisch.

Among the many others who have provided information and assistance for this series are Rui Aballe, Derek Allsopp, Vic Bilek, Dénes Bernád, Walter Bjorneby, Georges Bouche, Fred Butt, John Carlin, Cliff Carlisle, Steve Chaskin, Yevgeniy Chizhikov, Ron Wallace Clarke, Tre Colvin, Dr J.R. Crittenden Schmitt, Lewis Curtis, Ruud Deurenberg, Ken Duffey, Eugene Dvurechenski, Nigel Eastaway of the Russian Aviation Research Trust (RART), Leszek Erenfeicht, David Everest, Dan Ford, Urban Frederickson, Hugh Furse, Karl-Heinz Gansel, Dolf Goldsmith, Dr Ian Gooderson, Alexei Gretchikhine, Manfred Griehl, David Griffin, Bill Gunston, Joel Gurdebeke, Robert Hawkinson Jr, Henri Habegger, Hans Häfeli, Thomas Heinz, Dudley Henriques, Ian V. Hogg, Till Huber, I.J. Inauen of the Swiss Federal Military Library, Philip Jarrett, Orla Kragh Jensen, Jukka P. Koivusaari, Christian Koll, Lauri Koponen, Arthur Kramer, Yasufumi Kunimoto, Peter Labbett, Olivier Lefebvre, Robert Leiendecker, Jakob Lippert, Oleg Maddox, Tim Mason, Steve McGregor, Freddy Mead, Robert A. Mellichamp, Harald Mezger, Yves Michelet, Adam Millei, Marvin Morrison, Brady Mulhausen, Tero Mustalahti, Jim O'Brien, Merle Olmstead, Max Popenker, Ed Rasimus, Phillipe Regenstreif, Justin Riggir, Osmo Ronkanen, Henning Ruch, Yuji Sasaki, Alexandre Savine, Glenn Shiveler, James Spaw, James Sterrett, Peter Stickney, David Stone, Donald Thomas, Cecil Turner, Jakub Uchytil, Claudio Urruti, J.T. Valias, John Vasco, Peter Verney, Mirek Wawrzynski, David Watts, Harry Woodman (who kindly provided many illustrations and other material) and Les Whitehouse.

Thanks are also due to the companies and individuals who have given permission to use their photographic material.

Introduction

EVER SINCE THE FIRST AIRCRAFT STAGGERED PRECARIOUSLY into the air, thoughts were turned to their military potential. At first, this was envisaged as an extension of the existing use of balloons for observing enemy activities and directing artillery fire. It was soon realised, however, that if it was worth going to the trouble to collect such information about the enemy, it was equally worth trying to stop the enemy gaining similar information about one's own activities, and the notion of aerial combat was born.

The first air combats during the First World War were haphazard affairs; individual airmen took rifles, pistols and even shotguns aloft with them in the hope of taking some potshots at any enemy aircraft which might come within range. Behind the scenes, various designers were already working on more aggressive ideas for arming aircraft. Machine gun and even cannon installations were built and tested, and gradually found their way into combat. By the end of the war, the classic biplane fighter aircraft had evolved to a high state of effectiveness: agile and hard-hitting, typically with a pair of machine guns synchronised to fire through the propeller disk.

By this time, other aircraft (both aeroplanes and airships) had developed sufficient lifting power to be able to carry substantial loads of weapons with which to attack armies, warships and cities. Fighters were naturally assigned to attack these threats, sometimes with weapons and installations specifically intended to deal with them. Conversely, airships and bomber aeroplanes evolved defensive armament against the fighters.

Attention was not only paid to aerial targets. Some of the earliest projects during World War One envisaged airborne cannon as a much more effective way of attacking ground

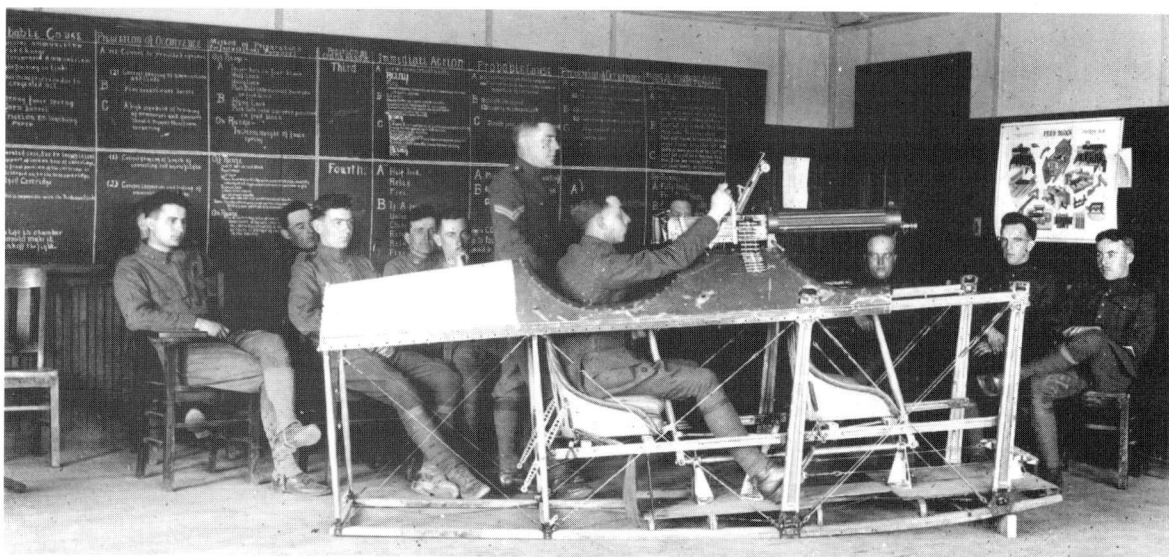

Gunnery class with a Vickers MG. (*Courtesy Philip Jarrett*)

targets than attempting to drop bombs on them. Specialist weapons, such as the recoilless Davis guns, were developed for this purpose, and some of them saw service. A parallel development was the armoured ground-attack aircraft, a concept which became much more important in the next conflict.

After the First World War, change was slow, with revolution giving way to evolution. Wartime designs, often produced in a great hurry, were refined and perfected. Experiments with unusual armaments took place in a leisurely way. By the early 1930s, the end of the period covered by this volume, aircraft and weapon design appeared to have settled into an established and little-changing pattern. This was the end of the first 'golden age' of aircraft and armament; within a decade, all would have changed.

The purpose of this book is to trace the parallel development of aircraft guns and the aircraft which have carried them. The aims are to describe and explain (in non-technical terms) the development of the guns and their ammunition, to examine which armament choices were made by different air forces at various times and how effective these choices proved, and to provide a complete listing of the gun armament fits of all combat aircraft which have seen service. The book is introduced by a technical summary describing the development of weapons and ammunition during this period; subsequent chapters are concerned with weapon installations, utilisation and combat experience.

Chapter 1

TECHNICAL DEVELOPMENTS

INTRODUCTION

BY THE TIME THE FIRST AIRCRAFT FLEW, THE GUNS WHICH would come to arm the first generation of warplanes were already well developed. However, it took a dozen years of experimentation and the pressure of war before aircraft and weapons were combined in a really effective way. The nature of aerial warfare – brief encounters at varying relative speeds, with targets manoeuvring in three dimensions – called for guns firing projectiles with a short time of flight to minimise aiming difficulties (i.e. fired at a high velocity) and capable of firing very rapidly to maximise the chance of a hit. In other words, aircraft and machine guns proved to be extraordinarily complementary, and progress in air warfare prompted the most advanced developments of the machine gun and its larger brother, the automatic cannon.

In order to understand these developments it is necessary to explain the characteristics of the various types of weapons and their ammunition. Firearms first emerged in the fourteenth century, but improvements over the next few centuries were slow and incremental. Gunpowder (a mixture of sulphur, saltpetre and charcoal) was poured into a 'chamber' at the rear of the gun and ignited to propel a projectile up a tube known as the 'barrel', from the resemblance to one of the earliest methods of constructing cannon – strips of metal surrounded by hoops. The only real developments until the nineteenth century were improvements in the quality of construction and in the method used to ignite the gunpowder, and the very limited use of rifled barrels (with internal spiral grooves) to spin the projectiles and thereby improve accuracy.

Progress needed to take place in three fields – metallurgy, engineering and chemistry – before recognisably modern weapons began to emerge during the nineteenth century. The quality and strength of metals were improved to permit guns to withstand the high pressures and temperatures needed to achieve high projectile velocities. The capabilities, precision and consistency of engineering improved

substantially to enable cartridge cases to be formed and complex mechanisms to be mass-produced. The introduction at the beginning of the nineteenth century of chemical primers (used to ignite the gunpowder) was also essential to the development of the machine gun. Finally, the invention towards the end of the century of smokeless propellants in place of gunpowder led to the production of high-velocity ammunition.

THE CARTRIDGE

OF ALL THE INNOVATIONS WHICH PERMITTED THE development of the machine gun, the most important was the metallic cartridge. Until the middle of the nineteenth century, gunpowder was still poured into the chamber, with the projectile pushed on top. This inherently prevented automatic handling of the ammunition and limited the rate of fire of weapons to, at the most, a few rounds per minute. The introduction of a metal (usually brass) case to contain the powder, into which was also fitted the projectile and the primer, led to dramatic alterations in gun design.

The metallic cartridge combines all of the elements of ammunition – primer, propellant, projectile – in one rugged and reasonably weatherproof unit. This speeded up loading and, in particular, greatly facilitated the design of breech-loading (i.e. from the chamber end) as opposed to muzzle-loading weapons. This is because the cartridge case, supported by the chamber walls, makes a gas-tight seal to prevent any of the burning propellant gasses from escaping through the breech to harm the firer. The ruggedness of the cartridge, or round of ammunition, made it eminently suitable for mechanical handling in order to speed the reloading process, and it was not long before the first machine guns appeared.

A particular cartridge is normally described by the calibre, or diameter of the barrel or projectile (not quite the same thing), or some approximation thereof. In order to

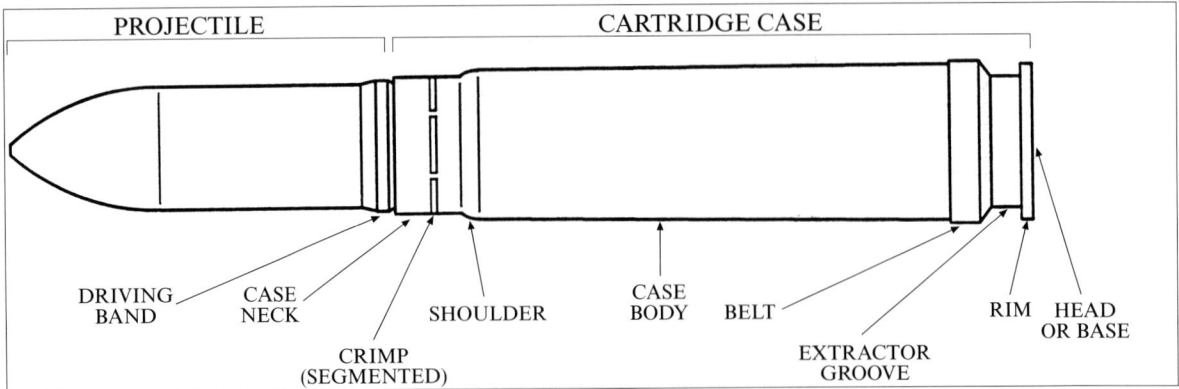

Elements of a cannon cartridge. *(drawing courtesy of J-F Legendre)*

distinguish between different cartridges of the same calibre, additional information is used which may be the nationality (e.g. .303" or .303 in – .303 inch – British), the gun it is most commonly associated with (e.g. 9 mm Parabellum or Luger) or the year of adoption (e.g. .30-06, adopted in 1906), but it is most commonly the length of the cartridge case (e.g. 7.92 × 57, the measurements being in millimetres). This method is so convenient that it is used retrospectively to describe cartridges which originally had different names; for example, the .303 in British is also known as the 7.7 × 56R, and the .30-06 as the 7.62 × 63. There are a few cases in which both the calibre and case length are the same, so some further identifier may be added for clarity (e.g. 20 × 110 Hispano and 20 × 110 USN).

Early cartridges had a flange or rim around the base, used to stop the cartridge from sliding too far into the chamber. Most military machine gun and cannon cartridges are now rimless, i.e. the rim is the same diameter as the case, separated by an extractor groove for the extractor to hook on to. This is usually the most convenient shape as it means that the cartridges can be slid lengthways out of a belt or magazine without the rim snagging on anything. Other rim forms have identifying letters added to the description: rimmed (e.g. 8 × 50R), semi-rimmed or semi-rimless (6.5 × 50SR) and rebated, i.e. with the rim smaller in diameter than the case body (20 × 70RR or 20 × 70RB).

Most aircraft guns of this period were adaptations of the standard army machine guns and were therefore chambered for whatever happened to be the national military rifle cartridge, normally of between 6.5 and 8 mm calibre. These later became known as rifle-calibre machine guns (RCMGs). There were some exceptions, however – a few larger-calibre heavy machine guns (HMGs) and some cannon. Incidentally, there is no hard and fast rule about the difference between HMGs and automatic cannon; national nam-

ing practices have varied. By more or less common consent, the term HMGs is nowadays applied to high-velocity machine guns with a calibre of between 12.7 and 15 mm. Current examples use bullets of similar construction to RCMGs (described below). Automatic cannon have calibres of 20+ mm and fire projectiles with separate driving bands instead of bullet jackets.

Cartridge case types (from left to right): Rimmed, straight (20 × 99R), Semi-rimmed (13 × 92SR), Rimless, bottle-necked (15 × 115 experimental), Rebated (20 × 72RB), Belted (13 × 93B experimental).

It is not easy to score hits in air-to-air shooting, in which both the attacking aircraft and the target are moving in three dimensions, probably having different directions and speeds. Projectiles take a measurable period of time to reach the target, during which it will have moved. It is therefore helpful to minimise the time of flight of the projectile, achieved primarily by firing it at a high muzzle velocity. However, muzzle velocities are generally improved by increasing the quantity of propellant, which requires a larger cartridge case. This generally requires a bigger and heavier gun, which is also likely to be slower-firing.

PROJECTILE DESIGN

THE STANDARD TYPE OF PROJECTILE OR BULLET USED IN machine guns is still known as 'ball' ammunition, even though it is no longer a round lead ball; it is elongated and pointed for better long-range performance, and covered with a jacket (usually of some alloy of copper and/or nickel). This remained in common use throughout this period, although the particular needs of air warfare saw the development during World War One of two variations on this – armour-piercing and high-explosive and/or incendiary bullets. Tracers (slow-burning chemical compounds) were also fitted inside the base of some bullets to aid aiming by making the flight of the bullet visible. Some tracers, especially those containing barium peroxide and magnesium, also had some incendiary effect. These specialised bullets had become common in air service by the end of the war.

Armour-piercing bullets were similar in construction to ball projectiles except that a hardened steel core was inserted, with the aim of doing more damage to engines and other robust parts of an aircraft. These were introduced into German and French air service in 1916, with British use following shortly afterwards. The German bullet was known as the SmK (*Spitzmunition mit Kern* – pointed bullet with core), the French as the *Balle Perforante*, while the British used several versions identified by 'AP' designations. The best of the AP bullets could penetrate up to 10 mm of armour plate at short range, but they wore barrels out more quickly.

Originally intended for shooting at tethered artillery observation balloons from the ground, explosive/incendiary bullets were subsequently adopted for aircraft guns. Their use was later extended to attacking airships; lighter-than-air craft were very difficult to shoot down (holes in the fabric caused only a very slow loss of gas), but they were filled with inflammable hydrogen, so finding some means of setting it alight was a high priority. Incendiary bullets were also found to be effective against aeroplanes, being able to set light to fuel systems and the normally fabric-covered wings and fuselages.

The development of incendiary and high-explosive bullets was complex, and can be considered in three phases. The first was their use in larger-calibre aircrew weapons – shoulder guns such as rifles, carbines and shotguns. Projectiles developed for such weapons were then used in some machine guns of 11–11.5 mm calibre. In parallel with this, the special projectiles were scaled down for use in rifle-calibre machine guns, which ultimately proved the most successful approach. An entirely separate line of development was followed in the case of cannon ammunition, which will be described in Chapter 3.

Incendiary and high-explosive (HE) bullets had a hollowed-out centre filled with a suitable compound. Some types of incendiary, such as the British Buckingham, which contained a phosphorus/aluminium mixture, were ignited on firing and burned slowly throughout their flight, while others ignited on impact. Most HE bullets were not purely explosive because the rifle-calibre ammunition was too small to carry an effective quantity of explosive; they were usually intended to burst violently in order to distribute the incendiary compound over a wide area. The British Pomeroy HE bullet, which contained nitro-glycerine and was purely explosive, was an exception, but the Brock, which contained potassium chlorate, and the RTS (RTS standing for Richard Threlfall and Sons), with both nitro-glycerine and phosphorus, had both high-explosive and incendiary effects. Use of these bullets was initially somewhat hazardous as the early versions had a reputation for premature detonations, and elaborate handling precautions were required.

.303 in cartridges: PSA (Pomeroy) Mk I, PSA Mk II, RTS Mk II, RTT experimental, R Mk 3 experimental.
(*Courtesy Peter Labbett*)

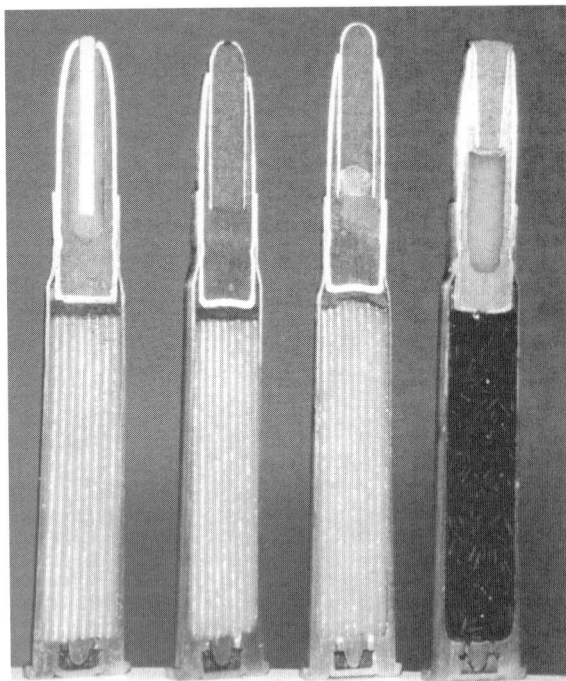

Sectioned .303 in cartridges: Brock incendiary, PSA Mk I explosive, PSA Mk II explosive, RTS Mk II explosive.
(Courtesy Peter Labbett)

Martini .45 in cartridges for aircraft gun use: Mk I incendiary (whole and sectioned), Tracer (SPG). (Courtesy Peter Labbett)

British bullets were made in .45 in (11.5 mm) calibre and even 12 bore (18 mm) early in the war for use in shoulder-fired weapons, the early .45 in tracer/incendiary being known as the 'Woolwich Flaming Bullet'. The .45 in ammunition was originally produced in the old, originally black-powder, Martini-Henry (11.5 × 59R) military calibre of Zulu War fame, and was used in single-shot Martini-Henry rifles or carbines. The incendiary used a pointed brass-jacketed bullet weighing 17.5 g, containing 3.2 g of incendiary composition and 1.3 g of priming composition. The bullet was considerably lighter than the original 31 g round-nose lead ball, which in conjunction with a 30 per cent increase in the quantity of cordite propellant raised the muzzle velocity from 400 to over 600 m/s. It was approved for service in 1914, but was initially known as a 'tracer', partly because it did emit a smoke trace but also out of sensitivity over the use of incendiaries which were of doubtful legality at that time.

Some British use was also made of Winchester Model 1886 .45-90 lever-action hunting rifles, although these were not formally approved for service. The ammunition was loaded with the Flaming Bullet or an SPG tracer bullet, and good results were reported in 1915. It should perhaps be noted that in the rather chaotic circumstances of the development of aerial weapons, the usual peacetime process of initial development, followed by approval for service, followed by issuing to units, was frequently bypassed, and some weapons were used which were never approved, or only approved some time later.

The British also experimented with tracer bullets in the Winchester self-loading carbines, both .351 in (8.9 × 35SR) and .401 in (10.3 × 38SR) calibres being in service in the French air force from early in the war.

The 12-bore (also known as .707 in) incendiary bullet for use in shotguns was of a similar design to the .45 in and was filled with yellow phosphorus mixed with metal filings. Although never fully approved for service, about 2,000 rounds were issued to the RNAS late in 1915 for emergency anti-Zeppelin use.

Even more remarkable was the 12-bore chain-shot loading. This consisted of seven lead balls strung along a 203 mm length of steel wire, with one heavy (15.7 g) and six light (3.5 g) balls, giving a total weight of 36.7 g. Muzzle velocity

.45 in MG cartridges (Gardner Gatling calibre) for aircraft use: Buckingham incendiary, SPG tracer, Pomeroy explosive, RTS explosive. (Courtesy Peter Labbett)

was about 300 m/s. The idea was that the chain would whirl around, damaging struts, fabric and propellers – a reversion to the original concept of chain-shot when fired from naval cannon in the days of sail. This was issued early in the war, although only finally approved in 1916.

Attention naturally turned to using the .45 in calibre ammunition in machine guns. In Britain, the concentration was on the old .45 in Maxims (long replaced in Army service by the .303 in Vickers-Maxim) which saw limited use in 1916 and 1917. A complicating factor was that some of the guns were in the Martini-Henry 11.5 × 59R calibre, while others were chambered for the .45 in Gardner Gatling case (11.5 × 62R), which caused some confusion. Ammunition varied: the Flaming Bullet was fitted, but so were Buckingham incendiary, Pomeroy and RTS explosive bullets and SPG tracers. As with the Flaming Bullet, the lighter weight meant that muzzle velocities were raised to around 600 m/s. Armour-piercing bullets were also developed in .45 in calibre.

More successful was the French development of a Vickers gun in their old 11 mm Gras rifle cartridge (11 × 59R), together with the Desvignes Mark XI incendiary bullet (which was actually a long-burning tracer), the resultant conversion thereby being known as the 11 mm or Gras Vickers. As with the British .45 in, the lighter bullet permitted a much higher muzzle velocity, in the region of 600 m/s. The French were the major users, although the USA adopted the weapon and ammunition in late 1917 (both being already manufactured there) and produced the weapons by converting some existing Vickers guns chambered for the 7.62 × 54R, a Russian order which had been cancelled following Russia's withdrawal from the war. The USA developed its own high-velocity loading with a tracer/incendiary bullet weighing 17.5 g. The guns could be fitted in place of any Vickers, but were reportedly not popular as the recoil was significantly heavier, causing more vibration when firing. However, these weapons were still much in demand at the end of the war, despite the development of similar ammunition for rifle-calibre guns, as the bigger projectiles permitted a much larger filling of incendiary and HE material. The USA continued experimenting with the 11 mm guns into the early 1920s, and manufactured over 500,000 rounds of ammunition for them.

During the war, attempts were made in various countries to combine the advantages of a large bullet with a modern, high-velocity cartridge, which would inevitably require a bigger gun. Germany came the closest with the 13 × 92SR calibre, initially intended for ground anti-tank and AA use in the Maxim T.u.F. gun, but also the basis of an experimental aircraft weapon, as described later. Britain developed in 1917 the rimmed .600/.500 cartridge, which was based on the .600 Nitro Express elephant-gun round, for both anti-tank and aircraft uses. By 1918 this had changed to a belted rimless case, and HE, incendiary, tracer and AP bullets were developed for it. In 1921 this adopted its final form with a rimless case as the .5 in Vickers (12.7 × 81), also known as the V/580 after the bullet weight in grains (37.6 g). The export version of this gun was chambered for a slightly modified 12.7 × 81SR (V/565), a cartridge which was adopted by Italy for its heavy Breda-SAFAT and Scotti aircraft machine guns and subsequently by Japan for its Second World War Ho-103 aircraft gun. The USA was also working on a .5 in cartridge at the end of the war, which emerged in 1919 as the famous .50 in Browning (12.7 × 99), although production ammunition was not formally adopted until 1923. Incidentally, contrary to many accounts, the .50 in cartridge case owed nothing to the 13 × 92SR; the German cartridge was studied during the Browning's development but rejected in favour of a scaled-up .30-06 round.

In spite of all of this activity, rifle-calibre guns were far more widely available and these provided the main focus for development during the First World War. The first rifle-calibre incendiary bullets – actually explosive/incendiary which detonated on impact – were introduced into Austro-Hungarian service in 1914 for ground-based anti-balloon guns. The Pomeroy, Brock and Buckingham entered British air service in .303 in (7.7 × 56R) calibre during 1916, the RTS in the following year. Germany followed suit in 1916/17 with 7.92 × 57 *Phosphor-F* bullets apparently based on the Buckingham, and Austro-Hungary produced improved ammunition in 1917. Tracer bullets in rifle calibres were also fielded; the first British attempt being the SPK of 1916, developed by Aerators Ltd of Edmonton. This was a solid copper bullet, bored out to accept a filling of 1.17 g barium peroxide (with 12% magnesium). The involvement of Aerators led to the SPK being dubbed 'Sparklet', the name of the mineral water sold by this company, although the official designation was the somewhat less handy 'Cartridge SA Tracer SPK .303 in Mark VII.T'. This was soon replaced by the SPG (adopted as the 'SPG .303 in (VII.G) Mark I.z') which used a bullet of more conventional design, somewhat easier to make, and carrying slightly more tracer compound, This could trace to over 700 m.

Although they were becoming widespread, there was still some nervousness about the hazards associated with the use of HE/I bullets. The British banned them from synchronised guns for some time, concerned about the consequences should one hit the propeller as a result of synchroniser failure (a not uncommon occurrence), and also by the fact that the Vickers guns fired from a closed bolt, increasing the risk of the projectiles 'cooking off' in a hot chamber. In Germany there were cases of spontaneous ignition of the ammunition in the magazines (particularly affecting the Fokker D.VII), an alarming prospect for the pilot.

THE GUN

SOME OF THE TECHNICAL TERMS USED TO DESCRIBE PARTS OF a gun have already been mentioned – chamber and barrel – and others are labelled in the diagram below. In principle a gun is just a tube closed at one end. Propellant in the closed end – the chamber – is ignited to produce rapidly expanding gases which drive a projectile up the barrel. This has two functions: it contains the expanding propellant gas behind the projectile to ensure that none of it is wasted, and it guides the projectile in a specific direction. In practice guns are more complicated than this, mainly because of the need to insert cartridges, fire them and then remove the empty cartridge case.

The need to load cartridges into the chamber means that there has to be an opening, or breech, in the rear of the chamber. The cartridge case obviously has to be held firmly in the chamber, otherwise it would depart rearwards under the pressure of burning propellant as the projectile travels forwards, so a part of the gun mechanism – the breech-block or bolt (or sometimes the 'lock') – has to be placed behind the breech at the instant of firing, which at this time was achieved by percussion, i.e. the primer was struck by a spring-loaded mechanical firing pin held within the bolt or breech-block. It then needed to be moved out of the way so that the empty case could be pulled from the chamber (by an extractor) and ejected clear of the mechanism (by an ejector) ready for the next round of ammunition to be 'chambered' (loaded into the chamber).

The speed which with the reloading cycle can be performed is defined as the 'rate of fire' (RoF), in rounds per minute (rpm) or sometimes rounds per second (rps). A high rate of fire is considered particularly desirable in an aircraft gun, as opportunities for firing, especially in air-to-air

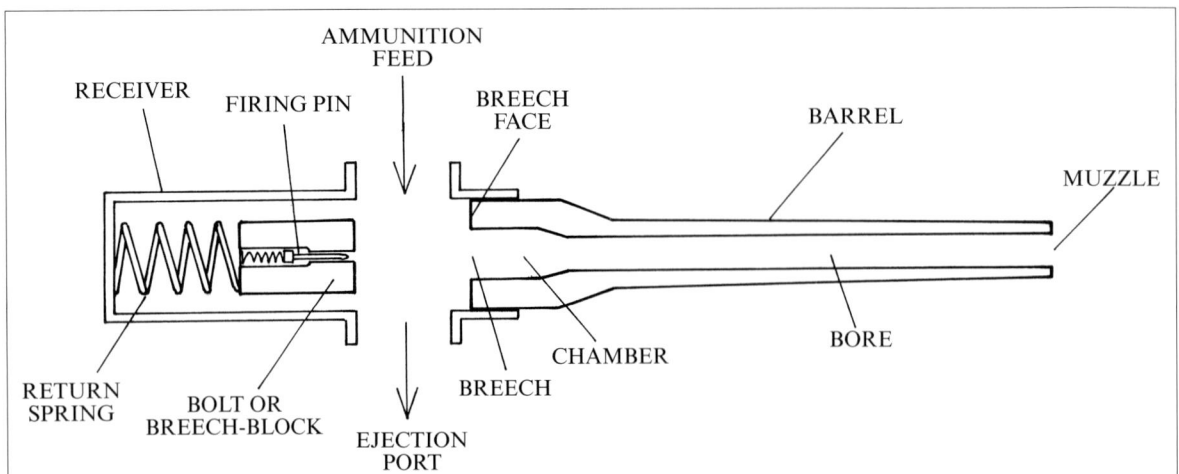

Basic elements of the gun (schematic).

combat, tend to be brief, and so it is important to maximise the chance of scoring hits. The rate of fire is primarily determined by the gun and reloading mechanisms, but it is also affected by the characteristics of the particular gun (new guns being 'stiffer' and tending to fire more slowly), the care put into maintenance and adjustment, the ammunition used, variations in altitude or ambient temperature, and in belt-fed guns the drag of the belt installation (which may reduce as ammunition is used up). For all of these reasons, quoted rates of fire are no more than averages. In addition, the need in some installations to synchronise the gun to fire through the propeller disk could significantly reduce the rate of fire.

MANUALLY-DRIVEN MACHINE GUNS: GATLINGS, HOTCHKISSES, GARDNERS AND NORDENFELTS

The first machine guns were not strictly automatic (i.e. driven by the force generated by firing the cartridge) as they were loaded and fired manually, by cranking a handle or lever. The first of these to be successful was the Gatling gun, invented by an American of that name, which was perfected in the mid-1860s. This was a rotary design, with several parallel barrels rotating about a common axis. Ammunition was held in a rack above the gun and dropped by gravity behind the breech of the barrel at the top of the gun, ready to be chambered. As the barrels rotated, the cartridge was gradually pushed into the chamber by the bolt until its barrel reached the bottom (6 o'clock) position, when it fired. Further rotation extracted and ejected the fired case until the barrel reached the top again, when it was ready for reloading.

Another type of nineteenth-century multi-barrel rotary gun was made by Hotchkiss and was designed as a refinement of the Gatling. It was known somewhat confusingly as the 'cannon-revolver', the modern meaning of 'revolver' being a weapon with several chambers but only one barrel. It was not a direct competitor as it was only ever available in large calibres of 37–53 mm. Each barrel was quite light, which came in useful during World War One, when surplus Hotchkiss cannon were dismantled in order to devise lightweight single-barrel guns for aircraft use.

The other notable manually cranked guns of this era were the Gardner and Nordenfelt, which differed in having fixed barrels mounted side by side, with the bolts being moved to and fro by a crank. The number of barrels could be varied according to requirements, which made these guns more flexible in design than the Gatling.

These manually cranked weapons were obsolete by 1900 (although some Hotchkiss guns remained in service for short-range fortress defence into the First World War) and none was used in aircraft, but the principle of directly driving the mechanism rather than relying on the force generated by firing the cartridge has certain advantages and has appeared in other forms.

SELF-POWERED GUNS

Since the invention of the Maxim gun in the latter part of the nineteenth century, the great majority of machine guns have been self-powered: that is, the reloading mechanism has been driven by a part of the force generated when the cartridge is fired. There are three basic ways in which this force has been tapped: directly, through the cartridge case being blown by gas pressure in the opposite direction to the projectile ('blowback'); recoil operated, in which the barrel is free to move rearwards under recoil, this movement being used to drive the mechanism; and gas operated, in which a portion of the high-pressure gas generated by the propellant is tapped from the barrel and used to operate the gun. All three types of mechanism were used in machine guns during the First World War.

An important issue in machine gun design is whether the gun fires from a closed or an open bolt. In a closed-bolt design, the 'ready to fire' position, in which the gun stops after each burst, is with a cartridge in the chamber and the breech closed. Open-bolt weapons stop with the chamber left empty and the breech open. The advantage of closed-bolt firing is that there is a minimal delay between pressing the trigger and firing, as only the firing pin is released. The problem is that after a long burst of firing, the cartridge left in the chamber can be heated up so much by the hot chamber that the propellant can detonate, with potentially serious consequences – a circumstance known as 'cook-off'. Obviously, an even greater risk accompanies the use of explosive projectiles. Open-bolt firing clearly avoids this hazard, and leaving the breech open allows the barrel and chamber to cool more quickly. The disadvantage of this, however, is that the timing of each shot is not usually so precise, so it may not be suited to synchronised installations; of which, more later.

THE MAXIM FAMILY

The Maxim was the first effective self-powered machine gun, invented in 1884 by Hiram Maxim, an American working in Europe who was subsequently granted British citizenship and knighted. It is a recoil-operated belt-fed design, relying on the short-recoil system in which the barrel and bolt are locked together and recoil for a few millimetres before the bolt is unlocked, the barrel movement is stopped and the bolt continues rearwards, extracting and ejecting the fired cartridge case and cocking the firing pin. The bolt is then pushed back towards the breech by a return spring, chambering the next cartridge as it does so, and is locked in place ready to fire again. The Maxim fires from a closed bolt.

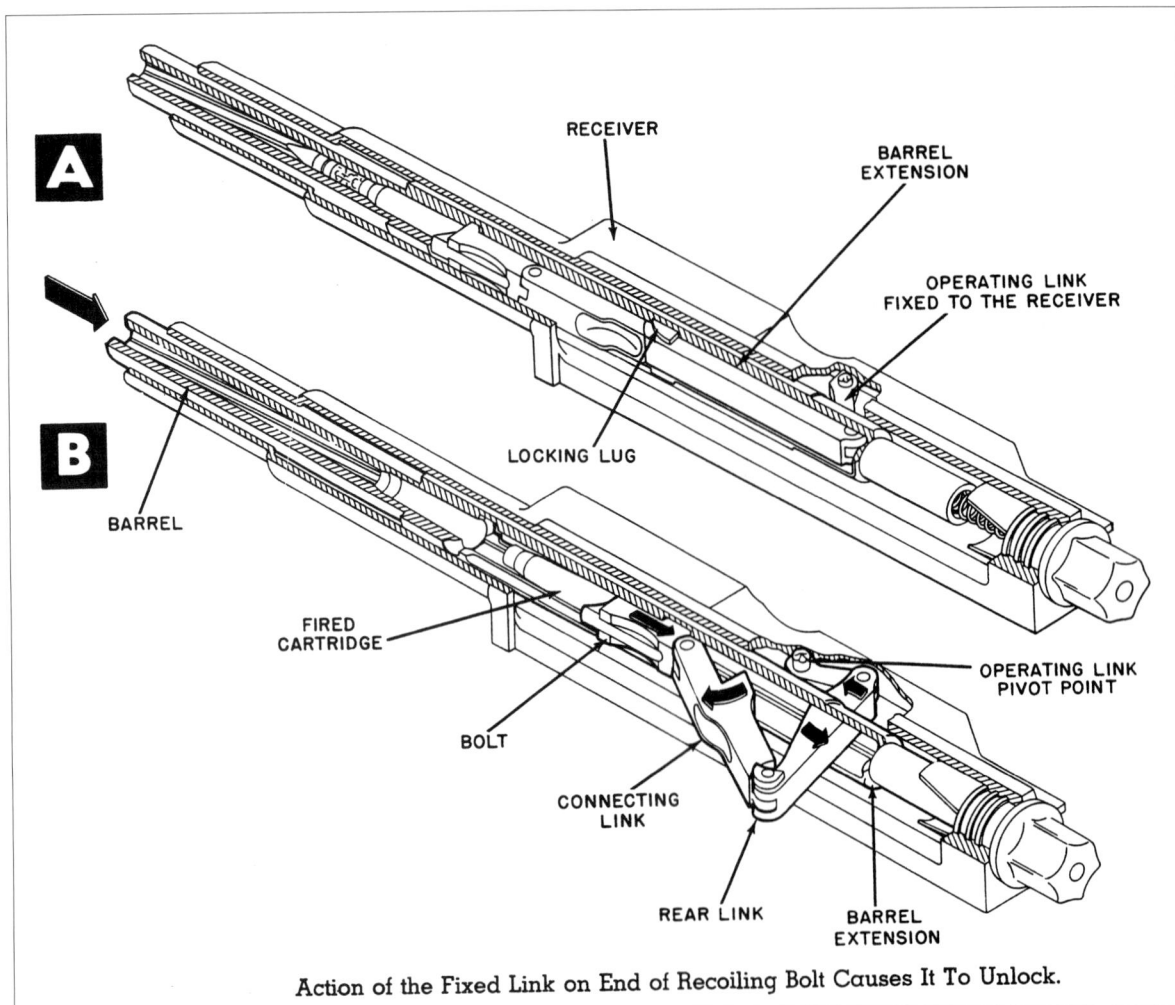

Action of the Fixed Link on End of Recoiling Bolt Causes It To Unlock.

Toggle-bolt short-recoil mechanism (Furrer). (BuOrd, USN)

The particular locking mechanism used by Maxim is toggle joint, similar to an elbow. The bolt is hinged half-way along, but remains rigid during firing. As the bolt and barrel recoil, a part of the mechanism forces the joint to bend, pulling the bolt face away from the breech, at the same instant that the recoil of the barrel is stopped.

The Maxim gun, or variants of the design, were in widespread use in several armies at the beginning of the First World War. The original Maxim gun was adopted by Germany (its most dedicated user) as the MG 08, in its standard 7.92 × 57 military rifle calibre, and by Russia as the M1910, in 7.62 × 54R. The Swiss MG 94 and MG 11 were chambered for their own 7.5 × 55 cartridge. The Maxim

had also been adopted by Britain, initially in .45 in calibre, but latterly in .303 in (7.7 × 56R). By the start of the war a redesigned and more compact version (which among other things turned the action upside down), originally known as the Vickers-Maxim and later just as the Vickers, was in service. However, the .45 in versions had not been forgotten, and saw limited use in aircraft.

At first, the Maxim family was not as popular as some other machine guns for use in aircraft, as they were bulky and heavy. The change came in 1915, with the demand to fix forward-firing guns whose shots could be synchronised to fire through the propeller disk without hitting the blades. It was found that the Maxim trigger mechanism, which controlled

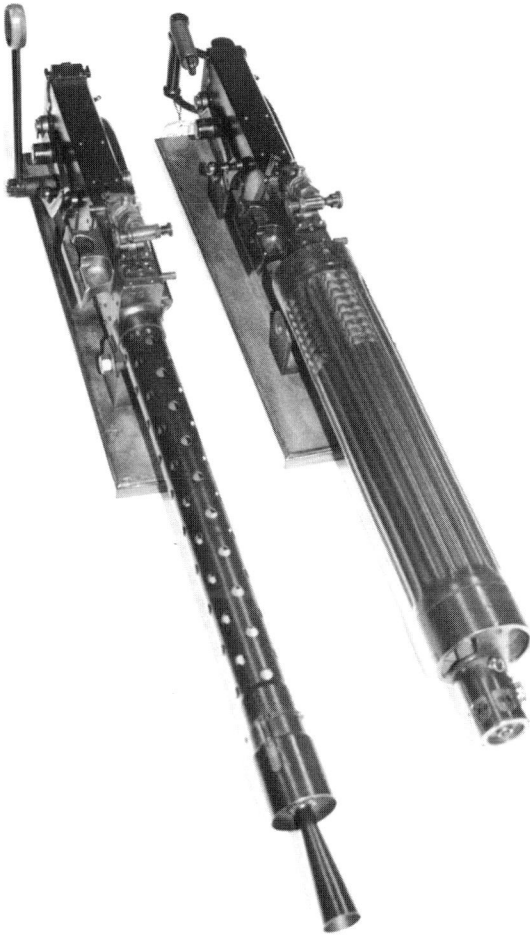

US 11 mm Vickers 'balloon gun'. *(Courtesy MoD Pattern Room)*

British .303 in Vickers Mk I (right) and Mk III. *(Courtesy MoD Pattern Room)*

the instant of firing very precisely, particularly lent itself to effective synchronisation, and variations of the basic design formed the most important fixed aircraft weapons during the latter war years and for some time thereafter.

As used by armies, the barrel of the Maxim and its derivatives was surrounded by a large-diameter water jacket to keep it cool during long bursts of fire. This was not necessary in the air as only short bursts were generally used, and in any case the airstream provided effective cooling. However, the barrel jacket could not be dispensed with as it provided a support for the front of the barrel as it slid to and fro, so at first the jacket was merely perforated at the front and sides to let the air flow through it. In several later versions in various air forces a slimmer, perforated jacket was designed.

The Vickers gun was developed through several Marks incorporating functional and production improvements, notably boosting the rate of fire from 400 to 850–900 rounds per minute (rpm) by means of the 'Hazleton booster', which was introduced in 1917. This utilised a device (known generally as a recoil intensifier, or muzzle booster) fitted to the muzzle which trapped some of the gun gas and used it to drive the barrel back more violently, in conjunction with an additional coil-spring recoil buffer which kicked the bolt back faster. Various other parts of the gun also had to be changed to enable it to withstand the more violent action. An $11 \times 59R$ 'balloon gun' version was developed in France and adopted by the USA, as described in the section on ammunition above. It was capable of 600 rpm.

As has been noted, aircraft guns of this period were prone to unreliability, and in the case of the Vickers the various reasons were codified as follows:

No. 1 Stoppage: spent cartridge is not ejected (several possible explanations, mainly caused by poor maintenance)
No. 2 Stoppage: chamber is fouled (case has separated, with part left in the chamber)
No. 3 Stoppage: a misfed round (usually owing to twisted belt or cartridge out of alignment in it)
No. 4 Stoppage: a misfired round (which may be a gun or ammunition fault).

The Mk II Vickers, which had a slim jacket, did not enter service until after the end of the First World War. The final British service version was the Mk III of 1928, similar to the Mk II but with a flash hider and other detailed improvements. The Vickers gun achieved commercial success post war, with the principal models being the Class E (fixed) and the Class F (flexible). The Class E was a version of the Mk II, while the Class F had an even slimmer jacket and was

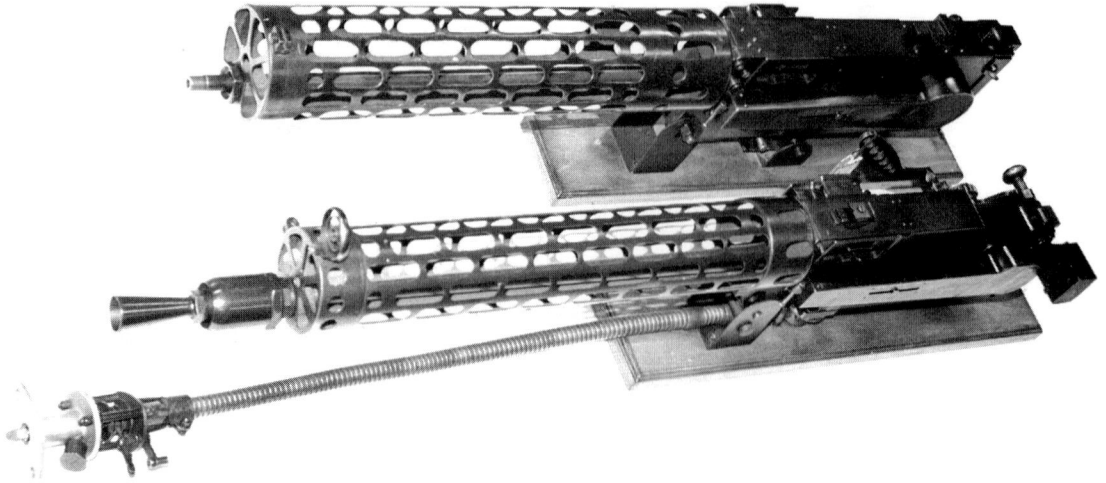

German 7.92 mm Maxims: LMG 08 (top) and LMG 08/15. (Courtesy MoD Pattern Room)

adapted to use the Lewis 97-round pan instead of a belt feed. The full magazine weighed 4.08 kg, compared with 3.29 kg for 199 rounds of belted ammunition used by other models of Vickers.

Germany similarly developed the MG 08 for aircraft use, along with its successor, the lightened LMG 08/15 (although these never achieved such a high rate of fire), and apart from early experiments these guns were the only types of fixed forward-firing aircraft guns used by the German air force. The L in LMG is variously stated as standing for '*leicht*' (light), '*luftgekühlt*' (air-cooled) or simply '*Luft*' (air). German Maxims were made in several factories, but these aircraft versions were all made at a government weapons factory in Spandau, a suburb of Berlin; the discovery of the name 'Spandau' on the gun's nameplate led the Allies to call it by this name, although it was not an official designation. Incidentally, 'Spandau' later became the Allied soldiers' name for any kind of German machine gun, a practice which still existed even in the Second World War, long after the last of these weapons had been consigned to museums. At the end of the war, the Maxim was further modified to the MG 08/18, a lightened air-cooled weapon with a slim jacket. Although designed as an infantry weapon, it did see some post-war use in aircraft. A more radical German redesign of the Maxim gun was the Parabellum (MG 14), a slim, light and fast-firing weapon. Production of this gun could not meet demand, so after some initial experiments it

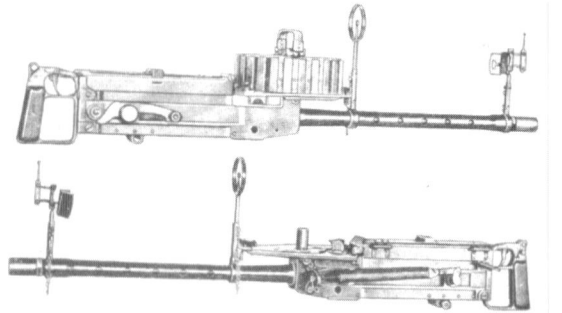

Two views of the Vickers Class F. (BuOrd, USN)

was solely reserved for flexible mountings, where its advantages were of most value.

Maxim-type guns were produced in a wide range of different calibres and used by many nations. As we have seen, Vickers kept developing their version of the gun and achieved many export sales around the world. Other nations that acquired Vickers guns went on to devise their own weapons based on it. In both Poland and Czechoslovakia in the 1920s, the Class E gun was rechambered to 7.92 × 57 calibre. The Czechs then devised a much-modified version of the Vickers, the CZ (*Ceska-Zbrojovka*) vz.30, available with either belt feed or a Lewis-type drum. In 1928, the Soviets introduced the Maxim-based PV-1 (*Pulemot Vozdushnyi* = aircraft machine gun), which became their standard fixed gun until the advent of the ShKAS. The Maxim operating principle was also adopted (albeit lying on its side) by the

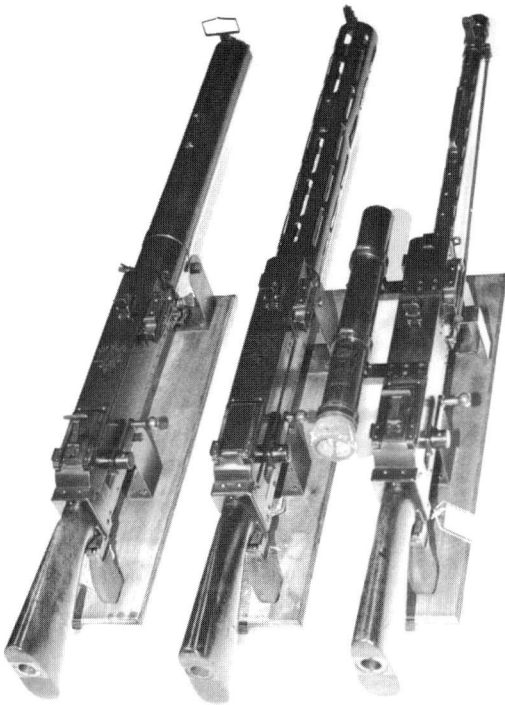

German 7.92 mm MG 14 Parabellums. From left to right: water-cooled, air-cooled, and MG 14/17 with 3× telescopic sight. (Courtesy MoD Pattern Room)

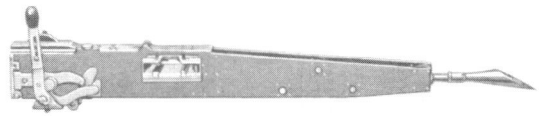

The Vickers Class B .5 inch gun. (BuOrd, USN)

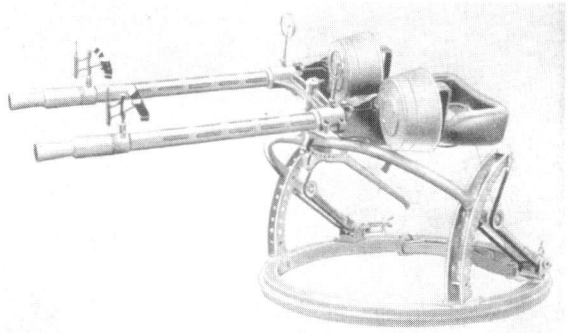

Late-model Madsen on a twin flexible mounting. (BuOrd, USN)

Swiss designer Adolf Furrer between the wars, and a range of guns in different calibres resulted. The belt-fed Models 1925 and 1928, in the Swiss 7.5 × 55 calibre, were speeded up for the Fl.Mg 29 aircraft version from 450–500 rpm for the ground gun to 1,100–1,300 rpm. This was available in two versions: a long-barrelled one, and a short-barrelled version incorporating a full-length barrel sleeve with a muzzle booster, to provide the more powerful action needed to pull long ammunition belts.

At the end of the First World War Germany was developing a large version of the Maxim, the MG T.u.F., for *Tank und Flieger*. This fired a powerful 13 × 92SR cartridge, essentially a scaled-up rifle cartridge firing a bullet four times as heavy, which was also used in the huge Mauser M1918 anti-tank rifle. The name, meaning 'tank and aircraft', described the intended targets, suggestions that it might also have been intended for fitting to aircraft being a claim made by the British after the war as an excuse to try to seize one of the weapons (military aircraft and their weapons being subject to confiscation by the Commission of Control under the terms of the Versailles Treaty). It was too

late to see action, only 24 of the 4,200 ordered being completed (by the *Maschinen-Fabrik Augsberg-Nurnberg*) but it can be regarded as the ancestor of all of the heavy machine guns that followed.

By the end of the war the RAF had also become interested in the development of a heavy machine gun in .5 in (12.7 mm) calibre, which could fire not only AP bullets with much better armour penetration than RCMGs but also large-capacity incendiaries. Much experimentation eventually led to the Vickers .5 in Class B, which was chambered for a new 12.7 × 81 cartridge. This was extensively tested but not adopted for aircraft use, although it was sold abroad in small numbers in a slightly different (12.7 × 81SR) export calibre. It is mainly of interest because the Italians, and subsequently the Imperial Japanese Army, adopted the 12.7 × 81SR cartridge for use in their own aircraft HMGs (the Breda-SAFAT and Scotti in Italy, the Ho-103 in Japan).

OTHER RECOIL-OPERATED GUNS

Not all short-recoil guns used the Maxim type of mechanism. Many different systems for locking and unlocking the bolt and breech were devised, including sliding, pivoting and rotating locks, all of them driven by the initial rearward movement of the barrel and breech assembly.

A famous short-recoil MG was the Danish Madsen, which was among the first light machine guns ever to see service, being introduced in 1902. It used a complex

Short-recoil mechanism. (*Courtesy: D.F. Allsop*)

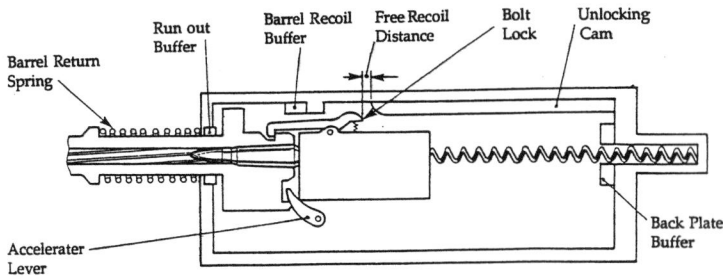

The barrel and breech block move into the forward position and a round is fed into the chamber

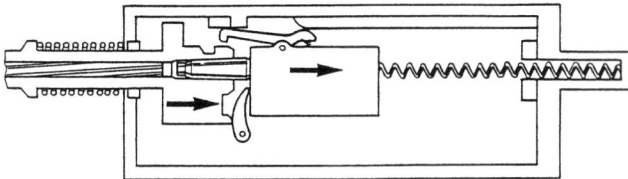

The round is fired and the barrel and breech block are pushed to the rear by the recoil forces. After a short distance they are unlocked and the barrel is halted. Additional momentum is given to the breech block by an accelerator lever before the barrel stops moving

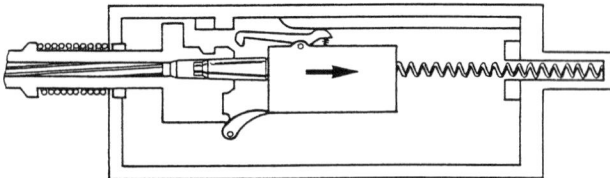

The breech block moves to the rear of the body of the weapon under its own momentum

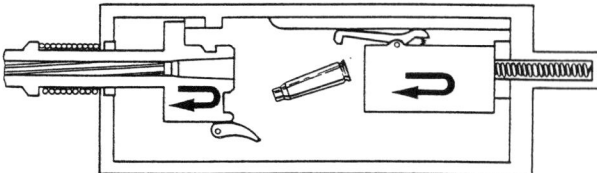

The spent case is extracted and ejected, the breech block is halted by the buffer and the barrel is held to the rear

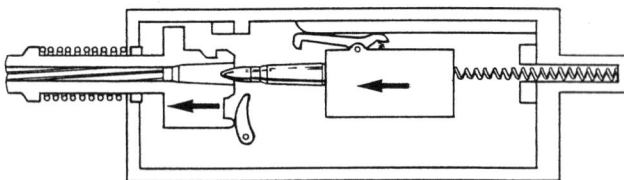

The breech bolt moves forward and chambers a fresh round

German Bergmann 7.92 mm MG 15nA flexible. *(Courtesy MoD Pattern Room)*

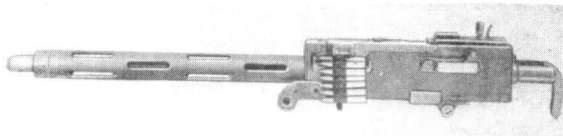

The early Browning Model 1918. *(BuOrd, USN)*

US Browning 7.62 mm Model 30. *(Courtesy MoD Pattern Room)*

A very early model of the .50 in Browning. *(BuOrd, USN)*

tilting-block locking mechanism. It was well suited to use in early aircraft by virtue of its light weight, air cooling and box magazine, although the rate of fire was low and the mechanism did not function well with rimmed cartridges. As an aircraft gun it was primarily used by Russia during the First World War, but it was also acquired by Austria-Hungary. The latter was not satisfied with the gun, because the ammunition capacity of the 25-round box was too small and the gun functioned reliably only when issued with ammunition of above-average quality. In the 1920s the firm decided to redesign the gun for aircraft use, converting it to belt feed and fitting a muzzle booster to increase the rate of fire to 1,000 rpm. The Model 1927, as it was called, achieved many sales for use in both fixed and flexible installations in a wide range of calibres, up to 11.35 mm.

Another variation used in this period was the rising-block lock, as employed in the Bergmann MG 15nA and the Browning MGs. In this design the barrel and bolt are connected by a locking piece which is cammed vertically upwards to disconnect them. The Bergmann was a modification of a ground-based gun, with the usual conversion from water cooling by means of a perforated barrel casing, in this case quite slim. Rate of fire was speeded up from 500 to 800 rpm. Being fairly light and compact, it was used to supplement the Parabellum as a flexible gun in both the German and Austro-Hungarian air forces, but was found to suffer from too frequent stoppages. Most were issued to the Army as a light infantry weapon. The Bergmann was tried in a synchronised installation in a Fokker B.II in 1916, but this did not prove successful.

John Browning, an American, had already invented various types of automatic mechanism before he designed the short-recoil machine gun that was to become most associated with his name. This first emerged in the M1917 RCMG in .30-06 calibre (7.62 × 63), followed a few years later by the M1921 HMG, the famous .50 in Browning, which fired a powerful 12.7 × 99 cartridge. Although the aircraft version of the M1917, known as the M1918, was ordered in large numbers, it reached service too late to see action in the First World War (although one was installed in a Bristol Fighter of the RAF in 1918). However, it became the principal US aircraft gun through the 1920s and 1930s as well as being widely exported. The big .50 M1921 saw very limited use, regular installations in aircraft not commencing until the development of the M2 version in 1933. The aircraft Brownings, like most of the others, fired from a closed bolt.

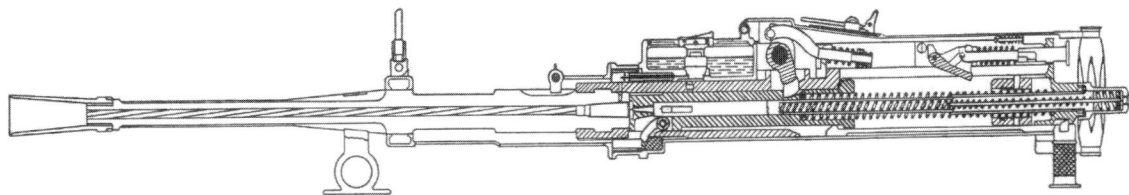

Sectioned drawing of a Fiat M1926. *(BuOrd, USN)*

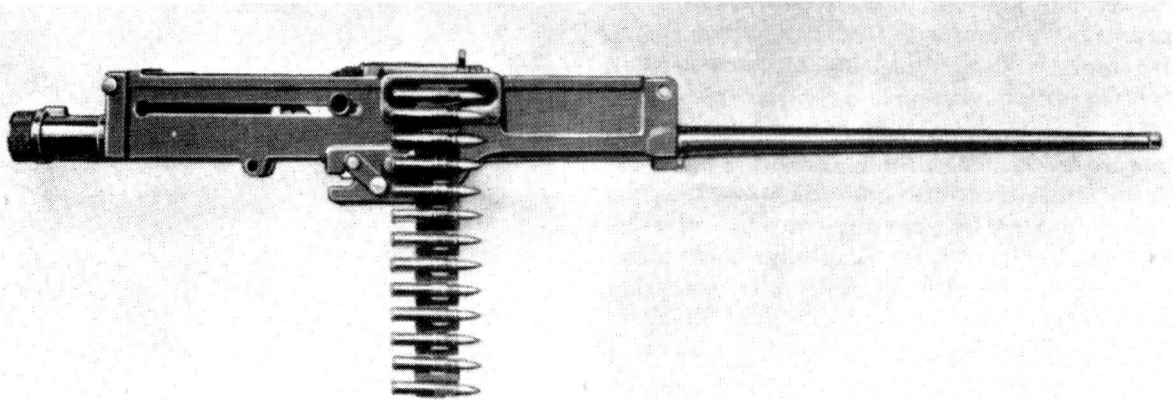

Fiat M1928. (*BuOrd, USN*)

The Italian firm of Fiat, which had for a long time produced the retarded-blowback designs of Revelli described
later, introduced in the M1928 gun a modified design by
Mascarucci; the changes turned the gun into a short-recoil
mechanism. The ground gun was produced in 6.5 × 52 calibre, but the aircraft version was made for the 7.7 × 56R
(British .303 in) cartridge already in service, converted to
belt feed and with the rate of fire increased to 800 rpm.

One famous gun which deserves mention even though it
was just too late to see service was the German Gast. This
was a twin-barrel gun with the actions of the two bolts
linked so that the recoil of one bolt drove the other forward.
By the end of the First World War this was achieving around
1,600–1,800 rpm, but the operating principle was not followed up until the late 1950s, when it emerged, in a rather
different form, in the Soviet GSh-23. The Gast is instantly
recognisable by the two big 180-round pan magazines,
mounted vertically on either side of the gun. A larger version, the 13 mm *Gast-Flieger* MG, used the same 13 × 92SR
ammunition as the T.u.F. and featured air-cooled barrels
and two curved box magazines above the action, but this was
only at the early experimental stage.

A more fundamental variation in recoil operation was
the long-recoil mechanism. This was similar to the short-
recoil described above, except that the barrel recoiled much
further, remaining locked to the bolt until the end of the
recoil stroke. The barrel was then pushed back 'into battery'
(i.e., into the firing position) while the bolt was held back,
the fired case being extracted and ejected at this point. The
bolt was then released to run forward, chambering a fresh
cartridge. The benefit of this mechanism was that the recoil
kick was spread out over a much longer period, converting
it into a smooth push which could more easily be absorbed
by the gun's mounting. The main disadvantage was that the

*Breech mechanism of the Gast, showing the pivoting link
between the bolts.* (*BuOrd, USN*)

large movements of the heavy barrel restricted the rate of
fire.

The characteristics of the long-recoil type of mechanism
meant that it was particularly suited to powerful cannon,
several examples of which are described in Chapter 3.
However, the system was occasionally used in smaller
weapons. After the war, the British firm of BSA
(Birmingham Small Arms) developed a .5 in calibre machine
gun, intended to be used in flexible aircraft mountings. Their
Model 1924 adopted the long-recoil mechanism in the interests of controlling the recoil from the relatively powerful
12.7 × 81 cartridge (this was initially slightly
different from the Vickers round, but the gun was later converted to accept the V/580). The low rate of fire, just
400 rpm, the size and weight of the gun and the limited

Long-recoil mechanism. (Courtesy: D.F. Allsop)

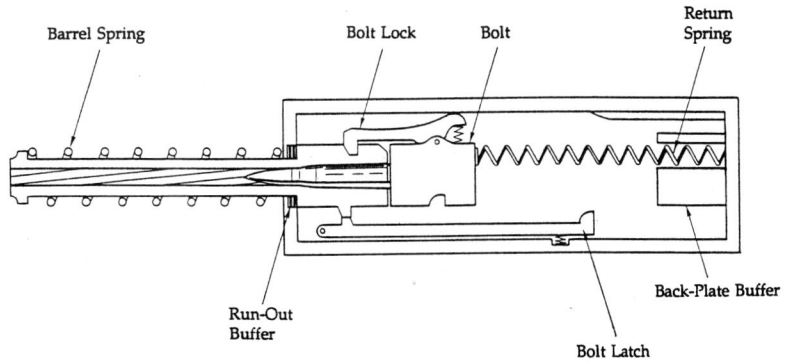

Barrel Spring   Bolt Lock   Bolt   Return Spring

Run-Out Buffer   Bolt Latch   Back-Plate Buffer

With the round chambered, the breech block is locked to the barrel. Upon firing the breech block and barrel are driven backwards

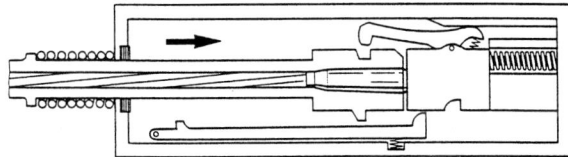

The breech block and barrel are slowed by the barrel spring and the breech block return spring. Towards the end of the stroke the breech is unlocked from the barrel

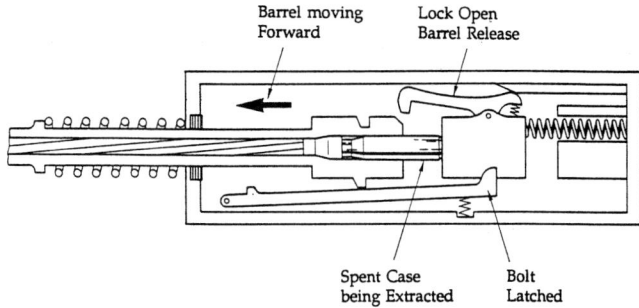

Barrel moving Forward   Lock Open Barrel Release

Spent Case being Extracted   Bolt Latched

The bolt is held to the rear and the barrel moves forward under the influence of the barrel spring. As the barrel moves forward the empty cartridge case is extracted and ejected

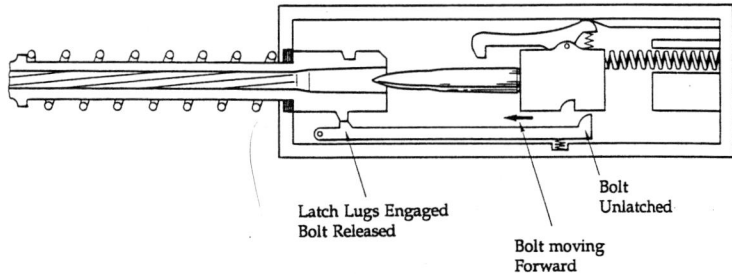

Latch Lugs Engaged Bolt Released   Bolt Unlatched

Bolt moving Forward

The breech block is released, a fresh round is chambered and the breech block is locked to the barrel

Gas operation. *(Courtesy: D.F. Allsop)*

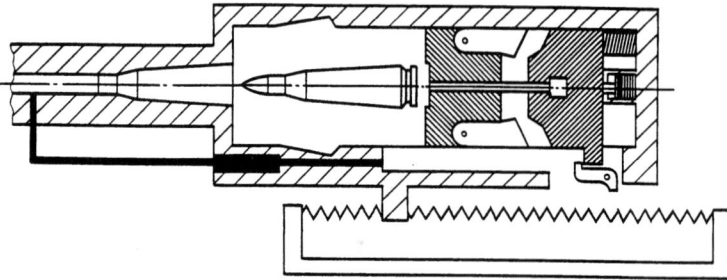

The cannon is ready to fire, the bolt is retained by the sear and the return spring is compressed. A cartridge is ready to be fed into the chamber

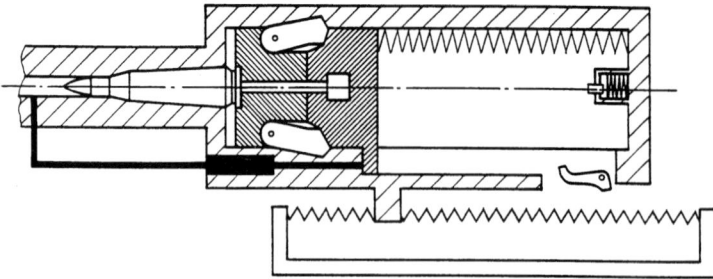

The trigger is released and the bolt feeds a cartridge into the chamber. The breech bolt locks to the barrel, the firing pin strikes the primer and the cartridge is fired

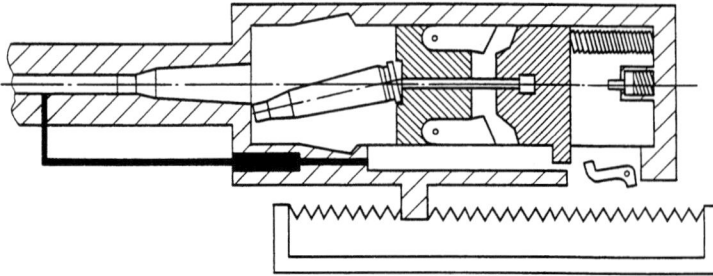

After the projectile passes the gas port, the gas piston unlocks the breech block from the barrel. Residual gas pressure accelerates the breech block after the bolt has unlocked. The empty cartridge case is extracted and ejected

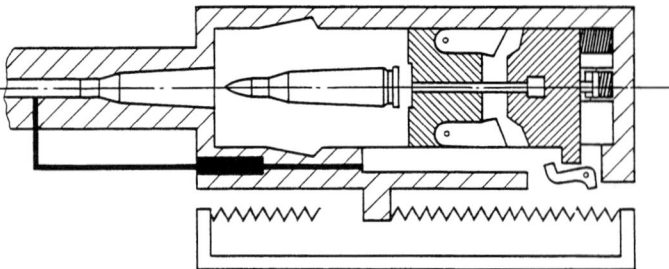

A fresh cartridge is chambered when the bolt is pushed forward by the breech block return spring

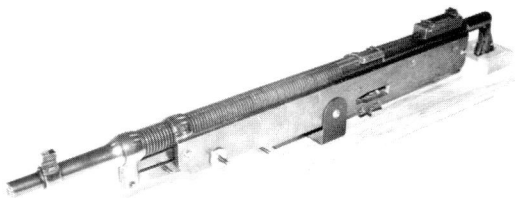

French .303 in Colt Model 1914. (*Courtesy MoD Pattern Room*)

US Marlin 7.62 mm M17. (*Courtesy MoD Pattern Room*)

Russian Marlin 7.62 mm. (*Courtesy MoD Pattern Room*)

capacity of the 37-round pan magazine led the RAF to reject it.

GAS-OPERATED GUNS

A constant rival for recoil operation has been the gas-operated system, which as its name suggests uses gas tapped from the barrel to drive the mechanism. This is usually achieved by allowing part of the gun gas to fill a cylinder located beside the barrel; the pressure of the expanding gas drives a piston down the cylinder, which in turn drives the usual unlocking, extracting, ejecting, cocking, chambering and locking cycle. The methods of locking the bolt are as varied as with recoil operation.

A benefit of gas operation is that the barrel is fixed to the gun, which makes accuracy easier to achieve. It is also possible to vary the amount of gas allowed through to drive the action, so there need never be any shortage of power (lack of operating power can be a problem with recoil-operated designs, particularly when they are belt-fed, so they are sometimes fitted with muzzle boosters in the interests of more reliable operation as well as a higher rate of fire). However, the gas-operated action can become clogged with powder residues and needs careful maintenance. Gas operation has become standard in infantry small arms, and recoil operation in the largest automatic cannon, but both mechanisms are still used in HMGs and light cannon.

One of the first gas-operated machine guns was an early RCMG design by John Browning, which was manufactured by Colt for the US Army and was therefore frequently known as the Colt-Browning. Its unusual feature was the use of gas pressure to drive a long, swinging arm under the barrel, which powered the tilting-bolt mechanism (and led to its nickname of 'potato-digger'). This mechanism had the benefit of providing a smooth operation, but as might be imagined the swinging arm was extremely inconvenient in an aircraft weapon. Despite this, the shortage of machine guns was such that some of the Colts were pressed into aerial service, particularly in Russia.

During the war a substantial redesign of the Colt took place, primarily concerned with replacing the swinging arm with a gas piston, resulting in the Marlin M1917 and 1918 RCMGs (there were only minor differences between them). These were most successful and were produced in large numbers for aircraft use in 1917 and 1918, before being gradually phased out in preference for the even better Browning M1918. They fired from a closed bolt, and were thus well suited to synchronisation.

The French firm of Hotchkiss favoured gas operation for its machine guns, utilising a gas piston to drive the mechanism. The gun commenced firing with an open bolt, the cartridge being fired automatically as soon as the bolt was locked in place. The first of these emerged at the end of the nineteenth century, and by the start of the First World War the *modèle* 1914 was beginning to enter French Army service in the standard $8 \times 50R$ calibre. It was a large and heavy weapon with a strip-type ammunition feed (see The Ammunition Feed, p.30) but despite this it was fitted to a few aircraft. Much more important was a lightweight version of the Hotchkiss, the M1909, developed for cavalry use as the 'Portative'. This was known to the USA (which used it only as an infantry weapon) as the Bénét-Mercié machine rifle. The aircraft versions were officially known as the '*Hotchkiss portative de cavalerie adapteé aviation*', or more simply as the 'Hotchkiss *Aviation*'. However, it also used a 24-round strip feed which was a considerable nuisance to the gunners, and the weapon was not as highly rated as the comparable Lewis gun. A 100-round articulated non-disintegrating steel belt, which could be wrapped around a spool, was later developed for this gun.

The Lewis gun was a light, gas-operated RCMG developed in the early years of the century by one of several American gun designers who achieved commercial success in Europe. It was originally intended as a highly portable weapon for army use, and was distinguished by two unusual features: the barrel was covered by a sleeve open at both ends (the idea being that the muzzle blast would cause cooling air to be drawn through the sleeve), and the ammunition was contained in a flat pan, rotated by the gun action. The sleeve was always a dubious idea and clearly unnecessary in aircraft applications anyway, so it soon disappeared, along with the longitudinal cooling fins which formed a radiator around the barrel. At least at first, this 'stripping' was unofficial, and some official concern was expressed about the removal of protection from the gas cylinder, and also the fact that the guns were no longer suitable for ground practice because of overheating.

The front of a Mk I Lewis gun sectioned to show the partly cut away finned radiator within the barrel jacket.
(*Courtesy MoD Pattern Room*)

The pan feed proved most useful, and in 1916 it was increased in capacity from 47 to 97 rounds by adding extra layers of cartridges. The gun used a rotating-bolt locking mechanism, like a bolt-action rifle, and fired from an open bolt which, in combination with its light weight and magazine feed, made it well suited to flexible mounting. However, like the Hotchkiss the gun fired automatically as the breech closed instead of being controlled by the trigger mechanism.

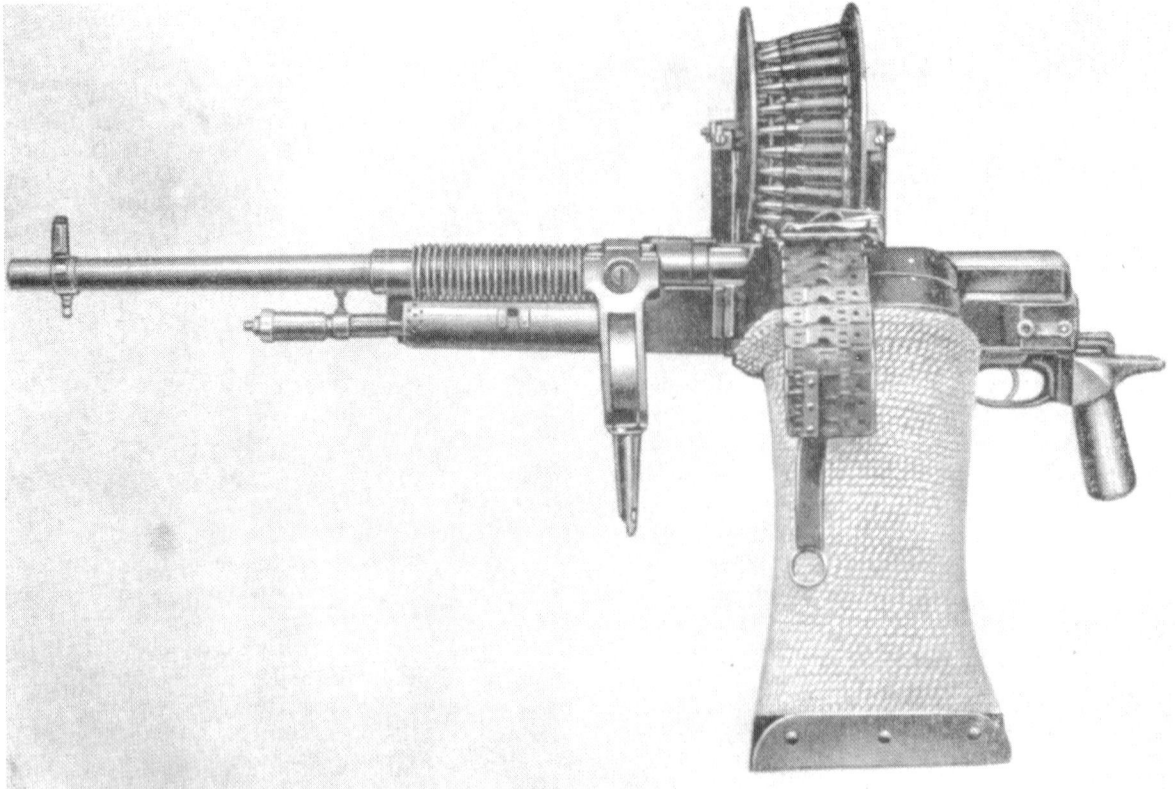

The Hotchkiss Aviation M1909. Note the ammunition spool and the bag for collecting empty cases. (*BuOrd, USN*)

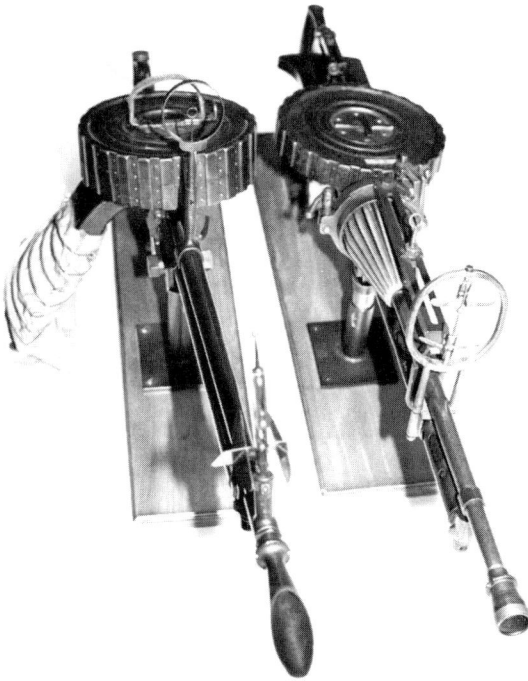

Lewis .303 in Mk III with 97-round magazine (left) and Italian pattern Mk I with 47-round magazine. Note that most of the radiator fins have been cut away. *(Courtesy MoD Pattern Room)*

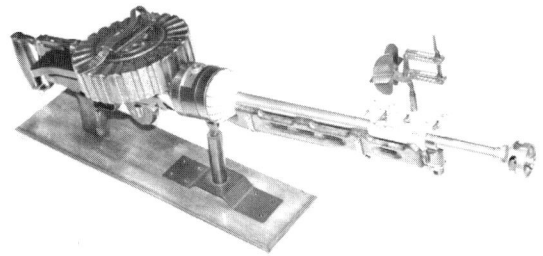

USN 7.62 mm Lewis Mk VI, converted from land pattern: note complex vane sight. *(Courtesy MoD Pattern Room)*

The slimmer jacket of the Mk II Lewis, compared with the Mk I in the background. *(Courtesy MoD Pattern Room)*

The Soviet DA. Note the bag for collecting spent cases. *(Courtesy RART)*

This meant that the precise instant of firing varied unpredictably, which made the gun unsuitable for synchronisation despite several efforts to achieve this.

The Lewis was first used by the British, as BSA had acquired a production licence before the war. It was extremely successful and was adopted by the USA in .30-06 (7.62 × 63) calibre and by the Russians in 7.62 × 54R, as well as being used by France, Italy and Japan in the original British .303 in (7.7 × 56R) calibre.

In the late 1920s, the Russians introduced the DA (*Degtyaryova Aviatsionny* = Degtyarev Aircraft) gas-operated gun, a variation of the DP light infantry RCMG in their usual 7.62 × 54R calibre. It resembled the Lewis in its pan magazine, but this was spring-driven rather than powered by the gun action, and had 63 rounds in three layers. The breech-locking mechanism was also different, utilising swinging locking pieces to hold the bolt in place. The gas piston pulled the locking pieces out of their places in the receiver, before pushing the bolt rearwards.

After manufacturing Lewis guns for the French air force the Darne company designed its own gas-operated aircraft gun, chambered for the 7.7 × 56R cartridge, which utilised a piston-driven pivoting breech-block mechanism. The M1918 model was too late to see action in the First World War but saw further development and extensive use in the inter-war period. The M1929 model, rechambered for the new French 7.5 × 54 round, was reportedly able to achieve up to 1,700 rpm, although in French service it was rated at 1,100–1,200 rpm, presumably in the interests of reliability and longevity. The gun's other claim to fame was its

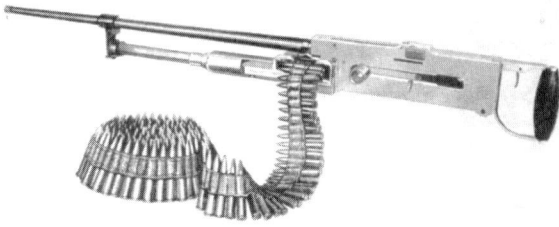

Early model of the Darne, the M1918, in .303 in British calibre. (BuOrd, USN)

Austro-Hungarian 8 mm Schwarzlose M07/12 on ground mounting. (Courtesy MoD Pattern Room)

rough finish, as the manufacturer saw no point in spending time and money on polishing except where this was functionally necessary.

Perhaps one of the unluckiest gun designers of the period was the British Col. Farquhar, who designed various weapons, including the Beardmore-Farquhar Aircraft machine gun. This was gas operated but unusual in that the action was not directly driven by the gas piston but rather via an intermediary spring. This greatly reduced the stresses and the recoil blow, and enabled a very light weight of 7.4 kg (complete with a 77-round drum magazine) to be achieved. The gun proved very reliable on test, the only criticism being its relatively low rate of fire, but the year was 1919 and nobody was buying new gun designs, so it became a footnote in armament history.

BLOWBACK GUNS

The simplest of the gun operating systems, in which the cartridge case is forced backwards out of the chamber by the expanding propellant gasses, is commonly known as blowback. To work, it requires the bolt to be unlocked from the barrel at all times, only held in place by the recoil spring and its own inertia, so that it is free to move backwards. In its simplest form, this mechanism is restricted to very low-powered cartridges because it is necessary for the bolt to hold the case in the chamber until the projectile has left the barrel, otherwise high-velocity burning gas will burst from the breech to the discomfiture of the firer. With high-pressure military rifle cartridges, the weight of bolt required would be so heavy that the rate of fire would be very slow.

Various solutions to this difficulty have been tried, because blowback weapons are attractively simple and cheap to manufacture. One is the retarded blowback, in which an additional mechanism resists the initial rearward movement of the bolt. The best-known military weapon to use this principle during this period was the Austrian Schwarzlose M07/12 RCMG. This utilised an elbow-joint attached to the bolt by one arm, with the other arm pivoted to a fixed axis on the receiver. The effect of this mechanism

was to force the initial rearward movement to operate under severe mechanical disadvantage, delaying the opening of the breech until the bullet had left the barrel. Even so, the cartridges it used were so powerful that the breech still opened too quickly. The solution was to shorten the barrel so that the projectile left the muzzle sooner, before the breech could open. This reduced the muzzle velocity; furthermore, the bolt weight required was so high that the rate of fire, at 400 rpm, was initially among the lowest of the RCMGs. Despite this, its ruggedness and reliability made it a popular gun in the First World War and it even saw service in aircraft.

The M07/12 was found to be sensitive to changes in atmospheric pressure, firing more slowly and finally stopping when the aircraft climbed above an altitude of 3,000 m. A set of modifications designed by Ir. Ludwig Kral raised the rate of fire to 630 rpm and the critical altitude to 5,400 m. A version specifically for aircraft use – the M16 – was developed, lighter and firing at 570 rpm. Continued development eventually saw the rate of fire of the M16A increased to 880 rpm, and raised its operating altitude to 7,000 m. But even in March 1918 fewer than 300 M16s were in service, and the M07/12 remained the numerically most important gun in the inventory.

The Fiat M1914 machine gun used another version of the retarded blowback mechanism, designed by Revelli, in which the barrel moved back a few millimetres to unlock the mechanism via a pivoting wedge, just as in a short-recoil action. However, as soon as unlocking was complete, the rest of the cycle was powered by blowback. The gun was originally made in water-cooled form for the infantry, and the ammunition feed was by means of a box with ten compartments, each holding five rounds. After the first five shots, the magazine was automatically moved sideways through the gun to line up the next compartment, and so on. For aircraft use, the water jacket was completely removed and a stronger barrel, with longitudinal cooling ribs, fitted. The gun retained the army's 6.5 × 52 ammunition.

The Italians developed another retarded-blowback gun, the SIA (Società Italiana Ansaldo of Turin), also in

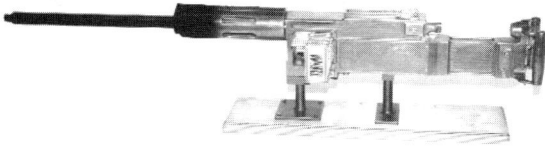

Italian 6.5 mm Revelli M1914. (*Courtesy MoD Pattern Room*)

Italian SIA on twin flexible mounting. Note the Revelli M1914 on the top wing. (*BuOrd, USN*)

being blown out of the chamber, so some form of waxing or lubrication for the cartridges is normally provided. Both the Revelli and the Schwarzlose incorporated a built-in oiler to oil the cartridges as they were loaded. This was a source of some discomfort when Schwarzloses were mounted in front of the pilot, who received a constant spray of oil in his face whenever the guns were fired.

An inter-war variation on this theme was the Italian Scotti M1928 gun. As with all Scotti designs, this used gas to unlock the breech-block via locking lugs on a rotating bolt head, after which blowback powered the rest of the cycle, as with the Revelli. This system had actually been pioneered by Mannlicher, who patented it in 1899, but Scotti made most use of it. Most Scotti designs were built by Isotta-Fraschini, and the aircraft RCMG was in the British 7.7 × 56R calibre, as this had become the standard air force round following widespread use of the Lewis and Vickers guns in the

Italian 6.5 mm Revelli M1914 magazine. (*Courtesy MoD Pattern Room*)

6.5 × 52 calibre. This was fed by a vertical box magazine and could be synchronised, although it seemed to be favoured more as a flexibly mounted gun, usually seen in pairs. This was entering production towards the end of the war, but the extent of its use is not known.

One problem affecting all blowback guns is the lack of positive extraction, i.e. the fired case is not pulled from the chamber by an extractor. The pressure inside the chamber is such that the case can 'stick' to the chamber wall instead of

Two of a kind: Swiss Flieger-Doppelpistole *(top) and* Italian Villar Perosa. (*Courtesy MoD Pattern Room*)

First World War. Unlike the Revelli, the Scotti fired from an open bolt and was thus favoured for flexible mountings.

A remarkable Italian retarded-blowback aircraft gun was the Villar Perosa, which was extremely small and light by virtue of being chambered for the little 9 × 19 Glisenti pistol round, dimensionally similar to the Parabellum (Luger) case but with a reduced loading. The gun, which fired from an open bolt, hardly needed the sophistication of a retarding mechanism, given the low power of the cartridge, and in fact this was quite simple, consisting of a slight cam-induced turning movement of the breech-block. In its aircraft installations the Villar Perosa was always used in pairs fixed together, although the guns operated separately. The very fast cyclic rate of 1,200 rpm per barrel gave an astonishing combined RoF of 2,400 rpm. However, the guns were fed by box magazines of 25 or 50 rounds, which gave a firing time of 1.25 or 2.5 seconds before the magazines needed changing. The low muzzle velocity and light projectiles severely limited the range and effectiveness of this weapon, which became much more useful when the two barrels were separated and each fitted with a shoulder stock, to create the first sub-machine guns. Immediately after the war the Swiss developed a very similar weapon, the short-recoil *Flieger Doppelpistole* M1919, in the 7.65 × 22 (.30 Luger) pistol calibre. It used basically the same short-recoil toggle-bolt action as the Luger pistol (similar in principle to the Maxim) and fired at 1,200 rpm per barrel from two 50-round magazines.

A different approach to the blowback mechanism was the advanced primer ignition, or API, blowback. This was only used in cannon calibres, however, so is described in Chapter 3.

THE AMMUNITION FEED

ONE OF THE CRUCIAL ASPECTS OF MACHINE GUN DESIGN IS the need for an automatic ammunition 'feed', or method of supplying cartridges to the breech. In the earliest guns this was achieved by gravity; the cartridges were held in a rack above the gun and dropped into place as required. Except for certain specialist installations this was clearly unacceptable in an aircraft which might be manoeuvring violently at the same time as firing, so a variety of other methods of holding the ammunition have been employed.

Simplest is the box magazine, not dissimilar to the gravity feed except that a strong spring is added to the end of the container or box, forcing the cartridges against lips at the open (gun) end which stop them from falling out (the cartridges being slid out lengthways by the gun mechanism for chambering). This design enables the box to be mounted to the side of or below the gun, although top mounting was generally preferred in larger weapons as gravity could then

British Lewis 97-round pan magazine, seen from underneath. (Courtesy MoD Pattern Room)

assist feeding. The problem with this design is that the box becomes very long if more than a few cartridges are carried (even though double-row boxes were developed to reduce the length), so more compact magazines were devised to hold a larger quantity of ammunition. These came in two forms – pan and drum magazines.

In the pan type (confusingly also sometimes called a drum) the cartridges are arranged in a circle, pointing inwards. Most pans contain more than one layer, further increasing capacity. These may be driven by a spring, or rotated by the gun action as it fires. In the drum type of magazine, the cartridges are held parallel to each other, in a coil arrangement. These are usually driven by a spring which is wound up when the drum is loaded. Pan and drum magazines remained popular in aircraft machine guns until World War Two, particularly in 'flexible' mountings in which the gun needs to move freely, because the gun and magazine form a self-contained unit.

The problem with all of these types of magazine is that their capacity was usually limited to a maximum of about 100 rounds, with only a few exceptions. For larger capacities, belt feed is employed. In this system, the ammunition is inserted into a belt (which can be of considerable length) which is pulled through the mechanism, normally by the action of the gun as it fires, with each cartridge being pushed or pulled out in turn. Early belts were of fabric, but this was inconvenient in aircraft, as the empty belt tended to flap around. Fabric belts were also subject to wear, lost their elasticity after a few fillings and absorbed moisture, which would often freeze at high altitude.

In an attempt to find a better solution, the metal disintegrating-link belt was developed in Germany midway through World War One. The cartridges were joined by separate metal links, which fell apart when the cartridge was loaded (non-disintegrating steel belts were also used but were less common). Unfortunately this initial design had weaknesses which discouraged the Germans and led them to revert to fabric belts for the rest of the war. The British and French, who examined the German disintegrating belt found on a Fokker captured in April 1916, initially copied the system with a few improvements, but these were also unsatisfactory until a major redesign in Britain by Prideaux produced the belt that then became standard for the Vickers aircraft gun. The German and Austro-Hungarians never copied this, possibly because of a shortage of the high-quality steel required; they tried to ameliorate the worst problems of fabric belts by soaking them in soap solution (which improved their reliability) and kept them out of the way by wrapping them around large reels next to the gun (one for the full belt, one for the empty one). This was an effective solution but very bulky, particularly in twin flexible mountings.

Some early aircraft RCMGs, notably the French Hotchkiss, used a strip feed in which cartridges were held by a rigid metal strip which was pulled through the gun as it fired. These had the disadvantages of box magazines but were less robust, and this system did not last long. Instead, the strips were hinged between each cartridge so that they could be wrapped around a feed spool as with the cloth-belt guns.

MOUNTINGS

THE FIRST WEAPONS CARRIED ALOFT WERE NOT FITTED TO the aircraft but held in the gunners' hands. It soon became clear that to stand any chance of hitting a moving target while trying to aim against the effect of the slipstream, it was necessary to gain support and steadiness by mounting the gun onto the aircraft. Two different classes of mounting developed, for fixed and flexible guns (the pedantic may argue that the term 'flexible' is inaccurate, as the guns themselves obviously remained rigid, but the term is in common use for guns that are mounted so that they can be swung by hand to aim in different directions).

Fixed guns were fired by the pilot, flexible ones by a gunner (or observer who acted as a gunner in an emergency, or in a few cases even by the pilot!). The first flexible mountings were simple vertical columns (also known as pintle or pillar mountings) located in front of the gunner in sockets to that the guns were attached by means of a joint that permitted movement in traverse (horizontally) and elevation (vertically). This was satisfactory for targets that were more or less in front of the gunner, but meant that to aim to one side the gunner had to lean right out of the cockpit on the opposite

side. However, they were retained to the end of the war in some large bombers in which the dorsal gun position had room for two gunners, using guns mounted on each side of the cockpit.

What was needed was a mounting that would enable the whole gun – and the gunner – to move around the cockpit so that for firing at targets to one side the gun would be mounted on the side of the cockpit with the gunner sitting or standing behind it. At first, this was achieved by using a cranked pillar (i.e. one which was bent so that by rotating it in its socket, the gun position could be altered) and/or by providing several sockets around a cockpit between which the gun or guns could be moved, but neither device was very convenient.

The solution was found in various types of ring mounting, in which a circular track was installed around the outside of the cockpit, with the gun being mounted onto a matching ring which rotated around the track. As an added refinement, these ring mountings also often had a facility for adjusting the height of the gun mounting, so the gun could more easily be aimed at targets above or below the aircraft. The mountings were manually operated, although some featured spring-loading to reduce the effort. Most of these mountings were for only one gun, but twin mountings did see service towards the end of the war despite the considerable physical effort required to operate them (when the first USA-built aircraft arrived in France, their ring mountings were replaced by French or British ones, as they were not strong enough to carry two guns). One of the best known of these mountings was the definitive British Scarff, but the original idea was patented in 1914 by Schneider, a Swiss engineer, and many different versions of the same basic idea were used.

A good view of the definitive Lewis gun – a Mk III with a 97-round magazine – on a Scarff ring mounting. (Courtesy Philip Jarrett)

Twin Lewis Mk II on a ring mounting, 1917. (Courtesy Philip Jarrett)

An early attempt at mounting a Lewis gun to the side of the aircraft, so that the magazine was in reach. (BuOrd, USN)

The mounting of fixed guns paradoxically posed far more difficult technical problems, except in the case of single-seat 'pusher' aircraft, in which the engine was mounted behind the pilot. In this case, fixing a gun to the front of the pilot's cockpit was very simple. However, most single-engined aircraft had front engines with propellers in front of the pilot. There were five ways of resolving this difficulty: to fix the gun to the engine and arrange for it to fire through a hollow propeller hub, to mount the gun so that it fired outside the propeller disk, to mount it to fire through the propeller disk and hope that the occasional bullet which hit the propeller would not do fatal damage, to improve on the second arrangement by fitting the propeller with deflector plates to protect it from bullets, and finally to connect the propeller and the gun so that the gun would only fire when the propeller blades were out of the way. The last solution, called 'synchronisation', was technically the most complex, but its advantages were such that it eventually became standard, with aircraft being equipped with synchronised guns up to the end of the propeller fighter era.

The first solution was only possible with in-line vee-engines with geared propellers. It was invented pre-war, being tested by Blériot in 1911 and reportedly by the already-mentioned Schneider in 1913. In the same year,

the Daimler engine works was granted a patent for a cannon firing through the hollow propeller hub of a geared engine. Rather surprisingly, this contained provision for the weapon to be aimed independently of the aircraft, by the rather awkward expedient of making the opening in the propeller shaft large enough to allow a limited range of movement. Otherwise the concept was sound, but its application on the wartime German fighters was hardly possible as their engines were either in-line six-cylinder units, or rotaries. Service use did not occur until 1917, when Hispano-Suiza developed a 37 mm cannon mounting for its V8 engine, as described in Chapter 3.

The second of the solutions had two variations. The first was to mount the gun within reach of the pilot (important to change magazines or clear jams), but aimed away from the propeller so that it fired at an angle to the line of flight. It was soon realised that this was unsatisfactory, because it made accurate aiming extremely difficult. By the second year of aerial fighting it had become clear that the best armament for attacking other aircraft was a gun fixed to fire forward, with the pilot aiming the whole plane at the target.

In biplane aircraft this could be achieved by mounting a gun on the top wing, above the propeller disk. The disadvantages of mounting a heavy weight at this location were resolved by fitting light machine guns, which were magazine rather than belt fed. This caused obvious problems when it came to changing the magazine, so later versions of these mountings, such as the British Foster, usually had provision for pulling the gun down towards the cockpit.

The best location for the guns, in terms of accessibility and weight distribution, was on top of the engine, right in front of the pilot. The first crude solution to the propeller problem – angled steel deflectors fitted to the propeller blades – worked, but did nothing for the aerodynamic

Detail of a Lewis gun (with 97-round magazine) fitted to a Martinsyde. Note the gate sight. (Courtesy Philip Jarrett)

A Hotchkiss Aviation fixed to fire forwards. Note the deflector wedges on the propeller, and the strip ammunition feed. (BuOrd, USN)

enthusiastic about this – worry about when the propeller was going to disintegrate cannot have been conducive to effective shooting – so it provided a further incentive towards the development of synchronised mountings.

The development of fixed aircraft weapons was delayed by a lack of official interest as well as by these technical problems. A good example of this was the attitude of Major Siegert of the German General Staff, who wrote a memorandum about the necessity of arming aircraft with a light, air-cooled machine gun. He dismissed fixed gun installations as he regarded them as undesirable from the tactical point of view, claiming that this would force pilots to fly towards the enemy and thereby throw away the advantage of speed.

SYNCHRONISATION SYSTEMS

THE FIRST DESIGN FOR A DEVICE TO SYNCHRONISE THE firing of the gun or guns with the rotation of the propeller was patented by the ingenious Franz Schneider, of whom we have already heard (although Blériot was also working in this field). However, his first patent in July 1913 was more precisely an interrupter rather than a synchronising gear; i.e. the mechanism prevented the gun from firing while a propeller blade was in front, instead of positively firing it when the line was clear. The latter approach was the method eventually adopted, although the term 'interrupter gear' remained in popular but inaccurate use thereafter. It should be noted that a synchronising gear effectively turned the machine gun into a semi-automatic weapon, as it only fired one shot for each firing impulse received. It seems that Schneider had thought of this method as well, so should not be denied the credit. His patent envisaged a flexible synchronised gun, albeit with a limited range of movement.

This was followed in April 1914 by the Frenchman

performance of the propeller. This method reduced the effective rate of fire owing to the loss of about 25 per cent of bullets deflected, and also incurred the risk of bullets being deflected back towards the engine, as well putting more strain on the propeller shaft from the impact of the bullets on the blades. Some propellers were specially designed for this purpose (they minimised the propeller area in the line of fire, which reduced the loss to ten per cent of bullets fired), but they were less efficient in doing their job. A more sophisticated alternative was to fit a supplementary rotating arm coaxial with the propeller, with wedges to deflect the bullets away from the propeller.

The alternative and even simpler solution was to do nothing to protect the propeller except bind it with varnished tape, calculating that in a typical action very few bullets would strike the propeller blades and two or three holes would not fatally weaken them anyway. Most pilots were not

Raymond Saulnier's patent mechanism which used an oscillating rod to fire the gun (a flexible link was also proposed). More significantly, Saulnier also built the first practical synchronising gear at this time, but suffered from applying this to a Hotchkiss, which was inherently unsuitable for synchronisation. Obviously discouraged by the results, Saulnier invented the steel deflector wedges as a simpler solution.

The Edwards brothers patented a synchronisation gear in Britain in the summer of 1914, but when they approached the RFC with it, they were told that the service did not have any money for that kind of development.

The first use of synchronising gear in aerial warfare did not occur until 1915, following the capture by the Germans in April of that year of a French aircraft using the deflector type of mechanism. The *Idflieg* (*Inspektion der Fliegertruppen*) sought a comparable system, and Anthony Fokker (who, although Dutch, had a factory in Schwerin, Germany) produced the first example of an aircraft fitted with a synchronising gear in May 1915. It seems likely that the *Gestänge-Steuerung* gear was actually designed by Heinrich Lübbe, an employee of Fokker's, based on Saulnier's patent. Initial versions used rigid connecting push-rods to fire the gun, but these proved troublesome (they were sensitive to temperature changes and would contract in the cold, preventing operation of the trigger), so flexible drive shafts were employed in later designs. The Fokker system remained predominant in Germany, but other synchronisation gears were also used, such as the Albatros-Hedtke fitted to all Albatros D aircraft until August 1917, when it was replaced by an improved version, the Semmler, fitted to the D.V.

At first, Allied efforts were hampered by the preference for using the Lewis and Hotchkiss *Aviation* guns, so much lighter than the Vickers-Maxim type. However, the mechanism of these guns was fundamentally unsuited to synchronisation as there was no positive trigger release: they fired from an open bolt, the primer being struck automatically as the breech closed. The time delay between the pilot pressing the firing button and the first shot being fired was typically about twelve times as long as with the Vickers-Maxim types, which was too long for the accurate timing required. For effective synchronisation the time between the trigger pulse and the moment when the projectile leaves the barrel (the lock time) is crucial. Because the propeller rotates over an important angle during this interval, this time needs to be accurately controlled. It also needs to be as short as possible, because the rotation speed of the propeller itself is not constant but dependent on engine rpm, and the longer the lock time is, the greater the variation in propeller travel will be. Little progress was made until the Vickers gun, which happened to have a positive striker release and was fired from a closed bolt, was modified for the purpose.

Testing gun synchronisation; note that the weapon is a Lewis, which does not give much cause for optimism!
(*Courtesy Philip Jarrett*)

The British, stimulated by the success of the synchroniser-equipped German fighters, started to develop their own gear in autumn 1915. First in the field was the Vickers-Challenger, introduced in March 1916 (the patent was applied for in January, well before the first Fokker with synchronisation gear was captured), but this experienced reliability problems and was replaced first by the Scarff-Dybovsky (a favourite of the RNAS), Sopwith-Kauper and other less common systems until the Constantinesco-Colley (or CC) hydrosonic gear entered service and rapidly became the standard thereafter.

Earlier systems had all used a mechanical linkage driven by a cam on the engine crankshaft (or in some cases the camshaft). The longer the distance from the gun to the propeller over which the linkages had to operate, the more

A stripped Sopwith Snipe Mk 1a forward fuselage, showing one of the Vickers Mk I* guns, CC Type B trigger motors (disconnected), the ammunition belt box and discharge chute for empty cases. (*Courtesy Harry Woodman*)

problems there were with backlash, wear, heating and cooling. Very careful maintenance was required to keep them functioning properly, and malfunctions were common. The use in the CC gear of hydraulic pipes to transmit the pulses, or percussive wave transmissions, permitted more precise control and thereby the highest rate of fire, helped by the fact that two firing signals were sent per propeller revolution. It should be emphasised that this was not a conventional hydraulic system: the liquid in the pipes did not move, but merely transmitted the sonic pulses at very high speed, the ingenious invention of George Constantinesco. It was theoretically capable of sending 2,400 firing impulses per minute to a two-gun installation, except that no gun at that time was capable of firing at such a rate. The first aircraft tests were in August 1916, but it did not go into service until March 1917. There were significant teething problems, but the British persevered, and the CC gear became their standard system until synchronised installations were abandoned in the Second World War. American and Japanese air services also adopted this system towards the end of the First World War, although the USA subsequently developed the Nelson gear which formed the basis for later designs.

The French copied the Fokker gear, appropriately modified for the Vickers gun (the only Allied gun suitable for synchronisation) which entered service in the summer of 1916. A later mechanism was designed by Marc Birkigt (who went on to design the Hispano-Suiza HS 404 cannon). The Italian Revelli could be synchronised, although it was not well suited to it. The Russians briefly used a Lavrov-designed gear to operate a Colt M1895 or Vickers attached to the Sikorsky S-16ser, but this only saw service in the spring of 1916 before being rejected as unreliable. Most other nations used British, French or German systems. The Austro-Hungarians had to develop synchronisation gear suited to work with the Schwarzlose retarded blowback gun. The Zaparka gear fired the gun on every fourth propeller revolution, and the quoted rate of fire dropped from 590 to 380 rpm (M16) or from 880 to 500 rpm (M16A). The mechanism could be relied on only within a band of engine revolutions between 1,000 and 1,600 rpm with the M07/12, and between 600 and 1,600 rpm with the MG 16. This explains the very prominent place given in the cockpit of fighters to a large engine tachometer. The Bernatzik and Daimler gear reduced the rate of fire even more – by 55 per cent in the case of the M16. However, the Daimler gear did have the advantage that the M16 could be safely fired from engine idle to 1,600 revolutions per minute, although the M07/12 was still restricted to a 1,100–1,600 rpm band. At the end of the war the Austro-Hungarian forces decided to standardise on the Priesel system.

As well as mechanical and hydraulic linkages, electrical synchronisation gear was developed in Germany and Austria-Hungary and tried before the end of the war. This used contacts on the propeller hub or shaft to send signals to a solenoid on the gun, which fired the trigger. LVG built forty C.IV planes fitted with a Siemens electrical gear, and the Aviatik company received instructions to fit fifty of their own systems to DFW C.Vs. Such systems were to become much more important in the next great conflict over twenty years later.

Synchronisation was the best solution available at the time to the problem of arming front-engined fighters, but it was not ideal. The gears were complex, and even the CC type required careful maintenance to keep them properly adjusted. When they failed, they sometimes resulted in the pilot shooting off his own propeller. Many Austro-Hungarian fighters were equipped with the Kravics propeller hit indicator, which consisted of electric wiring wrapped around the critical area of the propeller blades, connected to a light in the cockpit by a slip ring on the propeller shaft. If the light went out, the pilot knew the propeller had been hit!

A major contributor to synchronisation problems (and gun reliability generally) was ammunition quality, which tended to be variable during the war. In the *British Handbook of Aircraft Armament*, the notes on the Lewis gun contain the following:

Examination of Ammunition
Every round should be carefully looked over for dents, deepset caps, defective bullets, split cases &c., before it is placed in the magazine.

The best service test applicable to discover defects in shape is to use a spare Lewis gun barrel and drop each round into it in order to see that the cartridge enters freely. The rims should be examined to see that, as far as possible by eye, they are not too thick.

Several cases have been discovered in England of the cartridge containing insufficient or no charge, so that it would be convenient if the N.C.O. or man in charge of guns were able to test the comparative weight of each cartridge with a good one.

If possible U.S. ammunition should not be used as it has been found defective in various respects at this school.

Pilots frequently carried a mallet with which to hammer the loading lever in order to chamber a recalcitrant cartridge. In an attempt to resolve this, the British introduced in 1917 'Green Label' (or 'Green Cross') .303 in ball ammunition specifically for synchronised guns. This was taken from standard production lines, but carefully selected from batches that complied with tighter manufacturing tolerances and gave reliable ignition. This proved successful and was followed up in 1918 by establishing special production lines to make high-quality ammunition for this purpose. This was known as 'Red Label' (also as 'Special for RAF, Red Label', 'Special for RAF' and finally 'Special'), and ball, AP and SPG tracer ammunition were produced.

Synchronisation systems reduced the gun's natural rate of fire; by how much depended on a variety of factors. The first factor was a gun whose trigger mechanism could be controlled separately from the action of the bolt. As we have seen, the Lewis gun did not have this feature, and the initial efforts at synchronisation resulted in an RoF of only 100–150 rpm, less than a quarter of the normal rate. The later Alkan gear managed to increase this to 160–200 rpm, and a more thorough redesign of the firing mechanism by Hazleton did see some limited use, but by then the Vickers had been accepted as standard. The second factor was a precise and reliable synchronising gear. The more accurate it was, the lower were the safety margins required and the greater the number of degrees of the propeller disk available for firing. The third factor was the gun's normal rate of fire: the higher this was, the greater the percentage loss through synchronisation (other things being equal). The final factor was the number of propeller blades: the more there were, the more critical accurate timing became.

The rate of fire of a synchronised gun tended to be rather erratic because it varied with propeller speed. Theoretically, it was possible to achieve an ideal match between the propeller rpm and the gun's natural rate of fire, so that the gun was not slowed down at all. However, such harmony would obviously disappear as soon as the engine slowed down or speeded up. This particular problem was not solved until the adoption of the constant-speed propeller, which was uncommon until the late 1930s.

The effect of synchronisation on the rate of fire can best be explained by describing a simple system like that introduced by Fokker, in which one firing signal was sent to the gun for each rotation of the propeller. If the gun was capable of firing at 500 rounds per minute, then for propeller speeds of up to 500 revolutions per minute the RoF would be the same as the propeller rpm. However, as soon as the propeller exceeded 500 rpm, the gun mechanism could no longer keep up and could then only fire on every other rotation, so the RoF would drop to 250 rpm. It would then accelerate again with increasing propeller speed, but at half the rate, so when the propeller was spinning at 1,000 rpm, the gun would be back to firing at 500 rpm again. Once more, propeller revs faster than this would cause the RoF to drop, but this time only to two-thirds of the full RoF, as it would fire on every third rotation, so it would be achieving 330 rpm. As the propeller continued to accelerate to 1,500 rpm, the gun would be back up to 500 rpm again, and so on. Any quoted figure for synchronised rates of fire could therefore only be an average. It is worth repeating that quoted RoFs for unsynchronised guns were only averages also,

with the actual RoF for different examples of the same type of gun varying quite significantly, depending on age and maintenance. Any one gun might also vary in its rate of fire depending on the ammunition used, on the effect of the low temperatures experienced at high altitude in congealing the gun lubricants and of course on the variable G-forces consequent on manoeuvring.

More advanced systems like the CC and the later German types sent two firing signals per propeller revolution (logical with a two-bladed propeller, in which there would be two firing opportunities per revolution), although possibly at the expense of some reliability in these primitive early systems, as they would have to work twice as fast. In this case, the maximum RoF for our 500 rpm gun would be reached twice as often – at 250, 500, 750, 1,000, 1,250 and 1,500 rpm. A still more sophisticated variation was to use a 'critical sector cam', which instead of just sending a single firing impulse sent a continuous one during the 'safe' period when the propeller blades were out of the way. The effect of this was much less regular, with the gun firing in erratic bursts, but the average RoF was the highest of all.

In the vast majority of cases at this time, the engine drove the propeller directly, so the propeller revs were the same as the engine revs. Rotary engines ran at around 1,200–1,300 rpm, the six-cylinder in-lines favoured by the Germans at 1,200 rpm at the start of the war and 1,400–1,500 rpm by the end, the Hispano-Suiza used in the SPAD at 1,600 rpm, and the Rolls-Royce Falcon V-12 used in the Bristol Fighter at 1,800–2,250 rpm, depending on the version. In the case of geared engines (which saw relatively little use in the First World War, the main fighter example being in some installations of the Hispano-Suiza V-8) it was clearly the propeller rather than engine speed which determined the synchronisation conditions.

Taking all of this information together it becomes possible to understand the different national choices in regulating the gun RoF. With their in-line six-cylinder engines running at 1,400–1,500 rpm, the Germans' Maxim would have had to have been capable of about 800 rpm to take full advantage of a firing impulse every other rotation. It could not do this, so it made sense to adjust it to fire approximately every third rotation and thereby enjoy the benefits of greater reliability of both gun and synchroniser gear and reduced gun heating problems; the Maxim was in fact normally set at around 450 rpm. The introduction in 1917 of the Hazleton gear to the British Vickers enhanced the RoF to 850–900 rpm, which in combination with the fast-acting and more reliable CC gear would fire twice for every three rotations of a rotary engine, or every other rotation with the faster-running V-8 and V-12 engines.

A practical example of the effect of synchronisation is graphically provided by comparative tests held by the USN in 1926/7 of the .30 in M1921 and .50 in M1921, both on a test stand and in synchronised mountings. These also shed some light on the differences between claimed and actual rates of fire, and between different installations of the same gun. The .30 in had a claimed RoF of 1,200 rpm, but proved capable of between 800 and 900 rpm on the test stand. When synchronised, the RoF went down to an average of 730 rpm (a fall of about 15 per cent), with a range of between 667 and 818 rpm for different installations and propeller speeds. The .50 in had a claimed RoF of 600 rpm, and did rather well to achieve between 500 and 700 rpm, depending on the recoil buffer adjustment (although a contemporary British report put this at 400–650 rpm, the difference possibly caused by belt drag when installed), but this fell to an average of 438 rpm when synchronised, varying between 383 and 487 rpm. As the synchronised guns were adjusted for maximum RoF, this represented a reduction of around 37 per cent. It is possible that the heavier firing pin assembly resulted in a longer lock time, which as we have seen is critical to synchronisation.

ENGINE-DRIVEN GUNS

IT OCCURRED TO SOME DESIGNERS THAT IF THE FIRING OF machine guns needed to be physically linked to the propeller, it would be a logical progression, and in principle much simpler, to use engine power to drive the gun. The rate of fire would be directly linked to the engine and thereby the propeller speed, with none of the firing irregularities that accompanied synchronised systems. The most advanced design was developed in Austria-Hungary: this was the Gebauer, a twin-barrelled weapon which was successfully tested (on Aviatik D.I, D.II and D.III) and ordered in quantity, but appears to have been just too late to be used in the First World War, although a D.I armed with a Gebauer is claimed to have seen service with the Hungarian Red Airborne Corps post war. The Gebauer weighed 21 kg and could fire at up to 1,600 rpm. After the war, the Allies destroyed the manufacturing facility but Ferencz Gebauer recreated and developed his design, which went on to see service in two versions with the Hungarian air force in the Second World War.

Engine-driven designs were also produced by several German companies, namely Autogen, Fokker, Siemens-Schuckert and Wollerman; the Infantry Construction Bureau and the Aircraft machine gun Detachment at Döberitz also became involved. Fokker's design (which may actually have been by Lübbe) was also continued and patented post war but not taken further. Another Fokker development was a 12-barrel rotary gun, also externally powered, of which no details except a photograph survive. The Siemens-Schuckert weapon was sufficiently advanced in development

The neat lines of the Gebauer twin-barrel engine-driven gun (foreground) contrast with the bulk of the Gast. (Courtesy MoD Pattern Room)

to be installed in a Fokker D.VII, although the results of this experiment are not known.

In 1921 a Doctor Michaelis of Berlin was offering for sale an AGA motor-driven machine gun. It was of 7.92 mm calibre, and reportedly achieved between 1,000 and 1,200 rpm for a weight of 12 kg. However, with the exception of the Hungarian Gebauers, externally powered aircraft guns never saw service until the introduction of the American Vulcan M61 rotary cannon in the 1950s.

SIGHTS

THE PROVISION OF SUITABLE SIGHTS FOR THE NEWLY installed aircraft guns posed various problems which did not trouble the ground-based versions of the weapons. The operating environment included targets moving in three dimensions, a gun mounting subject to vibration, and little time to aim before firing. On the other hand, ranges were usually much shorter than ground-mounted guns were expected to achieve, so complex range adjustments were not needed. The basic requirement was therefore for sights which were large and clear, giving an unobstructed view, and easy to use.

The usefulness of a high muzzle velocity in reducing the projectile's time of flight has already been mentioned. At long ranges a high velocity also helps by flattening the trajectory, i.e. the curved path, caused by gravity, which the projectile follows through the air. Sights have to be harmonised so that the trajectory coincides with the aiming point of the sight at a particular distance. If the guns are fitted close to the sights this is not a significant problem except at very long range, or with a low-velocity gun which will have a strongly curved trajectory. However, if the guns are mounted some distance from the sights (either out in the wings, or considerably above or below the sights) then shooting at distances other than the harmonisation range will be less accurate.

With flexibly mounted guns, an additional problem arose; firing to one side meant that not only had the target plane moved on by the time the bullets arrived at its location, but this effect was exacerbated by the strong windstream blowing the bullets behind the direction of flight. Some form of compensating sight was therefore desirable.

The first and simplest form of purpose-designed sight for fixed guns was the gate sight, which emerged in 1915 and remained in use well into 1916. This consisted of a basic aiming mark at one end of the gun, and a frame, or gate, at the other. The frame could be adjusted in width to match the expected wingspan of a target aircraft at the preferred firing distance, typically 200 m. The pilot therefore simply had to line up the front and back sights and keep the target within the frame until the wings filled it. One difference in national preferences was that the Germans, who introduced the system, put the frame on the front of the gun and used the weapon's usual rearsight. The British tended to use the frame as the backsight.

The problem with the gate sight was that it gave no help to the pilot in estimating where to aim the sights in order to hit the target. In the case of an attack launched from directly behind the enemy this was no problem, as the pilot could aim straight at it. If the attack came in at an angle, however, the relative movement of the target had to be taken into account and the gun aimed ahead of the target; by how much depended on the angle of attack and the speed of the target. This was known as deflection or 'allowance' shooting. The rather crude solution to this problem was the ring and bead sight.

The bead was the rearsight, used to line up the pilot's head with the weapons. The ring was a metal hoop fixed near the muzzle of the gun, with vertical and horizontal bars forming a cross. At zero deflection (i.e. from directly behind) the pilot merely lined up the bead with the cross. In deflection attacks, the pilot would place the enemy plane on the rim of the hoop, so that the plane's nose was pointing in towards the centre of the cross. This gave a very rough compensation for deflection, but a high degree of pilot skill was required to achieve accuracy.

Optical sights, in the form of telescopes fitted with crosswires to provide an aiming mark, were available for ground guns and were tried in aircraft, but proved generally unsuitable as they had a narrow field of view and the magnification emphasised the vibration. However, in 1916 the British firm of Aldis produced a zero-magnification scope which proved very successful. It looked like a conventional telescope, 80 cm long and 5 cm in diameter, and included sighting elements engraved on glass within it, usually a pair of concentric circles. This arrangement had two benefits; the sighting elements and the target were both in focus simultaneously, and the pilot's head did not need to be precisely located in the centre of the sight, as the engraved markings remained on target even when viewed from a slight angle. The zero magnification dealt with the field of view and vibration problems.

The Aldis became the standard British sight (and was used by the Germans when they could capture them), eventually serving into the 1930s, but work continued to find better solutions. These were fruitless, as attempts, such as the Le Prieur Type A, to provide more sophisticated compensation for deflection were too complicated to use in the heat of battle. One development worth mentioning, however, was the reflector sight. This consisted of a glass screen, angled at 45° to the pilot's line of sight, so that sighting marks could be projected onto it by a bulb from below. This had similar advantages to the Aldis but was much more compact, and

A complex vane sight mounted to a 'stripped' Mk I Lewis, with the rear part of the radiator fins left in place. (Courtesy MoD Pattern Room)

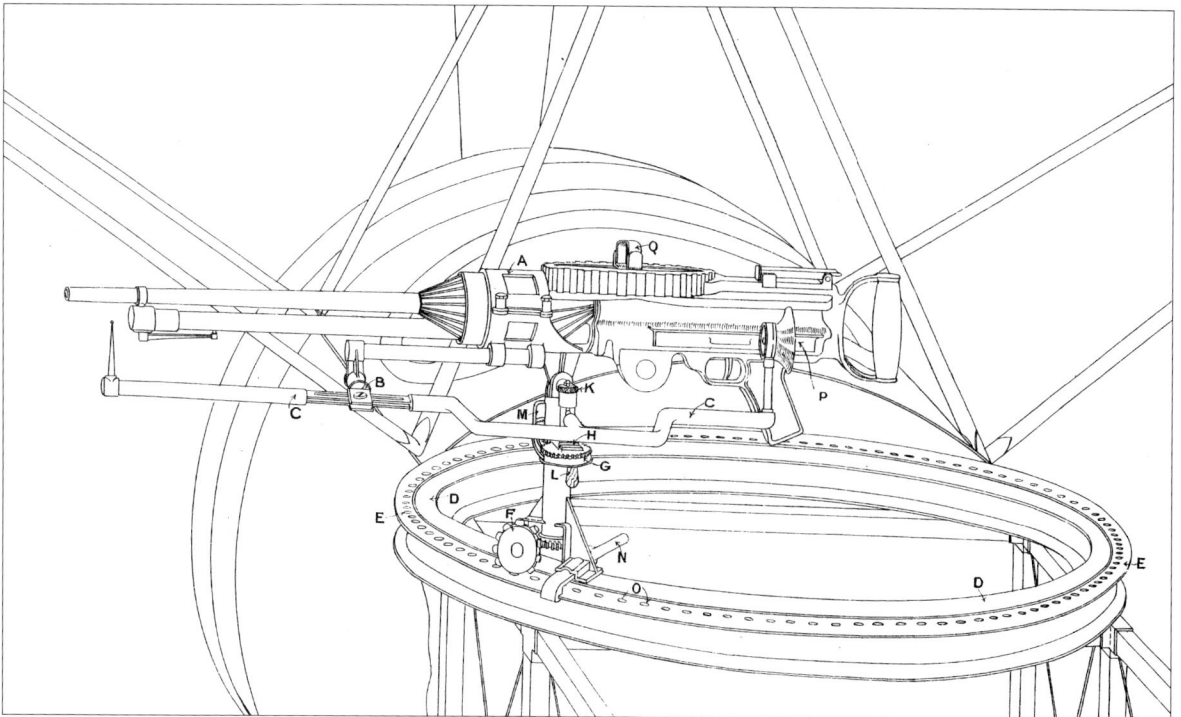

Drawing of a stripped Mk I Lewis on a ring mounting, with a Scarff Compensating Sight. (Courtesy MoD Pattern Room)

the diameter of the sighting ring could more easily be adjusted. The principle governing the reflector sight predated the war and was originally invented for artillery, but in 1918 an aircraft sight was developed by *Optische Anstalt Oigee* in Germany and had reached the field-testing stage by the end of the war, being installed (at least) on an Albatros D.Va and a Fokker Dr.I, as well as on flexibly mounted guns. The reflector sight was to become the most important type for most of the Second World War.

Flexibly mounted guns, in which weight was important, retained the ring and bead type of sight for much of the war, but the British developed modifications to allow for both deflection shooting and the cross-wind problem. These were nearly all variations of the same principle, and were known as vane sights (the original being the Norman Vane Sight, in service in 1917). In this, the rearsight was fixed but the foresight assembly, mounted near the muzzle and therefore out in the airstream, could pivot horizontally like a weather vane. The aiming mark was at the same end of the pivoting arm as the vane, and so the wind, in pushing the vane towards the rear of the plane, simultaneously moved the aiming mark in the same direction. This meant that the gunner had to swing the gun forward in order to line up the sight on the target, thereby automatically aiming ahead of the target aircraft to (it was hoped) the degree required to hit it.

A well-designed vane sight had the benefit of automatically compensating for the angle of fire and the aircraft speed; at higher speeds, the spring-loaded vane was pushed further to one side, while at shallower aiming angles the wind had less effect. The desire to achieve perfect compensation led to vane designs of ever-increasing complexity, but they worked well enough to survive into the Second World War, although curiously they were little used by the Germans.

A smaller version of the Aldis, just 25 mm in diameter, was developed for flexibly mounted guns. The correction needed for firing on the beam was achieved by a special geared mounting which altered the angle between the gun and the sight as the weapon was traversed. However, this could only be set for an average airspeed, as unlike the vane sight it did not automatically compensate for different airspeeds. A similar problem affected the Scarff Compensating Sight. This relied on a system of cogs and levers to move the sight bar. To get the correct angle of compensation, the gunner had to dial in the target's speed, his own speed and the estimated range. But in the heat of combat, this ingenious mechanism was far too complicated to be effectively used.

Finally, the night sights. The night-time Zeppelin raids on Britain prompted a response in the form of night-fighters with appropriate armament (usually incendiary bullets), but it was of course necessary to be able to see the sights in order to aim the guns. This was initially achieved by designing front and rear sights which could be illuminated by small red and green lights respectively, so that lining up the sights aimed the gun; the first of these was invented by A.E. Hutton in 1917. A variation on this, emerging later in the year, was the Neame sight, which was a ring and bead sight in which the foresight consisted of a hollow pillar with a bulb providing a spot of light through a pinhole at the top, while the inner face of the ring was illuminated by another bulb.

Chapter 2

PRE-WAR EXPERIMENTS AND THE
FIRST WORLD WAR

THE FIRST EXPERIMENTS

THE WRIGHT BROTHERS MADE WHAT IT IS GENERALLY recognised as the first manned, powered, sustained and controlled flight by a heavier-than-air aircraft on 17 December 1903. This flight spanned only 36.5 metres and lasted twelve seconds, but the brothers continued to perfect their aircraft, and on 5 October 1905 Wilbur Wright made a remarkable flight of 38 minutes over 39 km. The brothers were quick to understand the military potential of their invention, and entered in negotiation with the US government in January 1905. But their refusal to give demonstrations prior to the signature of a contract, and the great secrecy with which they surrounded their aircraft, encouraged scepticism. They made no flights at all between 16 October 1905 and 6 May 1908.

Meanwhile, progress in Europe had been more or less independent – steady, but slow. Alberto Santos-Dumont made a flight of nearly 60 m in October 1906, the first recognised flight in Europe, and Henry Farman managed a closed-circuit flight of 1 km in January 1908. In that year Wilbur Wright, visiting France with a number of aircraft, would amaze the spectators and silence his critics with flights of 66.5 and 124 km. One of the more notable aspects of the early history of aviation is that, after little progress for five years following the first flight by the Wright brothers in 1903, the world suddenly seemed to wake up to the possibilities of this new form of transport, and the pace of development accelerated rapidly. The centre of aeronautical progress was now shifting to Europe. On 25 July 1909 Louis Blériot (barely) crossed the Channel in his Blériot XI, an event that was recognised by many as indicative of the military value of aircraft. In the same year the first international air race was held, and the first aeroplanes were purchased for military purposes, by the USA and France.

The speed of development can be illustrated by a few European statistics. The longest recorded flight in that continent increased from 1 minute and 28 seconds at the start of

1908 to 2 hours 20 minutes by the end of the year, 4 hrs 20 min in 1909, 8 hrs 12 min in 1910 and more than 24 hours in 1914, with the maximum distance increasing from 1 km to 1,900 km over the same period. The aeroplane speed record went from 44 km/h in 1908 to 77, 109, 125, 170 and 204 km/h over the next five years, while the maximum altitude of 25 m achieved at the beginning of 1908 was increased to 110 m later that year, rising to 453 m in 1909, 3,100 m in 1910, and 7,850 m in 1914. The handful of practical flying machines in 1908 had increased to an estimated 2,000 aeroplanes in the world by 1913.

Perhaps the most remarkable pre-war aeroplanes were the Russian Sikorsky *Grand* of 1913, with four engines and a large enclosed cabin, and its immediate successor, the *Ilya Muromets*, which in February 1914 succeeded in carrying sixteen passengers for five hours at about 100 km/h, reaching an altitude of 2,000 m – a truly astonishing achievement only a few years after the first aeroplane flew in Russia.

The military possibilities of aeroplanes were apparent early on. The British novelist H.G. Wells published *The War in the Air* in 1908, describing future battles between fleets of airships and aeroplanes. Military thinking was not far behind. Armies had long valued the ability of tethered balloons to hoist observers up high enough to spot enemy activity and relay information about the accuracy of artillery fire. The aeroplane promised to extend the scope of such activities right over the enemy army, providing the kind of detailed intelligence which cavalry normally had to fight for.

Despite its slow start the US Army signed a contract for a Wright Model A biplane on 10 February 1908, the first ever contract for a military aircraft. Its flight trials began on 3 September, but it was not purchased until August of the following year. The first shots were fired from an aeroplane in August 1910, when an American soldier, Lt. Jacob Fickerl, fired a Springfield rifle from a Curtiss biplane. And at an airshow in the same year, Glenn Curtiss dropped

First attempts at firing from an aircraft: 1910 Boston-Harvard meet (C.F. Willard and Lt. Fickerl). (Courtesy Philip Jarrett)

dummy bombs. In June 1912 there was a demonstration of Lt.-Col. Lewis's new light machine gun which involved firing it from a Wright Model B at a ground target. The very first aerial combat seems to have taken place in Mexico in 1913, between two US mercenaries flying for different sides in an internal conflict. Both pilots fired pistols at each other until their ammunition ran out, to no effect.

In Britain the War Office had produced its first specification for a military aircraft in September 1908. It did not mention armament, or any military equipment other than maps and field glasses. The British set up an Air Committee in January 1912 to advise on the creation of a 'British Aeronautical Service'. At that time, there were believed to be nineteen aviators in the armed services, in comparison with 263 in France. This was clearly felt to be a serious situation: by April of that year, the Royal Flying Corps was established. During the course of the year, an aircraft selection contest was held at Salisbury Plain, the winner being a Cody biplane. In the Army manoeuvres in the following autumn, aeroplane reconnaissance was used to great effect by one side to win a convincing victory over the other. The losing commander was Lt.-Gen. Sir Douglas Haig, who ever after

US Army's first airborne machine-gun: a Lewis being held by Capt. C. Chandler in a Wright Bros biplane being piloted by Lt. R. Kirtland, on 7–8 June 1912. (Courtesy Philip Jarrett)

had considerable respect for the capabilities of the aeroplane.

The military use of the aeroplane had so far been envisaged primarily as reconnaissance, with some nuisance value being gained by dropping small objects on the enemy. The idea that weapons might be carried aloft to attack enemy aeroplanes did not immediately occur to many in the services; initially, it still seemed miraculous enough that aeroplanes could climb into the sky at all, let alone carry a warload. But it did not take long before some forward thinkers began to consider the possibilities of aeroplanes fighting each other. In 1909, Capt. H.G. Sargeant suggested that the ideal weapon for aircraft to use against airships or other aircraft would be a small-calibre cannon firing explosive shells with very sensitive fuses. Col. Capper of the Royal Engineers, which established an Air Battalion on 1 April 1911, had predicted in this year that if it was worth using aeroplanes to gather valuable intelligence, it would be equally worth trying to stop enemy aeroplanes from operating. In July 1912 a Vickers machine gun was fired from a British F.E.2. The officer who had defeated Gen. Haig in the 1912 manoeuvres, Gen. Grierson, foresaw the same future, as he stated in 1913: '... there is no doubt that before land fighting takes place, we shall have to fight the enemy's aircraft... Warfare will be impossible unless we have mastery of the air.'

The Admiralty was the first to issue a specification for an armed aircraft, when it signed a contract with Vickers in November 1912 to build a fighting biplane. The Vickers EFB.1 (Experimental Fighting Biplane No. 1), proudly named *Destroyer*, had a belt-fed Vickers gun installed in the nose, and was claimed to carry a generous 1,500 rounds of ammunition. It was shown at the Olympia Aero Show in London in February 1913, but never flew, being destroyed on its first attempted take-off. But Vickers persevered and produced the EFB.2 and EFB.3. These were refined and more powerful, two-seat pusher aircraft in which the gunner sat in front.

Different types of gun mountings were designed for this and the succeeding experimental machines, by the Admiralty as well as Vickers. The initial Admiralty mounting had the gun and gunner at each end of a curved cradle (rather like a see-saw) which could rock up and down to assist with aiming at different elevations. The Vickers design arranged for the gun to protrude through the nose, the opening being covered by a hemispherical shield attached to the gun, which moved with it in traverse and elevation. But this proved very impractical, as the gun was too far forward and too far below a comfortable line of sight of the gunner to be accurately aimed. This soon gave way to a simplified and more effective nacelle, in which the gun (still a Vickers) was raised towards the gunner on a faired pillar mounting.

Early in 1913, Maj. Sykes of the Military Wing of the RFC was calling for 'a two-seater fighting machine to carry a gun, ammunition, light armour and petrol for 200 miles', and a Grahame-White '1913 War Plane (Type 6)' was exhibited with a Colt-Browning Model 1895 mounted on a pillar. The British War Office published specifications for five categories of military aircraft in February 1914, following pressure from manufacturers who wanted to be able to compete with the Royal Aircraft Factory. Two of these, a single-seat Light Scout and a two-seat Reconnaissance Aeroplane, were to be unarmed. The three others, an armed Reconnaissance Aeroplane and two categories of Fighting Aeroplane, were to carry a pilot and a gunner. Fixed guns were not yet envisaged, and instead the specification demanded a clear field of fire up to 30 degrees from the line of flight.

In France, the Artillery selected a spotting aeroplane in 1909, and aircraft participated in manoeuvres in 1910, when the French Army established a *Service Aéronautique* and Lt. Féquant made the first photographic reconnaissance flight. Also in 1910, a Voisin with a Hotchkiss machine gun was displayed in Paris. By 1911 the French had over 200 aeroplanes available for their annual Army manoeuvres, demonstrating close liaison with the Artillery. In September of the same year, in the war between Italy and Turkey in Tripoli (Libya), four Italian officers made an average of seventy-eight reconnaissance and observation flights each, during which grenades were dropped (to little effect) and an airman was wounded by ground fire. Bombing contests were a frequent part of airshows in those days, and in 1912 the French instituted the Michelin Prize for bombing accuracy. The French and Spanish also used aeroplanes in North Africa, again dropping grenades, bombs and steel darts called '*flechettes*'. In 1913 the French sold six aeroplanes, equipped with Hotchkiss machine guns, to Romania. Defence was also being considered: the French were interested in armoured aircraft and in 1914 displayed three different models armoured against ground fire, but aircraft performance was inadequate to sustain the weight.

Initial German interest was mainly focused on the potential of dirigible airships, particularly the famous Zeppelins, and they were relatively slow to adopt aeroplanes. Zeppelin's LZ-4, his first really successful model, first flew in 1908 (the first of the wooden-framed Schütte-Lanz following in 1912), and for some years thereafter such airships had vastly superior endurance, range, altitude and load-carrying capabilities than the biggest aeroplanes. The German Delag company operated Zeppelin services between various German cities, carrying 34,000 passengers between 1910 and 1914.

As a result of this activity, German airships at first seemed to be a much bigger threat than aeroplanes. As early as 1912, concern was being expressed in both France and

Britain about the potential war-fighting capabilities of these huge craft, in which Germany held a massive technical lead. In manoeuvres held in that year, the French identified the aeroplane as having the capability of attacking airships, and in 1913 the Guerre 'incendiary arrow', a hooked, benzine-filled dart weighing around 1 kg, was developed specifically for that purpose. The British were contemplating 'sweeping' for airships using aeroplanes to tow bombs on the end of long wires.

However, the military use of aircraft was also investigated in Germany. In August 1912 the German *Aeroplanturnier*, held in Gotha, included bombing exercises and simulated attacks on airships.

In 1911, Ernst Euler patented an arrangement for a fixed machine gun on an aircraft. Euler's invention assumed a pusher design with a front-mounted elevator, and the machine gun was to be mounted low in the fuselage to clear the elevator. In 1912 August Euler had installed a machine gun in a pusher biplane for a demonstration to the authorities. In 1915 this had evolved in a single-seat pusher fighter, nicknamed *Gelber Hund* (yellow dog) and armed with an MG 08/15 in the nose. The aircraft was not accepted for service. Euler also developed a two-seat version of the same aircraft, with a gunner in the nose of an elongated nacelle, operating a Bergmann MG 15nA machine gun. This prototype was subsequently converted to have the pilot in front and a fixed Bergmann in the nose. At the same time the gunner behind him was raised to the top of a high streamlined pulpit, which spanned the gap between the wings and thus allowed him to fire rearwards, over the pusher propeller, with a single MG 14. This type failed to attract orders.

In 1914 Otto Schwade completed a small single-seat pusher aircraft, known as the *Kampfeinsitzer Nr.1*, with a Bergmann MG 15nA machine gun in the nose. But the development of this aircraft was quickly abandoned in favour of the *Kampfeinsitzer Nr.2*, still a pusher biplane and already obsolete when it appeared in late 1915.

Despite German emphasis on airships, their categories of aircraft proposed in March 1914 included a 'Type III' (intended for development in 1915 or 1916) which called for a 200 hp (and therefore twin-engined) three-man biplane equipped with machine guns to attack ground targets. This specification led to the development of the Gotha bombers.

The first attack by aircraft on naval vessels was made in 1913, when Greek aircraft unsuccessfully dropped small bombs in an attempt to hit Turkish warships in the Dardanelles during the First Balkan War.

By the beginning of the First World War in August 1914, Germany was able to mobilise 180 aeroplanes and twelve airships, France 136 planes and six airships, the Royal Flying Corps had 179 planes and the Royal Naval Air Service

(which had split off from the Army's RFC in July of that year) had 91. Russia boasted no less than 244 aeroplanes and fourteen airships, but Austria-Hungary had only 48. At that time, the US Army had just 23 military aeroplanes.

HAVE GUN, WILL FLY

Plenty of experience had clearly been gathered before the war in firing a variety of guns from aeroplanes. In the initial fighting, however, this had no place in senior military thinking, and planes were mainly restricted to the reconnaissance and observation roles, in which they soon showed their value, with occasional forays into bombing. A German *Taube* (ironically meaning 'dove') aeroplane bombed Paris at the end of August 1914, and Dover in October. The French formed the first bombing squadron, the *Groupe de Bombardment No. 1* (G.B.1) equipped with Voisin pushers, later in the same year. Despite this, it was not long before airmen of both sides started taking pot-shots at each other when the opportunity arose.

In these early encounters, a range of impromptu weapons was used. Strictly speaking, they were not aircraft armament but aircrew armament, as they were not fitted to the aeroplane but carried and held by their users. In the early months of World War One handguns achieved some popularity, particularly the early self-loading weapons such as the German Mauser C96 and P08 (Luger), the Italian Glisenti and the British Webley & Scott. These were very handy for an observer or even a pilot to use, and could fire several shots in quick succession. However, the low muzzle velocity and relatively light bullets meant that their range was very short and they were incapable of inflicting much damage. To bring down an enemy aircraft they really had to hit the pilot, but handguns are notoriously difficult to aim accurately, even on the ground against stationary targets.

Despite this, the first official victory of the RFC was scored on 25 August 1914, when three B.E.2as of No. 2 Sqdn forced a *Taube* to land after chasing it and, reportedly, firing at it with pistols (which probably failed to do any damage). The Germans landed safely, but the RFC pilots followed them down and burned their aircraft.

A few airmen took shotguns aloft. These had the merit of firing a spreading pattern of shot, greatly increasing the chance of hitting something, but the pellets were generally small and lost velocity quickly, so the effective range was very short. Most shotguns were also capable of only two shots before needing reloading. As we have seen, the British devised some special-purpose ammunition for their shotguns, including incendiary bullets and chain-shot.

The standard infantry rifle saw some early use. It was much more powerful than a pistol or shotgun, firing a relatively heavy bullet at a high muzzle velocity. It was capable of inflicting far more damage to aircraft structures and

First attempts at air weapons: Swiss Karabiner 11 in Blériot monoplane. (Courtesy Verlag Stocker-Schmid, Dietikon-Zürich)

Some of the cartridges used in hand-held weapons: the .455 in revolver, 9 × 19 P08, 7.63 × 24 Mauser C96, .351 in Winchester SL and .401 in SL.

systems and was also an inherently more accurate weapon to use. However, it was long and unwieldy to handle and slow to reload, as it was necessary to operate the action manually between shots. Shortened carbine versions, originally developed for cavalry, proved easier to handle in the cramped confines of a cockpit, but the other problems remained.

The particular requirements of aerial fighting led to the use of some unusual small arms which saw little employment in other fields of warfare. One of these was a throwback to the days of the American Wild West – the lever-action carbine made famous by Winchester. These guns were typically short and handy and could carry up to ten rounds of ammunition. They could be reloaded between shots much more quickly than the military bolt-action rifles, but most of them only fired low-velocity pistol ammunition. Versions were available for rifle ammunition, such as the .45-90 described in the first chapter, but these were proportionately longer and heavier and carried less ammunition.

More significant in the development of aircraft armament were various types of self-loading carbines and rifles; the user still had to press the trigger for each shot, but a much higher rate of accurate fire could be maintained. Some of these were simply carbine versions of the Mauser and

Two views of a Hotchkiss on a Deperdussin monoplane, mounted to fire over the propeller – not the most comfortable of firing positions. (Courtesy Philip Jarrett)

An early attempt to fit a Lewis gun to fire over the propeller of a Caproni Ca.20. (Courtesy David Griffin)

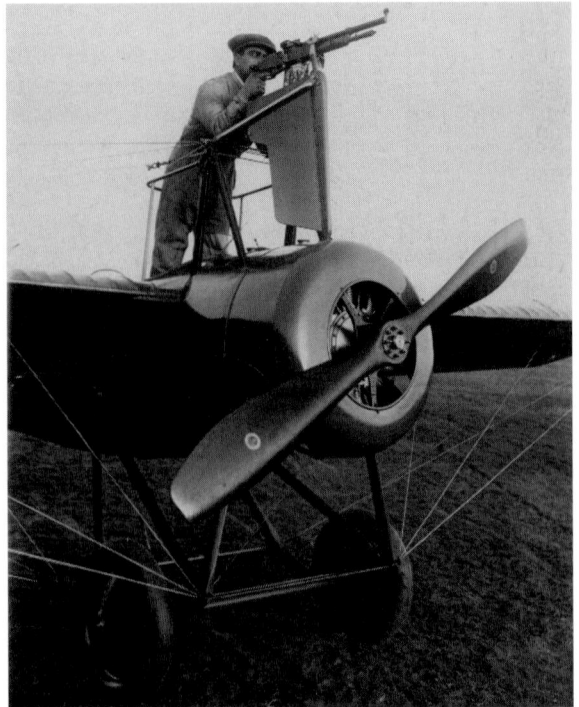

Luger pistols already mentioned. Fitted with longer barrels and shoulder stocks, they were far more accurate to use but still relatively ineffective. Others were civilian weapons firing medium-velocity ammunition, as made by Winchester in calibres .351 and .401 SL and used by France.

More important still were the purpose-built military self-loading rifles. These did not come into general military use until the Garand rifle was adopted by the US Army just before World War Two, but were in fact developed before World War One. They saw very little use in that conflict, partly because they were complex and expensive to make, partly because their relatively delicate mechanisms were poorly suited to the mud and dust of trench warfare. Such problems were of no concern to aviators, and these weapons were acquired and issued accordingly.

The German air force made most use of these, at first using the Mauser *Selbtslade-Gewehr Modell 15*, a short-recoil gun based on the pre-war C06 and C08 models. This used a ten- or twenty-round detachable box magazine, but it proved unreliable and was rapidly replaced by the Mexican Mondragon rifle in 7×57 calibre (as used by the Mexican Army) obtained from Switzerland where they were being made. The gun, which was gas operated, was available with a thirty-round drum magazine and was known as the *Flieger-Selbstladekarabiner Modell 1915* (FSK15), or air-man's self-loading carbine. However, this also proved unreliable and saw little use. The RNAS used the gas-operated Farquhar-Hill automatic rifle.

However, all of these were ungainly in use and hardly worth the effort of carrying aloft. It might be supposed that the carrying of such aircrew weapons ceased once suitable machine gun mountings became available, but in fact they were sometimes carried as auxiliary weapons late into the war.

LET THE ARMAMENT BEGIN

Early in the war, it became evident that it was not at all easy to shoot down one aeroplane from another, and two lessons were drawn. One was the desirability of using a machine gun in order to achieve the highest possible rate of fire. The other was the need to fit the gun to the aircraft in order to provide a steady mounting for more accurate aiming, rather than relying on the observer to hold the weapon; in the case of most machine guns, there was little choice in this as they were far too heavy to be fired without support anyway. Despite this, a few light machine guns were carried unmounted, such as the infamous French Chauchat in the Voisin 3.

Louis Strange of the RFC was one of the first in the conflict to fit a machine gun, a Lewis, to a Henri Farman plane, shortly after the war began. However, the extra weight prevented him from catching any enemy aircraft, and so the gun

was removed. A few aviators tried to install machine guns on tractor monoplanes. The weapon was supported by the tall 'cabane' struts that support the wire bracing of the wings, and if the gunner stood in his cockpit, he could fire over the propeller. Two Deperdussin TT monoplanes were delivered with such armament, but saw no combat. In Italy, a single Caproni Ca.20 was equipped in this way and was later claimed to have been the world's first fighter, but that saw no service either. Another pioneer of aircraft armament was Gabriel Voisin, the designer of a series of aircraft with push-er engines. His initial enthusiasm was for mounting large cannon, as described in Chapter 3, but although the military evaluated the type they preferred to place orders for the standard Voisin model 1913, powered by a 70 hp engine and, at least initially, unarmed. This changed in August 1914, when Voisin (inspired and supported by Capt. Faure) designed a tripod gun mount for the 8 mm Hotchkiss machine gun. In the Voisin 1913 the observer sat behind the pilot, so the gun was installed above the pilot's head; the observer had to raise from his seat to operate it. Six aircraft of Faure's escadrille V 24 were equipped in this way, but probably saw no combat.

The replacement was the 120 hp Voisin 3, with a redesigned all-metal fuselage, but an identical crew arrange-ment. On 5 October 1914 Joseph Frantz and Louis Quénault scored the first recorded air-fighting victory with a machine gun, by using an 8 mm Hotchkiss M1909 to shoot down a German Aviatik reconnaissance aircraft near Reims. This feat was followed on 22 November by the RFC, when anoth-er Aviatik was forced down by fire from a Lewis gun fitted to an Avro 504.

Even when the need to fit machine guns was accepted, it was still generally envisaged that aiming and firing would be the job of the observer, or gunner, not the pilot. The guns were therefore fitted into mountings that enabled them to swing as freely as possible in both traverse (horizontally) and elevation (vertically). As described in the previous chapter, simple pintle, pillar, column or spigot mountings were tried until the ring-type mounting was developed. The ring could rotate, enabling all-round traverse.

Achieving a decent field of fire for the observer was less easy. The tradition in most two-seater aeroplanes early in the war was to site the pilot (who in many cases was just the chauffeur) behind the observer, who was often in command. However, in most biplane designs this put the observer in between the wings, surrounded by wings, struts and bracing wires. Firing from this position was extremely difficult. The first solution to this problem was the 'pusher' aeroplane, in which the engine was placed behind the aviators. This meant that the observer was right at the front of the plane, with an unobstructed field of view (and fire) forwards, upwards and to each side. The first to make use of this layout to mount a

Vickers F.B.5 with Lewis gun. (RAF Hendon)

machine gun was the Vickers F.B.5 (the F.B. standing for Fighting Biplane), which became popularly but unofficially known as the 'Gunbus'.

The ancestor of the F.B.5 was the EFB.1 already described, which led to various experimental machine gun mountings. The F.B.5 eventually emerged with a simple mounting, fitted just above the nose fairing, and at the outbreak of war a number of these aircraft were in experimental service with both the RNAS and the RFC. When war broke out, more orders for small batches followed.

The Vickers RCMG proved something of a handful to operate, and after a few examples had been built (and seen action) the much lighter and handier Lewis gun was fitted instead. One of these aircraft tried to intercept a German Friedrichshafen FF22 seaplane flying up the Thames estuary towards London on Christmas Day 1914, but although the German was sufficiently alarmed to drop his bomb on Kent and retreat, the Lewis gun jammed, so a potentially historic battle did not occur.

Early in 1915 production F.B.5s began to arrive in France, and in July there were enough to equip an entire squadron. Some F.B.5s carried two Lewis guns, but the time-consuming development of a practical gun mounting was of far greater importance.

A number of F.B.5s were also built in France and Denmark (the latter were usually equipped with Madsen machine guns), but the type was already obsolescent, for the Fokker E fighters with their fixed armament were making their appearance. The slightly improved F.B.9 – still fitted with a gun mounting described as 'quite useless' in reports – appeared in 1916, but after a fairly short combat career it was relegated to training. In this role, many at last received Scarff ring mounts for their machine guns.

Work continued on the gun installations, and G.H. Challenger designed the first of the ring-type mountings, which emerged in the early summer of 1915. This was further refined to include a complex spring-type balancing system, but it was eventually replaced in British service by the Scarff type, which was introduced in 1916 and became the standard ring mounting thereafter.

The French Voisin and Farman pusher aircraft also enjoyed the important advantage that their forward-firing guns were more suitable for offensive tactics, but they had too low a performance to be good fighting machines, owing to the increased drag of the structure supporting the tail, and they could not be given an effective defence towards the rear. Some use was made of tall Étévé mounts to enable

Lewis Mk I on a Vickers-Challenger barbette in the nose of the prototype Vickers F.B.9. (Courtesy Harry Woodman)

the gunner to fire over the rear propeller.

At the time most German aircraft were of tractor design, with the engine in front and the observer sitting in front of the pilot. This made it very difficult to install armament. Early experiments with an Aviatik B.I added a machine gun and two tall pillar mounts, one at the left front and one at right rear of the observer's cockpit. To use the machine gun, the observer had to climb out of his seat and kneel on a platform. From this precarious position, he had not only to fire the gun but also to move it between the two posts.

Germany first came up with what now appears to be the obvious solution to the problem of defending two-seaters: put the pilot in the front cockpit of a tractor plane, allowing the observer to face rearwards, with an excellent field of fire covering the main directions of attack; above, behind and to each side (although not, in most cases, from below). The C type, armed with a Parabellum MG, was introduced in the summer of 1915 and established the classic two-seat single-engined biplane layout which endured until the late 1930s.

Other early experiments involved the French Nieuport

Two Hotchkiss guns: a strip-fed one for the pilot on a pillar mounting, and a bobine-fed gun on an Étévé ring mount for the observer. (Courtesy Harry Woodman)

10, a nimble two-seat sesquiplane (a biplane with a small lower wing) which came in different versions, with the pilot in the front or rear cockpit. This allowed a lot of variations in the installation of machine guns. On aircraft with the observer in front, a rear-firing gun could still be installed on

The problems of shooting from the observer's forward position in a B.E.2. (Courtesy Philip Jarrett)

a tall Étévé mount, but if the observer was in the rear seat a more conventional rearward-firing mount would be adopted. A very successful alternative was to fix a machine gun on the upper wing, angled slightly up to clear the propeller. The type had originally been intended as a reconnaissance aircraft, but in the autumn of 1915 it was increasingly employed as a fighter. In August 1915 two were assigned to the first French fighter unit, the *Groupe de Combat de Malzéville*, which also had a number of Caudron G.4s.

But the Nieuport was underpowered with a 80 hp engine, and the observer had to stand up to fire the machine gun; this was not only uncomfortable but also destabilised the aircraft. The solution was to operate the type as a single-seater with the observer's position faired over; and the addition of a Bowden cable to fire the machine gun turned the nimble Nieuport into a practical fighter.

In RNAS service some were equipped with a Lewis gun that was aimed sharply up through a hole in the upper wing, so that the ammunition pan and breech were within reach of the pilot.

Perhaps the most bizarre attempt to combine the virtues of the tractor layout with a forward gun position was the SPAD SA.2 of 1915, which housed the gunner with his

An unusual arrangement of guns on an AEG C.II in late 1915/early 1916. The upper gun is an MG 14 Parabellum, the flexibly mounted gun (on an AEG mounting) an LMG 08 with a stock and pistol grip. These weapons would typically be installed the other way round. (Courtesy Harry Woodman)

flexibly mounted gun in a 'pulpit' mounted ahead of the propeller. The pulpit was mainly held in place by struts running up from the undercarriage, and was inclined to become detached from the aircraft in adverse circumstances. Despite the obvious problems, 100 of these planes were constructed. A SPAD SG was tried with a fixed Hotchkiss in an

Lewis Mk I, with sawn-off butt and on a flexible mounting, in the nose of a Spad A2 in Russian service. (*Courtesy Harry Woodman*)

unmanned pulpit, and the Russians modified at least one SA to have three fixed guns. The British B.E.9 (a much modified B.E.2c) was also fitted with a pulpit, but fortunately only one was built.

Before examining later developments, it is appropriate to describe the official designators for the different classes of military aircraft used by the major powers in the conflict. The British used just four: B.E. for 'British Experimental' (originally 'Blériot Experimental'; pre-war tractor designs), F.E. for 'Fighting Experimental' (originally 'Farman Experimental'; all pusher designs), R.E. for 'Reconnaissance Experimental' (two-seaters) and S.E. for 'Scout Experimental' (single-seat tractor designs). These codes only applied to aircraft produced by the government-owned Royal Aircraft Factory (R.A.F.); other manufacturers invented their own designations.

The French codes included A for army co-operation including reconnaissance and artillery spotting, B for bombers (*bombardement*), C for fighters (*chasse*), and Ca for *canon* – aircraft equipped with large-calibre weapons, generally of 37 mm. The Germans had the most comprehensive list of categories, including A and B for early monoplanes and biplanes respectively, C for single-engined armed two-seaters, CL for lighter versions of these, D for biplane fighters (*Doppeldecker*), E for monoplane fighters (*Eindecker*), F for triplanes (later known as Dr for *Dreidecker*), G for large twin-engined bombers

(*Grossflugzeug*), J for armoured ground-attack planes, R for giant bombers (*Riesenflugzeug*) and W for seaplanes and flying-boats (*Wasserflugzeug*).

THE FIRST FIGHTERS

The performance disadvantage suffered by aircraft with pusher layouts prompted some pilots to find ways of mounting a gun on a single-seat, tractor-engined scout aeroplane. One of the first in the field was the persistent Louis Strange of No. 1 Squadron, RFC. He was the first to mount a machine gun – a Lewis – on top of a biplane's upper wing (in this case a Martinsyde S.1 Scout) fixed to fire directly forwards over the top of the propeller.

The early aircraft versions of the Lewis had only a 47-round drum (a double-stacked 97-round drum was introduced in 1916) which meant that the magazine had to be changed fairly often. In this first attempt at a top-wing mounting, this could only be achieved by the pilot undoing his seat belt, standing up in the cockpit and reaching up to unlatch and exchange the magazine. This process led to perhaps the most famous single incident involving aircraft guns in the entire war: while Strange was struggling to persuade a recalcitrant magazine to come off the gun, he lost control of his aeroplane, which promptly turned upside down, leaving the hapless pilot dangling underneath the plane, hanging on only by his grip on the magazine. Fortunately the magazine remained obstinately attached, and Strange managed to regain his seat and control of his aeroplane. He returned to earth safe and well, but presumably somewhat older than when he took off!

An alternative approach was tried by Maj. Lanoe Hawker of No. 6 Squadron, RFC, who fixed a Lewis gun to the fuselage of his Bristol Scout, angled to fire outwards in order to miss the propeller disk (one of many installations tried with this aircraft). This had the advantage of putting the gun within easy reach for changing magazines, but the disadvantage that aiming a fixed gun pointing in one direction while the aeroplane was travelling in another was a task beyond the capabilities of most pilots. However, Hawker was an outstanding pilot and shot down three aircraft on one day – 25 July 1915 – using this equipment.

It was the Frenchman Roland Garros who first fixed a machine gun to the engine cowling, directly in front of the pilot, clearly the best location both for reloading and for clearing any jams. The vexed question of how to avoid shooting off the propeller was addressed by the simple expedient of fitting steel wedges to the propeller blades, placed to intercept and deflect any bullets which might otherwise have struck the propeller.

The first aircraft so fitted was a Morane Type N 'Bullet', one of the sleek Morane-Saulnier monoplanes, which had a Hotchkiss *Aviation* installed. This was damaged before it could see action, and so the gun was transferred to a Morane Type L, with which on 1 April 1915 Garros shot down a German two-seater. This was followed by two more kills ten days later, but his success was short-lived, as on 19 April he was forced to land behind enemy lines.

The capture of the Morane caused great interest in Germany, and Anthony Fokker was asked to develop a similar device. However, under his direction a better solution was found in the first synchronisation gear to see service. The development of this gear was described in the previous chapter, so it will suffice to say that within a few days Fokker

put on a demonstration of an M.5 monoplane fitted with a synchronised Parabellum machine gun. (This aircraft was retrospectively known as the M.5K, and the armed version as the M.5K/MG). He was awarded an order for thirty aircraft, which received the designation Fokker E.I. It was to be several months, however, before the new fighter entered service in significant numbers, an event which was further delayed by a spate of synchroniser failures, causing the aeroplanes to shoot off their own propellers. A captured propeller with deflector wedges was tested in Germany, but failed because of the better armour penetration of the steel-jacketed German bullets.

Although the first victory scored by the new Fokker was by Kurt Wintgens on 1 July 1915, the beginning of what became known as the 'Fokker Scourge' is generally dated to 1 August, when Max Immelmann scored his first victory – a B.E.2c – followed shortly afterwards by Oswald Boelcke, his fellow pilot in *Feldfliegerabteilung* 62. By October, both had eight kills and the little Fokkers had begun to establish a four-to-one kill ratio over their enemies. The combination of the E.I and the new C-type two-seaters established a clear German superiority in air fighting which lasted for many months.

The great impact of the Fokker monoplanes was almost exclusively because of their revolutionary armament. The Fokker was not a great aircraft, and the reliability of aircraft, engine and gun installation left much to be desired. Fokker delivered only 54 E.Is, twelve E.IIs, 282 E.IIIs and 49 E.IVs. Because of slow deliveries and the inevitable losses, the number of operational aircraft at the end of 1915 was only about forty. They were flown by pilots who had to invent tactics and organisations for the new fighter, the first of its kind. The air force was well aware that the limitations of the Fokker E series would make their period of superiority short, and while they were being introduced into service it was already calling for better fighters, most of them

The Fokker E.III, showing the MG08 mounted over the engine.

biplanes with in-line liquid-cooled engines.

The synchronisation gear was still primitive and unreliable. The lubricant of the machine guns congealed in the cold air at altitude; the fabric ammunition belts absorbed moisture and froze. The varying quality of the ammunition was also a headache. Successful pilots took meticulous care of their equipment, checked every single cartridge before it was loaded in their ammunition belts, and devoted a lot of time to target practice. In a report on fighter tactics dated April 1918, Manfred von Richthofen put more emphasis on familiarity with the machine gun and shooting ability than on the skill of flying:

> *The main thing for a fighter pilot is the machine gun. He has to master it so that he recognises the cause of a gun jam. When I come back home with a jammed gun, usually I can tell the mechanics precisely what is the matter with it...*
>
> *I attach little significant value to the skill of flying itself. I shot down my first 20 when I still had the greatest difficulties with flying itself...*
>
> *I insist on target practice in flight and at high altitude in tight turns and at full throttle.*

A curious feature of the Fokker E-series was that they were delivered without normal gunsights. Instead, an adjustable head support was fitted, to bring the pilot's head to the correct position for aiming. Most pictures of the aircraft show what pilots thought about this feature: the headrests were removed and sights, of the frame and bead or ring and bead type, were installed.

The E.IV initially featured a three-gun installation tilted 15 degrees up, but the synchronisation mechanism often failed to function properly with three guns, and Fokker himself was embarrassed when he destroyed several propellers during demonstrations. The type usually flew with only two guns and with guns firing directly ahead. Overall the E.IV was a disappointment, inferior to recent Entente fighters despite the increase in firepower and a 160 hp two-row rotary engine. The period of Fokker superiority had passed.

DEVELOPING THE FIGHTER

THE ALLIES WERE NOT SLOW TO RESPOND TO THE GROWING crisis of German superiority, but the initial tools to hand were makeshift affairs. The RFC's Vickers F.B.5 Gunbus, already described, was no match for the Fokker, but this was followed in the summer of 1915 by the much better F.E.2b, which had the same two-seat pusher layout but much improved performance (further improved in 1916 with the much more powerful F.E.2d). The problem of the rear 'blind spot' was tackled in this aircraft by fitting a second flexibly mounted Lewis gun on the top wing, pointing to the rear;

First World War MG cartridges: Italian Revelli (6.5 × 52), Greek Mannlicher for Schwarzlose (6.5 × 54), 7.62 mm Russian (7.62 × 54R), American .30-06 (7.62 × 63), British .303 in (7.7 × 56R), 7.9 mm German (7.92 × 57), 8 mm French (8 × 50R Lebel), 8 mm Austrian for Schwarzlose (8 × 50R Mannlicher), Gras-Vickers (11 × 59R), 9 mm Glisenti for Villar Perosa (9 × 19).

French frontline units when the Fokkers made their dramatic appearance, because it was dangerous to fly. The aircraft were nevertheless taken over and flown by the RFC. A development with a 110 hp engine, the Type I, had a synchronised Vickers gun, but saw little service.

An alternative approach was used by the Airco D.H.2 fighter, designed by Geoffrey de Havilland. This adopted a pusher layout but with only one crew-member – the pilot – and with a Lewis gun mounted to fire forwards, fed initially by 47-round and later by 97-round drums. The gun was installed on a flexible mounting, however, clearly an impractical situation as the pilot could not be expected to fly with one hand and accurately aim with the other. Some pilots fixed the gun, but this met with official disapproval. The compromise was a spring clip that allowed the gun to be used as a fixed weapon without permanently fixing it. In this case, the relatively poor performance of pusher aircraft didn't matter much as the Fokker E.I was itself a low-powered and slow machine, so the little de Havilland, which entered service in February 1916, was able to compete on equal terms. The F.E.8 which followed it into service in August had a similar configuration, but by then there were better designs emerging.

The French used a mixture of two-seat Nieuport 10 (with a gun for the observer) and the little single-seat Nieuport 11 *Bébé*, which initially had a Hotchkiss with only 25 rounds,

Lewis Mk II on an F.E.2, with a Norman vane sight and collector bag, mounted on the goose-neck extension tube in the Anderson arch No. 10 Mk I mounting. The shoulder stock enabled the gun to be aimed more easily. (Courtesy Harry Woodman)

the gunner had to stand in his front cockpit and turn around in order to operate it. The pilot also had a couple of sockets for mounting a Lewis, one on each side of the cockpit.

Despite the pre-war patents, it was some time before the Allies fielded their own synchronised mountings. A contributory factor to this delay may have been the care with which the Germans guarded their secret; the E.I was not allowed to stray over Allied lines, and the first one was not captured until April 1916, nine months after the type entered combat.

The Entente powers attempted to counter the 'Fokker Scourge' in a number of ways. The closest equivalent was the Morane-Saulnier N 'Bullet', fitted with bullet deflectors on the propellers and armed with a Lewis or Vickers machine gun. The type was already being retired from

Details of a Lewis gun on a de Havilland No. 4 Mk I pillar mounting used in the D.H.2. The gun was often fixed in place. (Courtesy Harry Woodman)

For that over-the-shoulder shot: a Martinsyde Elephant in 1917. Note the Aldis sight and the handle for pulling down the Foster-mounted top-wing Lewis. (Courtesy Philip Jarrett)

Lewis gun on a French Moreau mounting, fitted to an RNAS Nieuport Type 11 in 1916. (Courtesy Harry Woodman)

and later a Lewis gun with a 47-round drum, mounted above the top wing as pioneered by Lt. Strange. The gun could be tilted backwards to replace the ammunition drums, but its position high above the pilot's head created some aiming problems and the recoil also affected aiming. The *Bébé*, which entered service in January 1916, proved the best answer to the Fokker *Eindecker*. More significantly, these aircraft were grouped into similar squadrons to counter the Fokker E.I units. A more powerful version, the Nieuport 16, was equipped with Alkan synchronisation gear when this became available.

The Nieuport 16 led to the 17, which had a larger wing and entered service in the middle of 1916. At last a synchronised Vickers, fed by a fabric belt, became the standard armament, although single or twin Lewis guns were fitted on the upper wings of some aircraft. The RNAS and RFC purchased a number of Nieuport 16s and 17s, considered far superior to the D.H.2, and the RNAS routinely equipped its aircraft with Lewis guns on Foster mounts instead of synchronised Vickers guns (possibly owing to concern about the reliability of early synchronisation gears).

The British also retained the top-wing mounting for a Lewis gun in aircraft such as the Bristol Scout and Martinsyde G.100 'Elephant', which also had a rear-firing

Sopwith 1½-Strutter, with Lewis gun for the observer and a Vickers on the cowling. (*RAF Hendon*)

gun for the pilot behind the cockpit. Later versions of this mounting, such as the Foster, which became the British standard, added the ability to pull the gun downwards towards the pilot to facilitate magazine changes and clearing jams. This incidentally also provided the option of firing upwards if required. However, it was difficult to replace the magazine against the force of the wind and even harder to push the gun back into position again.

A number of alternative approaches to aircraft armament were tested, mostly by individualistic designers. A curious solution was provided by the Mann & Grimmer M.1, flown in February 1915. This superficially looked like a conventional tractor monoplane, but the engine on the nose drove two pusher propellers behind the wings by means of a gearbox, extension shafts, and chains. The gunner sat immediately aft of the engine and in front of the wings, a position that gave a good field of fire. Only the prototype was completed.

Another alternative was investigated by Weymann and later by De Bruyère: a pusher fighter with the engine installed behind the pilot, but with a propeller behind the tail surfaces, driven by a long extension shaft. This avoided

the drag and weight penalty of a twin-boom or open lattice tail, but both designs failed. The Weymann W-1 of 1915 was to have two fixed machine guns, while the De Bruyère C1 of 1917 appears to have been designed for a 37 mm Hotchkiss.

The first Allied aircraft with a reliable synchronised mounting was the Bristol Scout D, which entered service with a single Vickers gun in March 1916, but by then the aircraft was outdated and unable to compete with the new German designs emerging. More successful was the Sopwith 1½-Strutter, not a single-seat fighter but a two-seat multipurpose aircraft, which also entered service early in 1916 and had a single Vickers combined with a Lewis for the observer. It became a test-bed for the various types of synchronisation gear then being developed, among them the Vickers-Challenger. The RNAS finally settled on the Scarff-Dibovsky gear and had this installed on its 1½ Strutters. The Sopwith-Kauper gear and (on a smaller scale) the Ross gear were also in use, presumably on aircraft delivered to the RFC or to France. The 1½ Strutter also had the Scarff No. 2 gun ring in the rear cockpit, which was welcomed as a breakthrough in the efficient installation of flexible guns. The 1½-Strutter was pressed into service as a fighter for want of a more specialised aeroplane, but was followed in September by the single-seat Sopwith Pup, which also had a synchronised Vickers.

Defending the rear: not the most comfortable of firing positions. Note the total of three Lewis MGs being carried by this F.E.2b in 1916. (Courtesy Philip Jarrett)

The Germans were not standing still, however. By mid-1916, German fighters were beginning to conform to a standard pattern, with a biplane layout, a single seat, a single tractor engine and two synchronised Maxim LMG 08/15 guns. The second half of that year saw the advent of the Halberstadt D.II (which had only one gun), and the Albatros D.I and D.II, which re-established the German superiority lost to the Nieuports and D.H.2s. Fokker produced biplanes of the D.I to D.IV series with one or two LMG 08/15s, but these proved uncompetitive.

It is worth noting that armament at this time was far from standardised, and there could be significant variations which often depended on the preferences of individual pilots. This particularly applied to light guns which could be easily attached, such as the Lewis, and the F.E.2d sometimes flew with as many as four of these guns, including one or two fixed to fire forwards.

The need to develop tactics for air fighting was also considered, and the RFC provided guidance in *Fighting in the Air*, published in 1916. Advice included, 'The only useful target to really attack is the Pilot himself', so attacking a pusher plane from the rear, or a tractor plane from the front, was not recommended as the engine would protect the pilot.

Pilots and observers are also advised to 'carry a primary and a secondary armament, i.e. a Lewis gun and a stripped rifle or pistol', although the reasoning behind taking a rifle seems somewhat curious: 'The rifle can be used for taking long shots, as it does not use as much ammunition at the same rate as the gun, and is just as unlikely to hit.' The author states that 400 yards (365 m) is the longest possible range to stand any chance of scoring a hit, but half that distance is the normal shooting range, and it is preferable to try to get within 50 m. Even so, 'Hundreds of rounds are fired every day at machines at ranges estimated at 50 yards [46 m] or less without doing any damage.' The harmonisation problem with top-wing-mounted guns is pointed out, in that the bullet trajectory will cross the line of sight at only one range (typically 180 m), otherwise being above or below, and this was held to be a serious disadvantage given the small size of the target – the enemy pilot. The British aces Albert Ball and James McCudden were still being cited in the Second World War as examples for fighter pilots to follow, because of their propensity to open fire at ranges of from 30 down to 15 yards (27 to 14 m).

This may have been because gunnery training in the RFC (indeed, all training) was very poor. In July 1915 the RFC ordered that all pilots and observers had to receive machine gun training, but little was done about it because a suitable training organisation did not exist. An attempt in 1916 to set up a gunnery school at Loch Doon, Scotland, did not succeed because poor weather conditions limited its usefulness. Even in 1918 some pilots 'completed' the aerial gunnery training course without ever firing a gun in the air. Aircrew trained in Canada received better instruction, as an advanced gunnery school was established there in June 1917.

Synchronised-gun fighters emerged from France in September 1916 in the form of the SPAD 7, which had a single Vickers gun with Birkigt synchronisation and proved highly successful (France had formally adopted the Vickers, in their 8 × 50R calibre). The SPAD 7, sturdy and with a powerful Hispano-Suiza (150 hp 8Aa or 180 hp 8Ab) engine, was a good match for the German fighters. Deliveries began in the autumn of 1916, but were far below expectation and unable to meet the huge demand for the type. The SPAD 7 was used not only by the French but also by the British, Italians, Belgians and Russians.

In the spring of 1917 the Germans regained air superiority, mainly thanks to the Albatros series of fighters, which outclassed the opposition. The Albatros D.I and D.II were biplane fighters with a highly streamlined plywood fuselage and a powerful liquid-cooled engine. The installation of two synchronised LMG 08 machine guns on these fighters established a classic pattern of fighter armament, and at least for some time gave the German air forces an important tactical advantage. The D.III adopted the sesquiplane arrangement

Sopwith Triplane with Vickers gun on cowling (note holes in front of jacket for air cooling). (Shuttleworth Collection)

of the Nieuport fighters, with V-struts connecting the upper and lower wing. These aircraft outflew and outgunned the Nieuports and D.H.2s, and their effectiveness was enhanced by organising them into fighter squadrons, *Jagdstaffeln*. For the RFC April 1917 became 'Bloody April', when losses reached the highest level of the war.

In 1917 the pace quickened, and the Allies at last began to adopt synchronised guns as standard, although initially often with only one gun instead of the pair fitted to German fighters. The aircraft ranged from the D.H.5 and Sopwith Triplane, each with one Vickers gun (in the D.H.5 this was experimentally tried at a fixed upward angle of 45°, and in a pivoted mounting allowing elevation to be varied between 0 and 60°), through the similarly armed French Nieuport 24 and 27.

An unusual combination was tried in the Austin-Ball A.F.B.1 of 1917, apparently proposed by the fighter ace Albert Ball. This had a Lewis gun on an upward-firing mounting, supplemented by another mounted between the cylinder blocks of the geared Hispano-Suiza vee-engine to fire through the hollow propeller hub.

The SPAD 7's obvious weakness was its armament of a single synchronised Vickers machine gun, although this was less of a handicap than it might appear, as the Vickers, which during 1917 was being fitted with the Hazleton booster, had a significantly higher rate of fire than the Maxim. There was some interest in installing a large-calibre cannon in the SPAD 12, as described in the next chapter, but a better option was the SPAD 13, armed with two Vickers machine guns. It was slightly larger than the 7 and powered by a 200 hp 8Ba engine. Unfortunately problems with this powerplant delayed the introduction of the SPAD 13 until the end of 1917. The SPAD 13 was selected by the USA to equip its expeditionary force, and many of the American aircraft (all built in France or Britain, because the planned licence-production in the USA did not start) were armed with two Marlin machine guns.

The RFC did order a small number of SPAD 13s. Meanwhile, the Royal Aircraft Factory had been asked to design a fighter around the Hispano-Suiza engine, of which the licence-production was being planned. Two design concepts were studied. One, named F.E.10, was a tractor aircraft with the pilot and his Lewis gun in front of the propeller in a 'pulpit', similar to that used by the French SPAD SA series

Lewis Mk II fitted to a Foster mount on an S.E.5a. Note the clamps for an Aldis sight. (Courtesy J.M. Bruce/G.S. Leslie/Harry Woodman)

than the SPAD 13. The decision not to fit an engine gun was fortunate, for problems with the licence-built engines were persistent until a direct-drive engine was adopted – the Wolseley Viper, a licence-built Hispano-Suiza 8Aa. This made the installation of an engine gun impossible. The Lewis gun on the upper wing could be used to attack enemy aircraft from below, where they had no defences, but a disadvantage was that it effectively limited firepower. When its ammunition drum was empty only the Vickers gun remained, for changing drums in combat (three drums were carried in the cockpit) was almost impossible. Pilots had to break off combat and reduce their speed and altitude to perform this difficult task. One report indicates that when the Lewis gun was fixed to fire forward, it was slightly depressed to cross the trajectory of the Vickers gun at around 50 m, but some factory drawings indicate that the guns were normally set parallel; as they were only about 80 cm apart anyway, this wasn't too much of a problem. It seems likely that many pilots decided on their own arrangements.

The pattern of two synchronised guns was followed by the Sopwith F.1, nicknamed Camel because of the bulge that covered the guns. The two Vickers guns (with 250 rpg), a powerful rotary engine, the pilot and the fuel tank were closely grouped in the front fuselage of a small biplane fighter. The result was a highly agile, unstable aircraft which was very effective in the hands of an experienced pilot, but dangerous to the novice. Lack of stability characterised many fighters at the time, and made them both tricky to fly and poor gunnery platforms. On the other hand combat ranges were short: the RFC set Vickers guns to converge at only 50 yards (46 m). In contrast, Manfred von Richthofen recommended that guns should be adjusted to be parallel out to 150 m. The Camel was originally fitted with Sopwith-Kauper synchronising gear, but this was later supplanted by CC gear.

Because its air-cooled rotary engine needed less warm-up time the Camel was a better choice as a home defence fighter than the S.E.5a. In this role, the synchronised Vickers guns were removed and replaced by two Lewis guns on the upper wing, on Foster mounts. This had important advantages for night operations, for the blinding muzzle flash of the guns was now outside the field of view of the pilot, and his forward view had been improved. Another factor was that the incendiary ammunition for use against Zeppelins was considered unsafe for use in synchronised guns. The RNAS used the 2F.1 version of the Camel as a shipboard fighter, and preferred the combination of a single Vickers (to port) and a Lewis gun on the upper wing.

The Morane-Saulnier AI parasol-wing monoplane, with one or two Vickers guns, entered service at the end of 1917 but despite being built in large numbers was not successful and saw little combat. The equally unconventional Bristol

of fighters. The other, the S.E.5, was a conventional tractor design, but the proposed armament was a single Lewis gun firing through the hollow propeller hub of a geared engine. For some reason, synchronisation was not considered at the time; or maybe the Lewis gun was being preferred. The prototypes appeared late in 1916 with direct-drive 150 hp Hispano engines, a synchronised Vickers gun, and a Lewis on a Foster mount on top of the upper wing. A large 'greenhouse' canopy was fitted, with the apparent intention of making magazine replacement easier by shielding it from the strong air current. But pilots disliked this because of its poor optical quality, and on most aircraft it was replaced by a small windscreen.

The first S.E.5s were delivered in March 1917. The S.E.5a, with a 200 hp engine, followed in June. It was probably the best British fighter of the war, fast and very strong, with good handling qualities and better manoeuvrability

M.1C monoplane, with one Vickers, was very fast for its power and received enthusiastic reports from test pilots, but it fell foul of Trenchard's prejudice against monoplanes and only saw limited service, in the Middle East.

For the next generation of fighters Sopwith produced the Dolphin and the Snipe. The Snipe retained the general layout of the Camel and the armament of two synchronised Vickers guns. An additional Lewis gun was evaluated on the prototypes, but it was not adopted. The Dolphin was a very different aircraft, powered by the Hispano-Suiza V-8 (unfortunately in a less than satisfactory geared version) and with a number of unusual features. The upper wing was lowered to the level of the pilot's eyes, so that he had a good view both above and below it, and two Lewis guns were installed on an open, tubular steel frame that replaced the centre section of this wing. Because the wing itself was set low, and the mounting of the Lewis guns did not raise them above the wing as the Foster mount did, these weapons could not fire directly ahead. They could be trained to some extent, but always pointed upwards at an angle of about 40 degrees or more to clear the propeller.

The purpose, of course, was to attack enemy aircraft from behind and below, but in combat pilots preferred to use their Vickers guns. As the Lewis guns hindered egress from the cockpit, only one was installed as standard; and this too was frequently omitted. In No. 87 Squadron a better use was found for the Lewis guns: they were mounted fixed on the lower wings, outside the propeller disk, and aimed to

Manfred Freiherr von Richthofen's Fokker triplane in 1917.

converge at 100 yards (91 m). It proved to be an effective and popular installation, although the ammunition drums could not be replaced when empty. Two decades were to pass before the RAF officially adopted a similar armament installation on a fighter. Despite its oddities, the ungainly Dolphin was an excellent fighter.

The French introduced the excellent twin-Vickers Nieuport-Delage 29 and the SPAD 20 (which had a rear gunner with one or two Lewis guns as well as two Vickers), but both were just too late to see action. The same fate befell the twin-Vickers Martinsyde F.4 Buzzard, which did achieve some overseas sales.

A Mk II Lewis gun on a Bristol F.2B. (Shuttleworth Collection)

A Lewis gun on a Bristol F.2B. (Courtesy Philip Jarrett)

The Germans introduced developed versions of the Albatros and Pfalz fighters, with Fokker (after a brief diversion to make the charismatic Dr.I triplane) producing the superb D.VII which entered service in May 1918. Lesser-known types introduced in that year included the Siemens-Schuckert D.III (one of which was flown by Ernst Udet, the ace who later became an important figure in Nazi Germany) and the LFG Roland D.VIb, both of which conformed to the two-gun biplane formula.

The entry of the USA prompted the Germans to strengthen their air forces. The 'America Programme' envisaged the production of 2,000 aircraft per month. They would need 2,500 engines, 1,300 fixed LMG 08/15 machine guns and 200 LMG 14 flexible machine guns. The aircraft themselves would have to be of new design if the qualitative superiority was to be won again, and in 1918 the *Idflieg* arranged three comparative tests for fighter aircraft. An armament of two synchronised LMG 08/15 machine guns was required, with 500 rounds per gun. Each gun weighed 11 kg, and its ammunition belt 12.8 kg, bringing the weight

of the armament to about a quarter of the specified 190 kg payload, including pilot and fuel.

The majority of the competing designs were tractor biplanes, although several monoplanes were submitted as well. The first competition was won by the Fokker D.VII, and the second by the Fokker E.V (later renamed D.VIII after a series of crashes because of manufacturing faults). The former was a biplane with a liquid-cooled engine, the latter a small and light parasol monoplane with an air-cooled rotary engine. The most advanced of all competitors was the Junkers D.I, an all-metal low-wing monoplane fighter with no external struts or bracing wires; a configuration about fifteen years ahead of its time. It did not win an order, because its novel construction prevented large-scale production, but its further development was encouraged.

The alternative to the fixed-gun fighter appeared to be the flexible-gun fighter, often powered by multiple engines and carrying multiple gunners, in a design optimised to enlarge the field of fire. The performance penalties were considerable and most of these aircraft remained pure experiments, but the failure of the concept would not prevent its revival in the 1930s and 1940s. In contrast, the powerful two-seat Bristol F.2A Fighter had one Vickers (two in the later

Schwarzlose M16 on a Fokker E series. (*Courtesy Harry Woodman*)

Revelli fitted over the top wing of a Macchi-Nieuport 11. (*Courtesy Harry Woodman*)

F.2B) and a Lewis for the rear gunner, and proved highly successful once it became realised that the best tactical employment was to use it as a fighter with a 'sting in the tail'.

OTHER NATIONS' FIGHTERS

ATTENTION HAS SO FAR CONCENTRATED ON THE MACHINES used by the Germans, French and British. Other nations were involved in the war, and although they often used machines acquired from the three major combatants, they also produced their own, some of which followed national preferences in armament.

Germany's ally, the Austro-Hungarian Empire, manufactured some German fighters such as the Albatros type, but also made their own aeroplanes, engines and armament for use in the *K.u.K. Luftfahrtruppen* (air force). The principal machine guns used were the Schwarzlose M07/12 and M16 in their own rimmed 8 × 50R calibre (not interchangeable with the French Lebel 8 × 50R), the latter having the big barrel jacket removed. Some use was also made of the Schwarzlose M12 in the Italian (Mannlicher Carcano) 6.5 × 52 calibre. Synchronisation gear was not available until late 1916 because of the difficulty in devising one suited to the characteristics of the Schwarzlose. Several different gearing systems were used but none was entirely reliable, leading to a loss of confidence on the part of the pilots. Use was also made of the Danish Madsen in the flexible role, chambered to take the German 7.92 × 57 ammunition, as the gun worked best with rimless cartridges.

Among the first of the Austrian fighters was the Hansa-Brandenburg D.I, a rather unconventional biplane armed with an unsynchronised 8 mm Schwarzlose in a fairing on top of the upper wing. This fairing was known as the VK canister. The standard version was the Type II VK, which held a Schwarzlose gun and 250 rounds of ammunition, while it also contained a gravity fuel tank. Sometimes two guns were installed in the canister. The Hansa-Brandenburg

D.I was also built under licence by Phönix, but was not very successful. The Phönix D.I combined its fuselage with new wings, a more powerful engine, and two synchronised Schwarzlose guns. It was a much better fighter, but deliveries started only in the spring of 1918. Very small numbers were delivered of the improved D.II and D.III. After the war, the D.III went on to serve with the Swedish air force. The other successful family of Austro-Hungarian fighters was entirely indigenous. The *Österreich-Ungarische Aviatik Flugzeugfabrik* (not to be confused with the German *Automobil und Aviatik AG*, which also built a number of fighters) produced the Aviatik D.I, which in prototype form had a single synchronised Schwarzlose but entered service in the summer of 1917 with two.

Russia also made much use of purchased equipment, particularly from France. Gnome and Hispano engines were built under licence, as were various types of aeroplanes, supplemented by direct purchases of French and British planes. The Russian planes tended to lag behind the latest developments on the Western Front, but this was balanced by the fact that the German and Austro-Hungarian forces also tended to use second-line aircraft on the Russian Front. The Russian Maxim was the standard machine gun, supplemented by the Lewis, Madsen and Colt-Browning guns in flexible and top-wing mountings. Unusually, the heavy Maxim was mounted on the top wing in some cases as well as being fitted in flexible mountings. Popular fighters were the Morane-Saulnier Type L parasol-wing and the Nieuport Type 11 biplane, both of which used top-wing mountings. Russia was also possibly the main user of the idiosyncratic SPAD SA.2 already described, with a Lewis gun in the front pulpit. Virtually all synchronised gun installations were in aircraft purchased from abroad; there were only seven Russian-made aircraft armed with synchronised guns on 1 April 1917.

Italy joined the conflict in 1915 on the Allied side. Heavy reliance was placed on the use of French fighters, and

Macchi began licence-production of the Nieuport 11 and 17 and later of the Hanriot H.D.1, a biplane fighter that had been rejected by the French military, which preferred the SPAD 7. The H.D.1, which entered service in 1917 and soon became the standard Italian fighter, was usually armed with a single synchronised Vickers gun, which was relocated to the centre from an offset position to improve aiming and give the pilot better access. The Revelli was also used, mainly in top-wing installations as it could only be synchronised with difficulty. The first Italian-designed fighter, the Ansaldo A.1 *Balilla*, did not enter service until 1918 and saw little combat. It was a conventional tractor biplane with one or two synchronised Vickers, probably using the Birkigt system.

The USA did not enter the war until April 1917, at which time the Army had fewer than 250 planes, all obsolete by European standards. There was also a strong emphasis on the observation role, probably because the development of military aircraft had been vested since 1907 in the Aviation Section of the Signal Corps (in France, aviation was organised under the Air Service of the American Expeditionary Force from June 1917). As a result, America was totally reliant on foreign fighters for the duration of the conflict, the most common types being the French Nieuports and SPADs, although the Bristol Fighter was also acquired. Vickers (made by Colt) and Lewis (made by Savage) guns were therefore standard equipment in the US .30 in calibre (7.62 × 63), which by the end of the war the Americans had speeded up to achieve 1,000 rpm and 800–850 rpm respectively. An 11 mm 'balloon gun' version of the Vickers was also made in the USA and was fitted to some Nieuport 28s (a plane which only saw service with the American forces). However, the indigenous Marlin Aircraft Gun Model 1917 was gradually introduced (and improved in 1918), and by the end of the war its eventual replacement, the Browning, was on the way. At first the Marlin was incompatible with the French synchronising connections in the SPAD, but modifications were made and by the end of the war SPADs could be fitted with Vickers, Marlin or Browning guns.

The first armed Japanese aeroplane was a copy of a Maurice Farman 1912 pusher, which was rebuilt after an accident in 1915 without the front elevator and with a machine gun in its nose. A further development was known as the Type Mo-4 (Mo for Maurice), and this could be equipped with a machine gun if necessary. The final version was the Type Mo-6, armed with a 7.7 mm Hotchkiss in the nose.

Defensive Fire

THIS SECTION IS CONCERNED WITH THE LATER DEVELOPMENT of flexibly mounted armament used in the defence of reconnaissance planes, bombers and airships. As described above, various trial-and-error attempts had resulted by mid-war in the ring-type mounting becoming adopted as standard. The major development after 1916 was the tendency to fit two machine guns to each mounting in order to double the weight of fire, presumably to restore parity with the twin-gun fighter armament which was becoming increasingly common. As with fighters, local modifications to armament to meet perceived needs or preferences also took place, so variations from the standard were often found.

For the first part of the war the most common type of aircraft was the single-engined, two seat reconnaissance plane, which was often used as a light bomber as well. The RFC was slow to change from its 'rear pilot' layout in two-seaters, so condemning the observer to a very limited scope for defensive fire. The B.E.2c of 1914 (which remained in service until 1917) and R.E.7 both adhered to this layout. Both aircraft were subjected to various expedients to improve their defence. The B.E.2c sometimes had up to four socket mountings located around the observer's cockpit, the gun or guns being moved between them as required, and some mountings were even provided for the rear cockpit to allow the pilot to join in. A 'cranked pillar' mounting eventually became more or less standard, but other variations included top-wing mountings, and up to four Lewis guns could be carried by these aircraft. The R.E.7 also featured many variations, including a flexible top-wing mounting, with a Scarff-type ring, to use which the observer had to stand up through a hole in the wing, and even a third cockpit behind the pilot for a second gunner. The Armstrong Whitworth F.K.3 (or 'Little Ack') of 1915 carried a Lewis gun on a spigot which moved along a gun rail – a U-shaped track that ran around the rear of the two-seat cockpit. (A similar system, a U-shaped track constructed of two metal tubes, would remain in widespread use on Austro-Hungarian aircraft until 1918, when the wooden Priesel gun ring was adopted.)

A transformation in British aircraft came in the spring of 1916 with the arrival of the Sopwith 1½-Strutter, which as previously described not only featured a rear observer with a ring-mounted Lewis gun but was also fitted with a synchronised Vickers for the pilot. It was immediately adopted by the RNAS, which used the Sopwith for both fighting and bombing, and it was also extensively used by the French. This was joined later in the year by the R.E.8 reconnaissance/bomber which looked much like the R.E.7 but was transformed by a seating arrangement and armament similar to the 1½-Strutter's. The Armstrong Whitworth F.K.8 and the fast Airco D.H.4 light bomber, both of which entered service in 1917, and the D.H.9 of 1918, adhered to the now accepted two-seat layout, and all of these had the synchronised Vickers and flexible Lewis combination. In

Twin Lewis mounting fitted to an R.E.8 in 1918. (*Courtesy Harry Woodman*)

complete contrast to these compact and agile aircraft was the massive Short Bomber, derived from the Short 184 torpedo-bomber seaplane. It was one of the largest single-engined planes of its time, with a wingspan of nearly 26 m, but it still had a crew of two and just one defensive machine gun. In the first example of the Bomber, the gun's ring mounting was unusually fitted to the rear of the top wing, and so the gunner had to stand to fire. Later production had a more conventional dorsal mounting.

The RFC was concerned about the training of gunners, and in 1917 the *Text Book on Aerial Gunnery* appeared. This contains some fascinating insights into the difficulties involved in air-to-air gunnery. Flexibly mounted machine guns were much affected by the movement of the aircraft, especially in turbulent conditions (particularly prevalent at altitudes of under 300 m), as well as by the difficulty of traversing the gun smoothly to follow a moving target. These problems led to a minimum group size (i.e. the measurement of the greatest distance between shots in a burst) at low altitude of 15 m at a range of 230 m; 'and this size of group has

Stripped Lewis Mk I on a de Havilland mount fitted to an F.E.8 in January 1916. (*Courtesy Harry Woodman*)

An MG 14 Parabellum mounted on an Otto C.I pusher. A collector bag is fitted to collect fired cases, which might otherwise fly into the propeller. (Courtesy Harry Woodman)

An MG 14 mounted on an Albatros C.III, showing how it could be raised to fire over the front wing. The pilot has a fixed LMG 08 in front of him. (Courtesy Harry Woodman)

often been greatly exceeded, even by an experienced gunner'. In smooth air, the group size could improve to 6 m at the same distance when firing at a target requiring no traversing, or 9 m with traversing.

The importance of constant training is emphasised in *Aerial Gunnery* to develop the skill of estimating the distance and direction of aircraft in order to judge the 'lead' required for deflection shooting. There are detailed instructions on how to obtain best use from the ring backsight and

LVG C.VI of 1917. (Shuttleworth Collection)

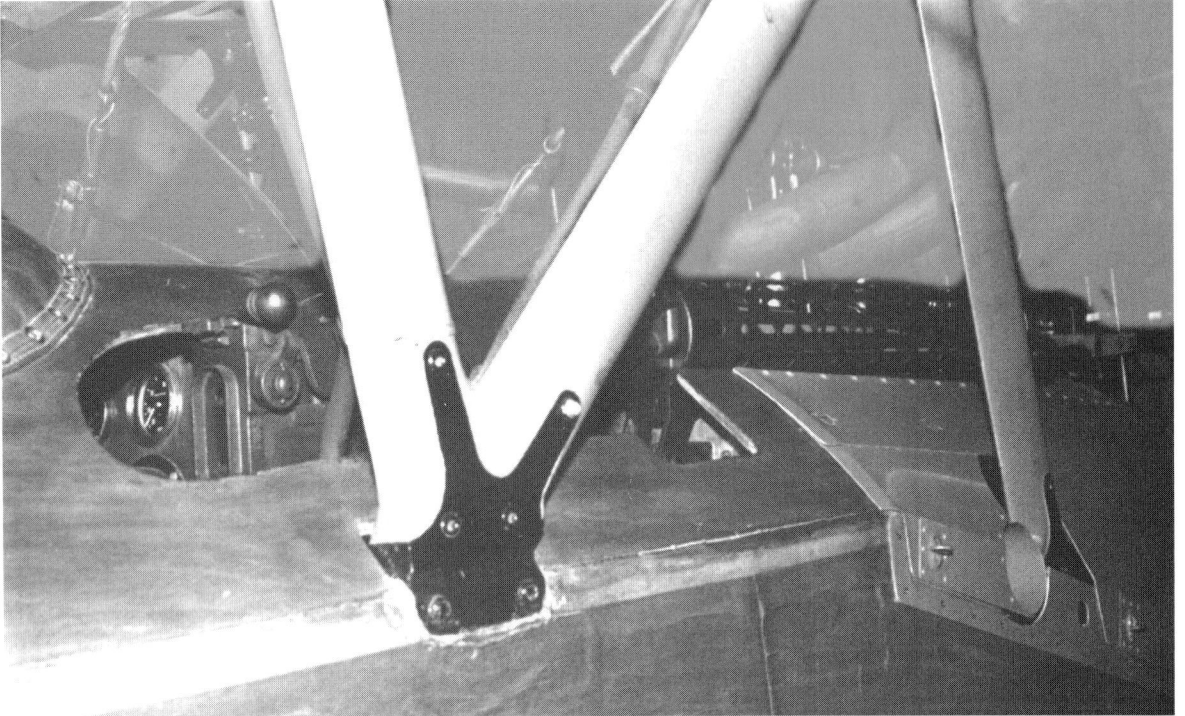

LVG C.VI showing LMG 08 (note rear of gun and cocking lever outside cockpit, to left of wing strut). (Shuttleworth Collection)

LVG C.VI showing MG 14 Parabellum. (Shuttleworth Collection)

Norman-pattern wind-vane foresight. About 180 m is held to be the ideal range for gunnery. The maximum range for opening fire under good conditions is stated to be 275 m; in contrast, it may be difficult for a gunner to hit a manoeuvring target at less than 90 m because of the rapid rate of angular change. It is suggested, however, that a light, agile scout should try to approach a larger plane to within 90 m, when 'he will usually have the big machine at his mercy', whereas 'the big machine having more guns and field of fire has the advantage at longer ranges'. This may seem surprising in the light of Second World War experience, but in fact the big German G- and R-class bombers proved tough and dangerous opponents, well able to look after themselves.

In Germany the aircraft of the C class were introduced in 1915 for armed reconnaissance. The first of these was the Aviatik C.I, which in its initial version still had the observer in the front of the cockpit, although it was a tractor biplane. Rails were installed at each side of the cockpit to carry a Parabellum, but the field of fire was very restricted, so the Rumpler C.I and Albatros C.I competitors were more successful. However, this layout was modified to a front-pilot configuration in the Aviatik C.Ia version in order to improve the observer's field of fire.

Almost all German single-engined aircraft were tractors, but exceptions were the Otto C.I, and the Ago Models C.I, C.II, and C.III of 1915–16, which were twin-boom pushers with the usual front-mounted gun. More conventional C-type aircraft were the LVG C.I-C.VIII series in service between 1915 and 1918 (the C.I was actually the first to feature the rear-observer layout, while a C.II was the first aeroplane to drop bombs on London, on 28 November 1915), and the contemporary AEG C.I-C.IV, DFW C.V, LFG Roland C.II, Rumpler C.I-VII and Albatros C.I to C.XII. Apart from increases in engine power, performance and bomb load, the later models usually carried two guns, normally a synchronised LMG 08/15 and a flexibly mounted Parabellum, but sometimes a Bergmann or even captured weapons (the Lewis being particularly favoured) were used instead. Some specialised versions of these aircraft, as well as the Halberstadt C.V of 1918, were used for high-altitude photographic reconnaissance.

The French produced a great variety of aircraft types, and like the British made much use of the single-engined pusher layout, retaining such aircraft in service for reconnaissance and bombing purposes well into the second half of the war. The Maurice Farman M.F.11 of 1914 was one of the first to carry a machine gun for the observer. It was acquired by the RNAS and used to carry out the first night-bombing raid of the war, attacking artillery installations near Ostend on 21 December 1914. Other pushers were the Henry Farman H.F.20 (the Farman brothers initially designed separately before combining their talents in 1915

The LFG Roland C.II, nicknamed Walfisch *(whale) because of its unusual fuselage shape, provided an exceptional field of view for the pilot and gunner.*

The Albatros C.III.

with the Farman F.40, also a pusher) and the Voisin series. A more modern-looking variation on the same pusher theme was the Breguet-Michelin family of bombers and fighters. All of these planes carried a flexibly mounted machine gun, initially a Hotchkiss but later a Lewis, although some of the Breguet machines carried cannon, as will be seen.

An unusual variation on the single-engined orthodoxy was the Caudron G.4, which was a twin-engined development of the single-engined G.3, featuring two low-powered

A Hotchkiss M1909 on a Voisin. Note the ammunition strips wrapped round a spool – and the handy bomb rack!
(Courtesy Philip Jarrett)

Another view of a Voisin fitted with the Hotchkiss M1909. (Courtesy Philip Jarrett)

wing-mounted tractor engines and a lattice tail. The pilot and gunner were seated back-to-back in a small fuselage pod, with provision for the installation of a machine gun in the front of the nacelle. Introduced in 1915, it was used by the British, Italian, Belgian and Russian forces as well as by France, and hundreds were made. It had a better performance than the Voisins and Farmans, but not sufficiently so to prevent it from rapidly becoming obsolescent; and then it turned out to have the same disadvantages. The G.4 was also produced in an armoured ground-attack version.

A complete contrast was the Breguet BR.14 of 1917, a conventional but large and powerful two-seat, single-engined tractor biplane. As well as carrying up to 300 kg of bombs, it was fitted with a synchronised Vickers on the port side of the fuselage, which in some cases was replaced, or possibly supplemented, by a top-wing-mounted Lewis. It also had one or two Lewis guns in a ring mounting for the observer, supplemented in a few later aircraft by a downward- and rearward-firing Lewis in the floor of the gunner's cockpit. It was roughly comparable to the equally successful British D.H.4, but the Breguet was larger and slower and carried a heavier bombload. It was partnered by the highly successful Salmson Type 2 reconnaissance plane, fitted with synchronised and flexible guns, of which some 3,500 were built (many being supplied to the USA), and the similarly armed Dorand A.R.1 and A.R.2 observation planes.

Following the G.4, Caudron produced the G.5, G.6, and R.4. Instead of the open lattice tail of the G.4, these twin-engined aircraft had a conventional fuselage, with positions for fore and aft gunners with twin Lewis guns each. From the moderately successful R.4 reconnaissance aircraft the R.11 was evolved, a more powerful development intended as a long-range escort fighter for bombers. The twin Lewis guns in fore and aft positions were retained, and a single downward-firing Lewis was added in the nose. The R.11s entered service in early 1918, to counter the increasing threat

A Colt-Browning on a Lecour Grandmaison mounting in the nose of a Caudron G.4. Note the box which contained the belt. A Lewis Mk I is visible behind the wings. (Courtesy Harry Woodman)

Nieuport with a defensive Hotchkiss M1909, with a spool for the ammunition strips. (Courtesy Philip Jarrett)

of German fighters against day-bombing attacks. They were used in mixed formations of Breguet 14 bombers and R.11 escort fighters, with a top cover of SPAD fighters. The greater range and endurance of the R.11 allowed it to escort the bombers over longer distances, but missions flown without the protection of single-seat fighters still resulted in high losses. Despite this the type was judged to be quite useful.

A wide variety of other single-engined reconnaissance/bomber types were produced by other nations, most of them conforming to the classic two-seat tractor biplane configuration, with the gunner in the rear cockpit, and sometimes a fixed synchronised gun for the pilot. Among these were the Russian Lebed 12 of 1916 and Anatra DS of 1917. Italy employed a range of aeroplanes in this category, including the S.I.A. 7B1, SAML S.1 and S.2 of 1917, and the Savoia Pomilio PE of 1918. The Ansaldo S.V.A.-series reconnaissance/bomber was unusual in being a single-seater, while other departures from the conventional were represented by the Savoia Pomilio S.P.2 pusher (normally one flexible RCMG, but some with 25 mm cannon) and the twin-engined S.P.4, with two gun positions. The Italian planes often had their flexibly mounted armament supplemented by the little 9 mm twin-barrel Villar Perosa, which was too light to have any impact on performance. Austria-Hungary used the Hansa-Brandenburg C.I and Lohner C.I of 1916, and the Phönix C.I and Ufag C.I of 1918. The USA acquired the D.H.4, and put it into production in America powered by the excellent American Liberty engine (also used in the British D.H.9A). The D.H.4 was the only US-built combat aircraft to see action, equipped with a pair of synchronised Marlin guns and one or two Lewises in the rear cockpit, and owing to protracted manufacturing problems, caused in part by the decision to alter the plane to use the Liberty engine, few reached the front before the Armistice.

It is worth noting that the visibility from many combat aircraft was very poor, and this could seriously affect gun aiming. Austro-Hungarian planes seemed particularly prone

Madsen mounted on a Russian Morane-Saulnier Type L.
(Courtesy V.B. Shavrov/Harry Woodman)

MG14 Parabellum with a spool for the cloth ammunition belt. (Courtesy Philip Jarrett)

Swiss 7.5 mm MG-94 in Häfeli DH-1. *(Courtesy Verlag Stocker-Schmid, Dietikon-Zürich)*

Schwarzlose M07/12 on an Aviatik Berg C.I in 1917. Note the tubular mount. *(Courtesy Harry Woodman)*

Schwarzlose M16 on a Hansa Brandenburg C.I. Note the type of ammunition belt spool. *(Courtesy Harry Woodman)*

to this: not only did they like to install a large tachometer in front of the windscreen, but their engines were mounted so high that the pilot had virtually no forward view and had to lean out of the cockpit to aim. On the Hansa-Brandenburg C.I, the line of sight was a small triangle bracketed by the fuselage to the left, the exhaust stacks from above and two struts on the right.

Madsen mounted on a Swedish Phönix. *(Courtesy Harry Woodman)*

MULTI-ENGINED PLANES

Despite the example set by the big Russian Sikorski aircraft before the war, aeroplanes with two, three or four engines were relatively uncommon in the First World War, although becoming increasingly important towards the end. Their main purpose was heavy bombing, and they were developed in response to a need to find some way of inflicting significant damage to an enemy who could not otherwise be reached across the miles of trenches and barbed wire which comprised the generally static front line. However, as we have seen, there were some exceptions to this general rule, with the notion of 'escort gunships', or 'air cruisers', attaining some popularity.

The first multi-engined bombers of the war were the big four-engined Sikorski *Ilya Muromets*. Some eighty of these were ordered, although the shortage of imported engines meant that there were many variations. The first of over 400 bombing missions (during which just two planes were lost) was made in February 1915. Defensive armament varied considerably, again depending on what was available, and is quoted as being between three and six guns, which could be Maxims, Lewises, Madsens or Colt-Brownings.

Next in the field were the Italians, with the Caproni series of three-engined bombers, which had a twin-boom configuration with the third engine being a pusher. These were the most successful of the big Allied bombers. The original Ca.1, also known as the Caproni 300 hp, was a biplane with twin tail booms, each containing a tractor engine, and a central nacelle with a pusher engine at the rear. Improved versions with a total engine power of 350 hp and 450 hp, respectively, were known as the Ca.2 and Ca.3. The first bombing raid was by Ca.2s in August 1915, and this model was progressively superseded by the Ca.3 and Ca.5 (although this last was unpopular because its engines were unreliable and relatively few were built) by the end of the

Ilya Muromets *Type Veh upper gun position, showing a Madsen (foreground) and a Lewis Mk I.* *(Courtesy V.B. Shavrov/Harry Woodman)*

Revelli *fitted in the nose of a Caproni Ca.3, on a Scarff-type mounting.* *(Courtesy Harry Woodman)*

war, by which time a total over 650 of the big biplanes had been built.

There were two defensive gun positions – one in the nose and an unusual one at the back of the upper wing. To allow the gunner to fire over the propeller to the rear, a tall cage-like structure was added behind the wings, on top of the rear engine, in which the gunner was entirely exposed to the elements. These positions initially had one Revelli RCMG each, but in some cases this was increased to twin mountings. A variation on this basic design was the significantly bigger Ca.4 of 1918 (able to carry twice the bombload of the Ca.3), which retained the same configuration except that it was a triplane. In place of the single rear gun position, there was a dorsal gunner's position in each tail boom, just aft of the wings, as well as a nose gunner. Again, the initial three-gun defence was later doubled by the use of twin mountings. The design was not as successful as the biplanes, and only forty-two of the huge triplanes were built (twenty-three of which were powered by American Liberty engines), but six of them were operated by the British RNAS, mainly

for night-bombing.

Next in the field were the Germans, with several different companies involved in building G- and R-class planes. The G series (*Grossflugzeug* = large aeroplane; they were initially known as K class, for *Kampfflugzeug* = battleplane) and the even larger R-planes (*Riesenflugzeug* = giant aeroplanes) all had their first versions flying in 1915, although service use developed slowly. The G class were principally made by AEG (*Allgemeine Elektrizitäts Gesellschaft* = General Electric Co. of Germany), Gotha (short for *Gothaer Waggonfabrik AG*) and Friedrichshafen, while all of the service R class were the Staaken series made by Zeppelin VGO (*Versuchs Gotha Ost*).

The first Gotha, the G.I, was a twin-engined biplane designed by Ursinus and flying in 1915. It had an unconventional appearance because of the attachment of the fuselage to the top wing while the engines were grouped close together on the bottom wing (later Gothas had a more conventional layout). This permitted a wide field of fire to the gunner, who had one RCMG in a flexible mounting. This plane, of which somewhere between twelve and twenty were built (although there was a maximum of six at the Front at any one time), was originally armoured and intended for attacking ground targets with machine guns. The first AEG and Friedrichshafen G.I planes (also twin-engined biplanes) were also flying in 1915. All of the early G planes were at first fitted with one or two RCMGs and used for a wide range of duties, including protecting friendly observation aircraft and attacking enemy ones, carrying out reconnaissance and, very occasionally, dropping bombs.

These early planes were not very successful, however, and much development was required before mass production was worthwhile. The most successful of the AEGs was the G.IV of 1916, of which nearly 500 were built. It was a

A Gotha bomber, showing the nose gun position.

conventional twin-engined biplane with an advanced appearance owing to its rounded, completely covered fuselage. It had a relatively short range and was mainly used for attacking military targets in rear areas of the battlefront. Defensive gun positions were in the nose and in the rear fuselage just behind the wings; this was to become the classic layout for a twin-engine bomber for the next two decades.

In the following year the Friedrichshafen G.III and the Gotha G.IV and the very similar G.V appeared. These differed from the AEG primarily in having pusher engines in the wings, with the propellers spinning uncomfortably close to the rear gunner. The defensive gun positions were the same, except that in the Gothas the rear gun position incorporated a ventral tunnel which allowed the gunner to fire downwards and to the rear (an idea copied in the Friedrichshafen G.IIIa). This permitted a lateral arc of 25 degrees and a vertical one of 60 degrees, and meant that it was no longer necessary to carry a separate gun firing through a hatch in the rear fuselage, a common expedient in earlier models of both types. On one aircraft, a captured Lewis gun was attached to the upper wing, pointing upwards; but it cannot have been more than a 'scare' weapon. The Gotha G.IV sometimes had a fourth MG mounted on a tall pivot between the bombardier and pilot. No more than thirty-six Gothas were at the Front at any one time. Thirty were supplied to Austria, which fitted them with Schwarzlose MGs. The Rumpler G series, which appeared in 1915, had a similar layout but only one gun position (in the nose) and were considered less successful.

The pusher propellers of the Friedrichshafen and Gotha bombers also had the disadvantage that any object spilled overboard from the cockpit would hit and damage them. For this reason the spent cartridges of the nose gun were collected in bags, instead of being thrown overboard. British aircraft had similar problems, especially if gunners allowed a Lewis ammunition drum to slip from their hands.

By far the most spectacular aircraft of the war were the German R-planes. These were intended for very-long-range bombing missions and were characterised not just by their size (which demanded at least three but usually four or more engines) but also by the requirement that the engines should be accessible for maintenance in flight. This led to some bizarre layouts, including central engine rooms in the fuselage driving wing-mounted propellers by extension shafts (SSW series and Linke-Hofman R.I), or four engines grouped in the nose driving a single, two-blade tractor propeller of enormous size (Linke-Hofman R.II). However, the only successful ones were the Staaken series, built by Zeppelin.

The first Staaken, the VGO I, first flew in 1915 and featured three engines – two pushers in the wings and a tractor in the nose. Gun positions were provided in the noses of the engine nacelles. The VGO III and succeeding R.IV had coupled engines, giving a total of six. In the R.IV, defensive armament had been carefully considered and consisted of four different positions accessible to the flight engineers in the wing-engine nacelles; two were forward-firing in the front of each nacelle, and the others were on the top wing directly above the nacelles and reached by ladders. In addition, there was a wide dorsal position in the fuselage aft of the wings, capable of taking two gunners, each with a gun on a pillar mounting on the side of the cockpit, who could also use a ventral position under the fuselage. The R.V had five engines (one in the nose, four coupled units in the wings, this time with tractor propellers) and emerged in 1917. It had gun positions in the rear of the engine nacelles, and in the '*Schwalbennest*' (swallow's nest) mountings on top of the wing.

So far, only single examples of each type had been built. The only Staaken to go into 'quantity' production (eighteen were built) was the R.VI, which differed in having four engines in two wing nacelles in a tractor/pusher arrangement, which subsequently became standard. In this variant, the nose engine was deleted, leading to some changes to the armament. A nose gun position was provided, together with the previous dorsal and ventral positions. The official German specification interestingly called for an armament of three Lewis guns, as these were lighter than the German guns. In service, the nose and dorsal mountings often carried twin guns. A few of these machines were also equipped with top-wing gun positions above the engine nacelles. The first of the R.VIs was accepted into service in mid-1917, the last being completed in July 1918.

The next production model was the R.XIV, which had the nose engine restored to provide a total of five. This again dictated changes to the armament, which consisted of six guns – one in each of the upper-wing positions and two in the dorsal and ventral positions. Only a handful were made, one of which was shot down in August 1918. Examination of the wreckage revealed a mixture of Lewis and Parabellum guns.

The Gotha and Staaken bombers were well known in the UK as they took over from Zeppelin airships the role of bombing attacks on the British Isles. Although London was first bombed from an aeroplane by a single-engined LVG C.IV in November 1916, the first major attack was made against London in daylight on 25 May 1917 with a mixed force of twenty-two G and R class, but due to weather problems Felixstowe was attacked instead. In June 1917 Gothas started to bomb London. The big bombers later switched to night bombing after suffering heavy losses to the British defences (a total of twenty Gothas were shot down, eight by fighters and twelve by AA fire, compared with thirty-six which crashed in Belgium), so a night interception school was established in the UK.

At first, attacks on the R-class caused some confusion to British fighters, as their wingspan was so much greater than the G-class planes that they filled the sights at a much greater distance, causing the fighters to open fire too soon. Neither plane was easy to shoot down as they carried armour protection for vital areas, and their defensive armament was as heavy as that of the attacking fighters. Government permission had to be obtained to use Brock and Pomeroy bullets against them, due to concerns that Germany would regard the use of such bullets as infringing the St. Petersburg Convention. In 1917 the RTS bullets, with improved incendiary performance, were also issued to home-defence squadrons.

Experiments with fixed, upward-firing guns were conducted, as this was considered to be a more effective form of attack at night. Initially a Martinsyde G.102 was fitted with three Lewis guns firing at an upward angle of 47 degrees, and this was followed by an F.1 two-seater from the same company which carried two guns fixed at a similar angle. However, the experiments did not achieve any successes although their main proponent, an innovative officer called Murlis Green, continued to argue their merits after the war. Despite all of the problems, the Gothas were ultimately mastered. On the night of 19/20 May 1918 thirty-eight G class and three R class raided England. Six Gothas were shot down; three by fighters and three by anti-aircraft fire.

The British also became interested in heavy bombers, but only two types saw significant service: the Handley-Page O/100 which entered service in August 1916 (remarkably, its initial specification was written in September 1914), and the improved O/400, with more powerful engines, which reached squadrons in April 1918. This original 1914 specification for the Type O/100 did not specify much in the way of defensive armament: a service rifle and 100 rounds of ammunition! On the other hand it did require the generous use of manganese steel armour plate to protect the engines, radiators, fuel tanks, crew compartment, and bomb bay. The prototype carried some armour and a single machine gun, but production aircraft omitted the armour and instead had conventional nose and dorsal positions, and a ventral gun. The O/100 initially entered service with the RNAS but was subsequently ordered also by the RFC.

Both bombers were conventional twin-engined biplanes which carried four or five Lewis guns in the usual nose (one

Stepping up the firepower: a twin-Lewis mounting. (Courtesy Philip Jarrett)

or two), dorsal (two, one each side on pillar mountings) and ventral (one) positions. Both also had folding wings to aid hangar stowage. A total of forty-two O/100s and over 550 O/400s were built, with over 250 of the latter in service at the end of the war.

In 1917 German attacks on Britain prompted the creation of a strategic bombing force to retaliate. The Independent Air Force, part of the new RAF, consisted of heavy O/100 and O/400 night-bombers and fast single-engined D.H.9 day-bombers. In a foreshadowing of events during World War Two, daylight operations without fighter escort resulted in heavy losses, while night attacks encountered navigation difficulties. Nevertheless attacks on Berlin were planned, and the large four-engined Handley Page V/1500 bomber was ordered for this purpose.

One other British heavy bomber to see limited service was the Blackburn Kangaroo, converted from a seaplane in 1918. This twin-engined biplane was mainly used on anti-submarine duties, with some success, and carried the light armament of just two guns. The twin-engined Boulton & Paul Bourges and four-engined Bristol Braemar triplane, both of 1918–19, used Scarff-ring twin guns in the nose. The Bourges had a similar installation in the dorsal position, but the wider Braemar had two transversely moving pillar mountings, plus a ventral gun. Neither saw service. At the end of the war, two potent aircraft were just entering service – the twin-engined Vickers Vimy and the massive four-engined Handley-Page V/1500. The former (principally famous for being the first aeroplane to fly non-stop across the Atlantic) normally carried one or two Lewis guns on a Scarff ring in the nose, plus a ventral gun. A dorsal Scarff ring for one or two Lewis guns could be installed, but was not usually fitted. The V/1500 had five Lewises: a twin Scarff mounting in the nose, two single dorsal guns on side pillar mountings, and a single on a Scarff ring in the extreme tail, aft of the tailplane.

The French principally relied upon the Caudron series of twin-engined biplanes for their heavy bombers. The R.4 of 1915 had the conventional nose and dorsal gun positions, each with twin Lewis mountings. Another aircraft in the same category was the Letord 4 of 1917, with the same armament.

The USA had selected the Martin MB-1 for its heavy-bomber role, but as with other US aircraft, the war ended before it could see action, and it was only built in small numbers. Up to five RCMGs were normally fitted.

THE FIGHT AGAINST AIRSHIPS AND OBSERVATION BALLOONS

TETHERED OBSERVATION BALLOONS HAD BEEN USED SINCE the nineteenth century in order to extend the range of vision of army observers, particularly during static warfare and especially to correct the aim of artillery fire. They were therefore ideally suited to use on the Western Front in the First World War, which was for the most part a static conflict in which artillery played a dominant part. Needless to say, the enemy on both sides found such observation inconvenient and took steps to curtail it. Artillery fire from the ground was tried but was largely ineffective since aim correction was difficult to judge. Aeroplanes therefore became the favoured means of destroying balloons.

The development of the Zeppelin airship raised altogether more serious fears, with images of fleets of the vast machines cruising deep into enemy territory and bombing the population into submission. These were realised (albeit on a much smaller scale) on 19–20 January 1915, when two Schütte-Lanz airships (L3 and L4) attacked coastal towns in England, and on 31 May of that year, when LZ 38 dropped 270 kg of HE/I bombs in the first Zeppelin raid against London. The first bombs had actually been dropped from a Zeppelin in September 1914, when LZ 17 dropped three bombs on Antwerp. This was followed up by bombing raids on the Eastern Front about three months later. It was essential to discover an effective means of countering these raids, and while AA artillery was used, aeroplanes were the obvious answer.

There were particular fears over the efficiency of airships for naval reconnaissance. Admiral Jellicoe of the British Grand Fleet was extremely concerned about the tactical advantage given to the German High Seas Fleet by the use of Zeppelins to keep track of, and report back, his own fleet movements, and he encouraged various means of attacking them. As on land, gunfire was tried, and high-angle guns were fitting to a wide range of ships – including submarines. As on land, these attempts saw little success, with only the Navy's L 7 and the Army's LZ 85 being shot down by warship fire. Aeroplanes again became the favoured weapon, with the added complication of how to launch and recover the planes at sea.

Balloons and airships had various characteristics in common, when considered as targets. Both were large and stationary or slow-moving, and so easy to hit. However, riddling them with machine gun bullets did little damage as it took a long time to deflate a balloon or a Zeppelin gas bag, so they could generally sail on regardless. Their main weakness was the gas which held them aloft – hydrogen. By itself it would not burn, but when mixed with oxygen from the air it was extremely inflammable. Much effort was therefore expended in finding ways to set these craft alight, which involved two stages: tearing open the fabric to release hydrogen into the air, then igniting the resulting mixture. The techniques used by aeroplanes can generally be divided into three: non-gun weapons, large cannon and incendiary bullets for machine guns.

The non-gun weapons were of two types. First were the explosive or inflammatory darts. The Guerre incendiary arrow of 1913 has already been mentioned but it was not the only one; the Ranken explosive dart (invented by Engineer Lieutenant Francis Rankin) was also issued. This was a long, slim tube with a sharp iron point, and was filled with HE and black powder (the latter intended to add some incendiary effect). The dart fell stabilised by a small rubber parachute, then lodged itself in the fabric of the airship with three sprung arms, which triggered the fuze when they were forced open by the impact. Ranken darts were carried by RNAS aircraft in canisters of twenty-four or fifty and were intended to be released at between 20 and 200m above the target. One success was achieved with this weapon by a BE.2c (L 15, in April 1916) but another attempt in August 1916, when a Bristol Scout attacked the L 17, was unsuccessful. The problems are not hard to see. It was difficult enough for most aeroplanes to catch the fast-climbing Zeppelins with their excellent altitude performance; getting above them to drop a dart on them was much more difficult. Furthermore, Zeppelins had separate gas bags inside their structure, so a hole in the outer fabric would not have produced a gas leak.

There was one spectacular success with the bombing technique: in June 1915 Cooper bombs, dropped from an RNAS Morane-Saulnier Type L, were used to destroy LZ 37, though this was achieved entirely by chance as the pilot was on his way to bomb airship hangars when he spotted the Zeppelin at low altitude below him.

More promising were the French Le Prieur incendiary rockets, which resembled large versions of commercial fireworks. Up to eight per plane were carried by Nieuport 11 and other fighters, mounted on the outer struts connecting the two wings. On 22 May 1916 at Verdun, a co-ordinated attack on the German balloon line in support of an infantry attack succeeded in shooting down five out of the six balloons then aloft. However, the rockets were wildly inaccurate at much beyond 400 m and, against airships, had to be fired from above; a particular problem since their installation seriously reduced the performance. A number of RNAS Sopwith Pups, carried on board ships, were fitted with eight Le Prieur rockets each, but none ever had the opportunity to fire them at an airship.

The use of large-calibre cannon proved ineffective. This left rifle-calibre incendiary and/or explosive ammunition, which was generally preferred to cannon or rockets as it was more accurate and had a much higher hit probability. The development of incendiary ammunition for anti-Zeppelin purposes actually commenced in the UK before the war in .45 in (11.5 mm) calibre for use in the obsolete single-shot Martini-Henry carbines. Early British night-fighters carried

these guns, or American Winchesters in .45-90 calibre, and even 12-bore (18 mm) shotguns, firing incendiary bullets. There are no reports of any successes with these weapons, though they were occasionally fired at Zeppelins. They were also issued in France, for anti-balloon duties.

Later on, incendiaries and HE bullets became available in .303 in (7.7 mm) calibre, although concerns that this ammunition might contravene international agreements prohibiting munitions that might cause unnecessary suffering held up their use until 1916, and even then they were restricted to home-defence applications. Their use was not entirely successful; they were sometimes fired without result and it was found that extreme cold at high altitude affected their performance, so magazines were heated (but not too much!). It was also feared that the Brock and Buckingham bullets were unable to set light to the huge volumes of hydrogen which may even have had the effect of extinguishing them as it was the hydrogen/oxygen mixture that burned, not the hydrogen alone. The RFC tended to use the Pomeroy while the RNAS preferred the Brock, but in all cases the .303 in calibre was felt to be marginal, and larger bullets were considered to be more effective.

The HE and incendiary bullets tended to be used with top-wing-mounted Lewis guns for several reasons; it was initially felt dangerous to fire explosive/incendiary bullets through the propeller disk in case the synchronisation malfunctioned, there was also the risk of 'cook off' of the sensitive projectiles in the closed-bolt Vickers, and the usual Foster mounting enabled the Lewis to be pulled down so that it could fire straight up – a major advantage when trying to catch Zeppelins. The guns were also lighter than the Vickers, an important factor when performance was so marginal.

The British experimented with .45 in calibre Maxim guns, but the most successful large-calibre machine gun was

F.E.2b of No. 51 (HD) Squadron, being flown as a single-seat night-fighter for home defence. Note the two different versions of Lewis gun. (Courtesy Philip Jarrett)

A second view of the F.E.2b night-fighter, showing how one of the guns could be elevated for upward firing.
(Courtesy Philip Jarrett)

An F.E.2b converted as a night-fighter, with two Lewis Mk IIs linked to a searchlight. The 'propeller' under the nose is presumably a generator for the searchlight, driven by the airstream. (Courtesy Philip Jarrett)

An F.E.2b with two Lewis guns. (Courtesy Philip Jarrett)

the French-developed 11 mm balloon gun version of the Vickers, as the larger bullets enabled more incendiary material to be carried. In October 1918 the British placed an urgent order with France for fifty conversion kits to fire the 11 × 59R loaded with Devignes tracer/incendiary bullets, plus a million rounds of ammunition (and belt links from the USA). The French stated they could only supply 21 guns as their supply was insufficient to meet their own demands. At that time, the French had 700 of these guns, the Americans 130 and the British only fourteen.

The need to attack airships bombing England at night called for different characteristics from those of the front-line fighter. Manoeuvrability was unimportant, but stability was valued. For this reason, the very stable, easy-flying Avro 504 trainer and the B.E.2c were adapted from their usual roles to become night-fighters by having a Lewis mounted on the top wing, and in some case their front cockpits replaced by a fuel tank (these versions being designated the Avro 504C for the RNAS and the 504D for the RFC). These were not too successful because of their inadequate performance (although LZ 34 was shot down by a B.E.2c in

A water-cooled MG 08 as used on German airships.
(*Courtesy MoD Pattern Room*)

The upper nose position of a German Army Zeppelin in 1915, showing MG 14 Parabellum guns, fitted with water-cooling jackets. (*Courtesy Harry Woodman*)

November 1916), and they were eventually replaced by more powerful fighters and fast bombers from the Western Front.

Aircraft used for the night defence of England were characteristically equipped with the top-wing Lewis guns, as well as or instead of the usual synchronised Vickers, right to the end of the war. Apart from the advantages already given, the muzzle flash of the Vickers tended to spoil the pilots' night vision; less of a problem with the top-wing mounting. The night-fighter version of the Sopwith Camel had both Vickers guns removed in favour of two top-wing mounted Lewis guns on Foster mountings, with the cockpit moved to the rear. This had the additional benefit of greatly improving forward visibility, normally blocked by the 'hump' over the guns. Later on, flash hiders were developed for the Vickers guns.

Eventually, these better-performing aeroplanes armed with machine guns firing incendiary ammunition proved to be the answer to the Zeppelin threat, with some seventeen being destroyed in the air by aircraft or AA guns. The airships were not entirely helpless; they had gun positions in various locations, such as platforms with two or more RCMGs high above the nose, reached by a long ladder from the gondola, and positions in the extreme tail aft of the fins. The one notable aspect of the weapons used was that the water-cooled version of the Parabellum was preferred. This was to minimise the risk of heat from an intensively used gun barrel igniting the hydrogen which was sometimes released from the airship.

Despite this, bombing raids on England became too costly. The first airship shot down over England was SL XI on the night of 2/3 September 1916. Three more were shot down over the next four weeks, plus two more at the end of November, and at the end of 1916 the German Army gave up its airships to the Navy. The Navy persevered with occasional raids on England (about fifty airships were in service at the end of 1916), using airships developed to operate at higher altitudes, despite losses which included five out of eleven Zeppelins being shot down in one raid, on 19 October 1917. The last raid was on 5 August 1918, when LZ 112 was shot down by a D.H.4. More than 50 per cent of the airships used by Germany in the war were lost in action or through accident, with 40 per cent of the crews being killed.

ALL AT SEA
THERE WAS EARLY INTEREST IN OPERATING AEROPLANES AT sea. The first take-off from, and landing on, water was by Frenchman Henri Fabre in a seaplane in March 1910. In the same year, the American Eugene Ely flew a plane off a warship platform, and in the following year landed on one – a much more difficult feat, which became even harder as aircraft size and performance increased. Also at the beginning of 1911, Glenn Curtiss made the first powered flight from water in a flying-boat.

As on land, reconnaissance was the main reason for wanting aeroplanes to operate at sea. Navies were particularly interested as they could locate enemy warships at much greater distances than traditional cruisers. At 1,000 m altitude it is possible on a clear day to see over 100 km, and in favourable conditions mines and submarines could also be spotted. Speed in reporting the findings of reconnaissance aircraft was much more important than on land, because the position of ships could change quickly and unpredictably, so there was much concentration on the development of airborne wireless to achieve this. British, French and German naval manoeuvres held in 1913 all successfully used aeroplanes for reconnaissance. Artillery spotting for naval guns was also foreseen in 1914, and happened for the first time a year later in the Dardanelles campaign.

Later on, the submarine threat favoured the use of airships (dirigible or not), as these could accompany coastal convoys and hover over the suspected position of a submarine. Flying-boats were sometimes fitted with heavy armament for use against U-boats, but experience showed that the main value of anti-submarine aircraft was in keeping the U-boats below the surface, which greatly restricted their speed and field of view, so armament was often left off in the interests of extending patrol endurance.

At first, naval aviation consisted of seaplanes or flying-boats using coastal waters or lakes, supplemented from August 1914 by seaplanes aboard specially fitted ships, which used cranes to lower them into the water and haul them back up again. This clearly required calm water to work, which was only occasionally available in the North Sea, and was inconvenient because the ship had to stop for both manoeuvres. Later, both land-planes and seaplanes were flown directly from ships, either from specially designed platforms which could be rotated to turn the aeroplane into the wind for take-off or, on larger warships, from platforms fitted to gun turrets, which could be trained in the required direction. An alternative approach sometimes used was to take off from platforms towed behind smaller ships, usually destroyers.

Such operations were greatly helped by the fact that most First World War aircraft had very low take-off speeds, so required only a short run in addition to the wind created by the ship's forward motion. However, there were no facilities to land aircraft on the ships again, so if they were land-planes (often preferred because of their superior performance as they were not burdened by bulky floats) they had to ditch in the sea at the end of their mission. This led to the development of proper aircraft-carriers, with flying-off and flying-on capability, and HMS *Argus*, the first of these, joined the RN in September 1918. All credit to the Frenchman Clément Ader, the aviation pioneer, who astonishingly suggested in the 1890s the development of the flat-topped aircraft-carrier, including the use of elevators from the hangar and of folding wings for the aeroplanes.

Many seaplanes consisted of land-planes fitted with floats, which was an inexpensive solution, whereas flying-boats were unique designs. Fighters like the Sopwith Baby and single-engined bombers such as the Breguet 14 were all fitted with floats. However, some floatplanes were purpose-designed, and the Hansa-Brandenburg W 12 single-engined two-seat floatplane fighter of 1917 was particularly effective.

An unusual feature of the W 12 was the vertical tail fin, which projected below the fuselage rather than above, providing a remarkably clear field of fire for the rear gunner, a detail retained in the W 29 monoplane which entered service in 1918.

Other floatplanes used by the Central Powers included the Gotha WD series, both single-engined (with one flexible gun) and twin-engined (with two guns in nose and dorsal positions) and the Hansa-Brandenburg KDW single-seat fighter, with two synchronised guns. The Friedrichshaven FF 29, 33, 39, 49 and 59 series of patrol/reconnaissance floatplanes were all single-engined biplanes. From the FF 33b onwards, the observer was housed in the rear cockpit with a flexibly mounted gun. The FF 33e achieved fame as the aircraft carried by the *Wolf* commerce raider, and carried a radio instead of a gun. Later versions saw the restoration of the gun, with provision to fire forwards and upwards between the wings, and in some cases a synchronised gun was fitted as well.

To some extent the choice between flying-boats and seaplanes was affected by national preferences. Flying-boats were generally preferred in larger sizes, although a floatplane version of the huge Sikorski *Ilya Muromets* flew in 1914. The German Navy had no flying-boats in the First World War as they relied on Zeppelins for long-range naval reconnaissance. In an unusual variation, the USA favoured single central floats integral with the fuselage, probably because they were easier to launch from catapults.

When war broke out in 1914, the American firm of Curtiss was building the H-1 America flying-boat, designed for an attempt at the first transatlantic crossing, to be financed by Rodman Wanamaker and flown by Lt. J.C. Porte of the Royal Navy. War prevented this, but the RNAS bought a military version of the aircraft, the H-4 America. On its arrival, Porte discovered that the hull of the H-4 was too weak and insufficiently seaworthy for operations in the North Sea, so he redesigned it to created the Felixstowe F.1, named after the Naval Air Station where this work was done. The Curtiss H-12 Large America suffered from the same problems, and with a new hull and British engines became the F.2 of 1916, which became the workhorse of British coastal aviation. There were gun positions in the bow, in a dorsal position in the fuselage, and behind two waist windows; the engineer and wireless operator also acted as gunners. Another gun could be installed in the cockpit, so that the aircraft could carry up to seven Lewis guns if twin guns were installed on the nose and dorsal mounts. The heavy armament was necessary, for on their patrols the flying-boats encountered German seaplanes. Despite the firepower and careful formation flying of the flying-boats, the smaller and more agile seaplanes seem to have had the upper hand.

A partially stripped Lewis in an FBA. (Courtesy Philip Jarrett)

Experiments were conducted with 'fighting tops' – gunner's nacelles attached to the upper wing, at the position of the first pair of struts outboard of the engines. With twin Lewis guns on a Scarff ring in each nacelle, this substantially increased firepower, but nevertheless it was not a success. The fighting tops cost 10 knots in speed, and the gunners in them were unable to communicate with the rest of the crew. The F.3 and F.5, slightly larger and usually carrying four guns in three positions, followed in 1917. One US-built version of the F.5 had a Davis gun, while another for Japan was fitted with a 1 pdr gun of unspecified type.

Not all flying-boats were large. The Austro-Hungarian Lohner L of 1915 was a three-seat single-engined biplane which carried one Schwarzlose gun. The Italian Macchi L.1 was based on a captured version of this, and normally carried a Fiat RCMG in the flexible nose mounting. The Macchi L.3 (later redesignated M.3) was a new design which emerged in 1917. It carried a flexible 7.7 mm Fiat gun or a light cannon, and was followed into service by the similarly armed M.8. The M.5 and M.7 of 1917 and 1918 were single-seat fighter flying-boats, with pusher engines and one or two fixed 7.7 mm Vickers guns. In the Mediterranean, Austria-Hungary and Italy operated small flying-boat fighters, with a flotation hull and biplane wings, usually with the engine installed as a pusher engine, high above the hull between the wings, to keep it clear of the water. The armament was installed in the bow, usually single or twin Schwarzlose guns in the case of Austrian aircraft and Vickers guns in Italian aircraft.

The French also favoured small single-engined flying-boats with pusher engines. The most common types were the Donnet-Denhaut family, which first entered service in 1916 but continued to be developed until 1922, by which time over 1,000 had been built, and the similar but smaller FBA series, also built in large numbers. The smaller aeroplanes carried just one Lewis gun in a bow mounting, but the larger of the Donnet-Denhauts were fitted with up to four guns in bow and dorsal positions.

Some aeroplanes were designed to stow easily on board ship, such as the Short Folder floatplane of 1913 and the Short 184, in which folding reduced the span from 19 to 5 m. Smaller aircraft generally didn't need folding wings, but the Beardmore W.B.III of late 1917 was developed from the Sopwith Pup specifically for shipboard use, with retractable or jettisonable undercarriage to prevent overturning on ditching. The later W.B.IV and WB.V only reached prototype status. The W.B.IV had the 200 hp Hispano-Suiza engine mounted aft of the cockpit, driving the tractor propeller by a long extension shaft. This made it possible to seat the pilot in front of the leading edge, so that he had an excellent view. The potential of the configuration to mount a cannon firing through the propeller hub was not exploited; armament consisted of a synchronised Vickers and a Lewis, mounted on a tripod in front of the cockpit. The W.B.V had a conventional engine installation, with a geared Hispano-Suiza in the nose. It was intended to carry a cannon firing through the propeller hub, but this was quickly discarded in favour of a Vickers and a Lewis.

The navalised Sopwith Camel, the 2F.1, did not have folding wings but did have a removable rear fuselage. By the end of the war, the Sopwith 1½-Strutter was used as general observation/spotter plane on RN warships, and some of them were fitted with detachable wings. The Parnall N 2A Panther was specifically designed for this role, and although too late for the war served until 1924. Its rear fuselage could be folded sideways.

The gun armament of naval aircraft did not vary significantly from that of land-planes, although RNAS fighters

Sopwith Pup cockpit showing a Vickers gun. (Shuttleworth Collection)

differed from the RFC's. The RNAS chose the Sopwith Pup to succeed the Baby as its fighter, but replaced the Vickers gun with a top-wing Lewis, possibly to save weight in order to enable the little planes to climb fast and high enough to tackle the Zeppelins, but also so that the gun could be aimed vertically to attack from below. For the same reason, the navalised Sopwith Camel lost one of its synchronised Vickers in favour of a top-wing Lewis. Two Zeppelins were destroyed by shipboard RNAS aircraft: L 23 in August 1917 by a Pup flying from a platform on the light cruiser *Yarmouth*, and L 53 by a Camel flying off a high-speed lighter towed by a destroyer. Aerial combat was rare between naval aircraft (excluding those RNAS fighters which operated over the Western Front), and so the pressures to increase armament and fit armour were not as great.

By the end of the war naval aircraft were demonstrating that they posed a greater threat to warships than merely spying on them. In August 1918 six British MTBs (motor torpedo-boats) were destroyed by machine gun attacks from German seaplanes in the Heligoland Bight. Even larger ships were no longer immune. Torpedo-carrying aircraft were in service by 1918, and only three years later the US General William Mitchell bombed and sank the ex-German Dreadnought *Ostfriesland*. The ship was moored and undefended, but this feat presaged future developments.

Naval aviation was very strong by the end of the First World War. On 1 April 1918 (when the RNAS merged with the RFC to form the Royal Air Force) the RNAS had nearly 3,000 aeroplanes as well as eleven airships, of which eight were rigids. At the end of the war, the German Navy had nearly 1,500 aeroplanes and nineteen airships, France 1,260 and 37, the USA 2,100 and twenty, Italy 630 and 36, and Austria-Hungary about 250. Despite all of this activity, it should not be forgotten that the difficulties and dangers of naval aviation were considerable at a time of limited navigational equipment, and many aeroplanes disappeared without trace over the sea.

THE DEVELOPMENT OF SPECIALISED GROUND-SUPPORT AIRCRAFT

AS SOON AS MACHINE GUNS WERE FITTED TO AIRCRAFT, the possibility of using them to attack ground troops arose. They obviously had the ability to attack soldiers where they would normally be safe – in their trenches – as well as being able to launch attacks against supply columns moving materials and reinforcements to the front line. Such attacks were only sporadic in the early war years. The first planned, large-scale use probably took place at the start of the Battle of the Somme in July 1916, when the RFC sent eighteen aircraft on observation/attack missions over the trenches. The Germans called these attacks 'punishment', or *Strafen*, from which came the term 'strafing'.

Ground-attack missions became much more common in 1917 in further fighting on the Somme. The RFC used Nieuport and F.E.2b fighters in May, carrying 20 lb (9 kg) bombs in addition to machine guns, to break up German troop formations. In the Ypres fighting of that year waves of aircraft delivered low-level attacks, and close co-ordination with the Army was quickly developed. Missions included the strafing of enemy airfields, troop movements and transport, including trains. The RFC distinguished between trench strafing (equivalent to the modern Close Air Support) and ground strafing (now known as Battlefield Air Interdiction).

At this time, ordinary fighters and two-seaters were used, some of which were considered to be particularly well suited to the task (or perhaps just not as good at air-to-air fighting). It seems likely that, as in the Second World War, air-cooled engines were found to be more suitable because of the vulnerability of engine cooling systems to small-arms fire. An example was the RFC's D.H.5, which had the benefit of good visibility provided by its backward-staggered top wing. On 23 November 1917 these aircraft were used to strafe artillery positions in support of a tank attack. The British also introduced the concept of dive-bombing to increase the accuracy of delivery of the small bombs carried by their fighters.

Attacks on front-line troops were highly effective at first, breaking up infantry attacks and seriously affecting morale. However, soldiers gradually learned that they could fight back with machine guns and other small-arms, and trench strafing then became much more dangerous. Loss rates increased and some important victims were claimed; the Italian ace Francesco Baracca was killed while strafing. At Cambrai, the RFC suffered 30 per cent casualties *per day* during ground-attack missions, with similar figures during the German offensive in March and the offensive at Amiens. No. 80 Squadron was in action from early March 1918 to the end of the war. It lost 168 officers during this period, on an average strength of 22. The morale problem then began to affect the pilots tasked with ground attack rather than the troops they were attacking. Consideration was given to providing the aircraft with armour protection, and even of developing specialised ground-attack types.

The Germans and the British adopted different approaches to the design of specialised ground-attack aircraft. The British had primarily been using single-seat fighters, so they thought in terms of armoured versions of the same general configuration. An experimental armoured Sopwith Camel T.F.1 (Trench Fighter) was produced early in 1918, fitted with three Lewis guns, two pointing downwards and one on the top wing. Vickers built the F.B.26A Vampire, one of the last pusher designs of the war, fitted with over 230 kg of armour plate and three Lewis guns in the nose, but by then the Sopwith Salamander had already been selected, specifically designed for ground attack with nearly 300 kg of armour; it emerged just too late to see action. It was equipped as standard with the usual twin Vickers, albeit with 1,000 rounds of ammunition per gun, but various additional experimental installations were reported, including up to eight downward-firing Lewis guns.

The last aircraft completed by the Royal Aircraft Factory was the A.E.3 Ram, an indirect development of the F.E.9 pusher fighter, intended as a specialised ground-support aircraft. It had an angular nacelle constructed of steel armour plate, with double walls in front and at the bottom. There were two Lewis guns in the nose, which offered limited movement, but it was so constructed that the guns could fire vertically downwards. For defensive purposes a third Lewis gun was mounted on a tall pillar behind the gunner. Thirty-two ammunition drums were provided. The A.E.3 was tested at the front, but did not find favour.

The Germans started from the experience with low-flying infantry contact patrols (*Feldfliegerabteilungen-Infanterie*) to

Three Schwarzlose M16 guns in a downward-firing installation for ground attack. The aircraft is an Austro-Hungarian Brandenburg C.I. (Courtesy Harry Woodman)

collect information about battlefield activities to help commanders understand what was happening. These tasks were primarily carried out by the C-type two-seat planes described above, which also became used for ground attack in the defensive battles of summer 1917.

In turn, the lighter and faster CL types were developed in 1917 for the *Schutzstaffeln* (known as *Schustas*, or protection squadrons). The CLs were good fighters despite being two-seaters and were used as armed escorts for reconnaissance aircraft as well as for ground attack. Armament was the usual one or two synchronised forward-firing LMG 08/15s, with a flexibly mounted Parabellum for the observer. The first of the CL-category aircraft was the Halberstadt CL.II, which entered combat in the second half of 1917. It was armed with one or two fixed guns and a flexible gun in the rear cockpit. The Hannover CL.II and CL.III sported a remarkable biplane tail, designed to increase the field of fire of the rear gunner by reducing the span of the tailplane.

These were conventional tractor biplanes, but the Junkers CL.I was different: an all-metal low-wing monoplane without any struts or bracing wires. It proved fast and strong, with the rear cockpit providing an unparalleled field of fire for the gunner, but only a few reached the front by the end of the war. Many of the *Schustas* were reorganised from November 1917 into *Schlachtstaffel* (*Schlachtstas*, or battle squadrons) for supporting infantry, and these units went into action towards the end of the Battle of Cambrai, in which they successfully aided the German counter-attack. They would often make low-level attacks behind the lines in order to catch Allied troops unawares and in the open.

The most specialised class of German ground-attack aircraft were the armoured J-type two-seaters, such as the AEG J.I and Junkers J.I which were used to equip *Infanterieflieger* units. The Junkers J.I biplane of late 1917, nicknamed the 'furniture van', was the first operational all-metal plane, having 5 mm of chrome-nickel steel armour covering the crew positions and engine. It proved difficult to shoot down, particularly since its powerful engine gave it a performance close to that of fighters. It was fitted with two forward-firing and one rear-firing machine guns as standard, with two additional guns angled to fire downwards as an option.

The Germans also experimented with the concept of the armoured ground-attack fighter, the *Panzer-Einsitzer*, given the function letters DJ to indicate its combination of fighter and ground-attack properties. This aircraft would need to combine armour and the carriage of light bombs with adequate performance for fighter-vs-fighter combat. AEG built first a triplane, then a biplane aircraft; the latter became the DJ.I. Of all-metal construction with fabric-covered wings and a dural-skinned fuselage, it had twin synchronised LMG 08/15 guns. Testing was under way when the war ended.

The German attacks of March 1918 were supported by CL and J planes, and countered by British fighters dropping bombs and strafing. RFC doctrine saw Camels and Bristol Fighters being mainly used for ground attack, covered by S.E.5a and Dolphin fighters. The air attacks proved very effective (particularly against horses, which panicked), but the RFC suffered heavy casualties once more as the non-specialised aircraft were not really suitable for the task. This conflict saw the first successful anti-tank missions, when the aircraft of 34 (Bavaria) *Jagdstaffel* attacked a column of advancing British tanks, stopping them with machine gun fire.

The French used bombers for ground attacks; for example Breguet 14 aircraft were active on both 4 June and 27 October 1918 in bombing troop concentrations out of artillery range, putting the forces out of action. Apart from the D.H.4, the US Army used mainly French aircraft for bombing and close support, such as the Breguet 14 bomber and the Salmson 2A2 for infantry contact patrols. Ground-attack aircraft also showed their worth away from the Western Front, with the retreating Bulgarian Army suffering heavy losses when caught in the open in Macedonia in September 1918, and the Austro-Hugarian Army being similarly mauled by the RAF a month later, following the battle of Vittoria Veneto.

The most dramatic example of the capability of ground attack occurred not in Europe, but during the British Palestine Campaign of 1918 against the Turkish Empire and its German allies. The RAF and the Australian Flying Corps were heavily involved in ground-attack missions both before and during this campaign, using Bristol Fighters, S.E.5a and D.H.9 aircraft. Adopting a strategy eerily reminiscent of the Gulf War of 1991, they attacked German airfields and air forces in July and August 1918 to reduce their ability to interfere, followed up by air attacks on ground positions. The ground campaign started on 19 September 1918 and led to an immediate Turkish retreat, with aircraft bombing and strafing the retreating army. Most destruction occurred at Wadi Zeimer on the 19th, where a large force was trapped in a defile, and at Wadi el Far'a on the 21st, where 44,000 rounds of machine gun ammunition were fired in ground attack, effectively destroying the Turkish Seventh Army. Descriptions of the scene after the attacks are full of awe at the scale of the death and destruction. Hardly any aircraft casualties were experienced, despite attacks being made at less than 30 m, because the Turkish morale collapsed in the face of the bombing and strafing and there was no effective resistance. Air strikes continued to great effect for the rest of the campaign, and Damascus fell on 30 September. It was the first campaign which could be said to have been won from the air.

Chapter 3

AIRCRAFT CANNON DEVELOPMENT
AND USE, 1914–32

THE RIFLE-CALIBRE MACHINE GUN WAS THE SUPREME air-fighting weapon during the 1914–32 period, but some nations put a great deal of effort in developing weapons of 20 mm and larger calibre. It should perhaps be noted that although the French used the term '*canon*' and the Germans '*Kanone*', no such term was in use for British weapons at that time; they were simply known as 'guns'. However, the more modern term 'cannon' will be used, as at present, to describe all of these large-calibre weapons.

Aircraft equipped with cannon were never available in large numbers, and most weapons developed saw little more than experimental use. Most of the guns used were manually loaded and a few were recoilless. Automatic aircraft cannon were only just achieving service status at the end of the war, and their development saw only very gradual progress until the 1930s. However, these weapons represent a fascinating side-branch from the main trunk of armament development, which was only to come to fruition during the next great conflict a quarter of a century later.

AMMUNITION

IT IS WORTH STARTING BY COMMENTING ON THE LEGAL status of the explosive and incendiary ammunition. The signatories to the Declaration of St Petersburg in 1868 renounced the use of any projectile weighing under 400 g which was either explosive or 'charged with fulminatory inflammable matter'. At that time, the appropriate calibre for 400 g shells was 37 mm, which accounts for the popularity of this calibre for decades thereafter. This limitation was generally adhered to until 1914. However, as we have seen, tracer, explosive and incendiary bullets were all developed and used even in rifle calibres during the First World War. After the fighting was all over, it was decided that the legal position should be clarified, and so in 1922 a Committee of International Jurists met at the Hague to consider a set of rules for aerial warfare. They decided that the use of tracer,

incendiary or explosive projectiles by or against aircraft was not prohibited. This draft Convention was never formally ratified, but everyone thereafter behaved as if it had been, albeit with a degree of nervousness in some quarters.

Projectiles used in cannon were quite different in form from those used in machine guns. They were made of steel, and except for a few specialised armour-piercing types, were hollow in order to contain high-explosive (HE) or other contents. Non-explosive AP types were known in the UK as 'shot', hollow HE projectiles as 'shells'. The steel bodies were too hard to be gripped by the rifling, so they were fitted with one or more 'driving bands', usually of copper. The HE shells needed to be detonated once they hit the target, so they were fitted with a fuze which normally incorporated mechanical safety devices to prevent detonation until after the shell had left the barrel. There were two basic types of shell: nose-fuzed and base-fuzed, the latter usually being semi-armour-piercing, so needing to have a hard point. One notable development was the extremely sensitive British No. 131 fuze, which had a flat nose covered with a metal foil which easily broke to detonate the shell on impact with fabric. It was fitted to several types of 37 mm and 40 mm shells, principally for use against airships.

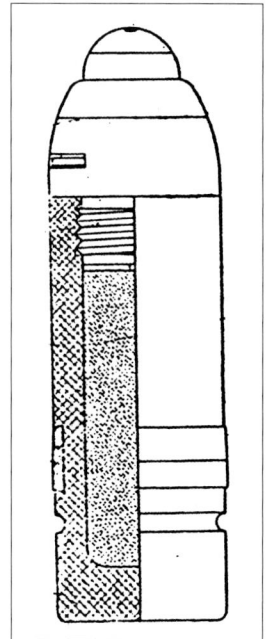

Sectioned Italian 25.4 mm HE shell. (*Courtesy Harry Woodman*)

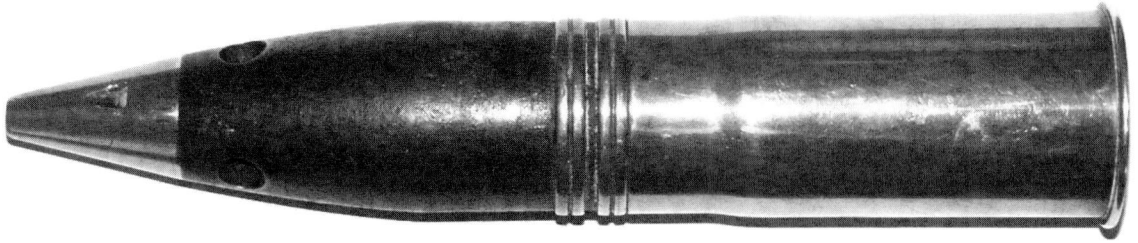

37 × 94R Hotchkiss cartridge with incendiary projectile; note the holes in the nose for the flames to escape. This shell was also fitted to the 37 × 201R. (Courtesy John Carlin)

The French and Italians used some incendiary shells for cannon which had large holes drilled near the nose of the shell. The shock of firing triggered the fuze, igniting the long-burning incendiary which flamed out of the holes as the shell flew towards its target; it must have been a spectacular sight at night!

An unusual variation in large-calibre projectiles was the use in a few French and Italian aircraft of canister shells, which were filled with a quantity of small balls just like a

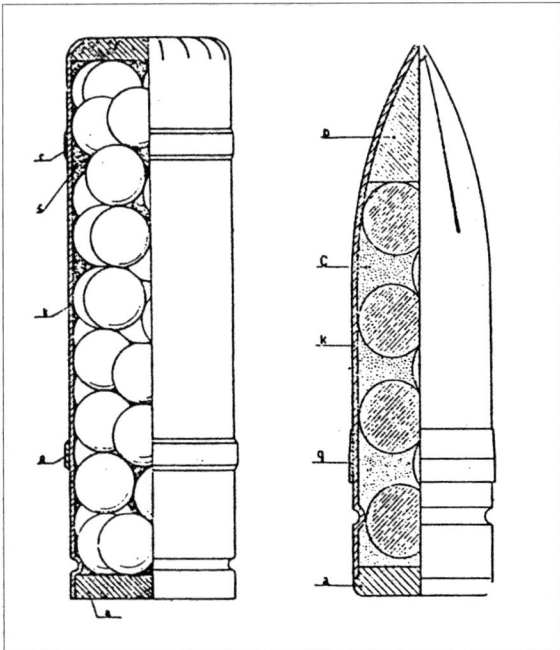

Two contrasting Italian styles of canister or case-shot projectiles for aircraft cannon: the 37 mm (left) and 25.4 mm. (Courtesy Harry Woodman)

giant shotgun. These had to be used with smooth-bored barrels, as rifling would have disturbed the pattern of shot. Little use was made of them, at least in part because of the need to reload the cannon by hand.

MANUALLY LOADED CANNON

The smallest calibre of cannon available before the First World War was 37 mm, because of the international agreement already mentioned. Most of these guns were substantial weapons intended for naval or artillery-type mountings and too heavy to be realistically carried into the air, but some lighter guns were devised which were more suitable for the purpose. The guns described in this section were all manually loaded, i.e. each cartridge was inserted into the breech by hand and the breech closed before firing. Some, but not all, featured automatic breech opening and ejection of the fired case immediately after firing, powered by the recoil, a feature known in artillery terms as 'semi-automatic'.

The first of the French 37 mm airborne cannon was the powerful M1902 'Tube canon', which fired a 37 × 201R cartridge. This was originally designed as a sub-calibre training device for fitting into the barrel of large naval guns (it economised on full-calibre ammunition), so needed to have a recoil-absorbing mounting added to it for use in aircraft.

The other common French aircraft weapon in this calibre was the short-barrelled naval Hotchkiss M1885, chambered for the low-velocity 37 × 94R cartridge. The M1885 was later modified with a smooth-bore barrel to fire the 'shotgun cartridge' shells in some fighters.

The Italians used the M1885 (as did various other nations) and also developed their own Vickers-Terni aircraft gun around the more powerful 37 × 201R cartridge. They referred to these guns as the 37/20.6 and 37/40 respectively, after the barrel lengths in calibres (i.e. the 37/40 barrel was 37 mm × 40 = 1,480 mm long), although the French used two different barrel lengths with the M1885.

Another gun to see service in French fighters was the SAMC, chambered for the usual 37 × 94R cartridge, which had a five-round vertical-feed ammunition hopper to simplify the manual reloading process.

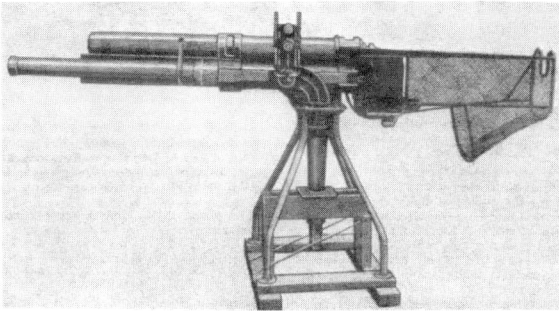

A French 47 mm cannon. (BuOrd USN)

A 47 mm Hotchkiss (produced by dismantling the old rotary cannon) saw limited use by the French, and even a 75 mm gun was tested (with a reduced muzzle velocity to limit the recoil).

The British made hardly any use of manually loaded cannon, except for the Davis guns mentioned below. An exception was the 1.59 in Vickers-Crayford (originally known as the 1.45 in Vickers Light Gun), which had the attraction of being very small and light for the calibre. This became popularly known as the Rocket Gun, after an early misunderstanding as to the nature of the weapon; in fact it was a conventional gun firing a 40 × 79R cartridge (a shortened version of the common 40 × 158R naval AA round). It was fitted with an imposing muzzle brake to reduce the recoil, as it was intended that the mounting would be interchangeable with the .45 in Maxim which Vickers then had in hand. Although the Crayford was approved for air service in 1917, the simple, artillery-type manual breech mechanism was so slow to reload that the gun saw little use.

A more powerful British weapon was the semi-automatic

37 mm Obukhov naval cannon modified for aircraft use, in the Obukhov works at Petrograd, May 1917. (Courtesy Harry Woodman/B. Stepanov/A. Alexandrov)

2 pdr Mk V, of which 40 examples were ordered 'off the drawing board', also in 1916. In this case, the 2 pdr naval AA case was extended to 40 × 240R, raising the muzzle velocity to 700 m/s. Initial enthusiasm soon waned, and the order was reduced to only two guns, but in March 1918 the delivery of the first gun was still awaited. It was expected that the gun would weigh 133 kg and that the ammunition would be fitted with the sensitive No. 131 nose fuze.

The Russians did produce small numbers of one locally designed gun, the 37 mm Obukhov, named after the steelworks near St Petersburg where the gun was built. It was produced just before or during the First World War, and reports indicate that ten were sent to the Baltic Sea Division in 1917 and probably a similar number to the Black Sea Division. Ten were still on charge at the Krasnoyarsk hydro aviation base in 1919. No data have survived, except that it was available with case-shot ammunition and in 1917 work was under way on a timed-fuzed shell.

Other manually loaded weapons were tried in various nations, but little if any information has survived about their characteristics, so they will be dealt with in the section on the applications of these guns.

THE DAVIS RECOILLESS GUNS

Early aircraft were very frail and found it difficult to cope with the recoil as well as the weight of a powerful, large-calibre cannon. There was therefore much interest in the recoilless gun (RCL) developed by the USN Commander Cleland Davis, which was available in three sizes: 2 pdr (40 mm), 6 pdr (57 mm) and 12 pdr (76 mm). There are also reports of an earlier 1½ pdr (37 mm) test model. The Davis guns had a breech that was open to the rear and used the counterweight principle, in which the cartridge fired a weight (normally lead shot) to the rear which was equal to the projectile weight, cancelling out the recoil.

The lack of recoil force meant that the Davis guns could be made very light (although long, as they effectively had two barrels, back to back) and also only needed a light and simple mounting. However, the cartridge cases were very big, as RCLs required much more propellant, and reloading was cumbersome and very slow. It was achieved by unlocking the two halves of the gun, then pulling the rear half backwards before rotating it along an axis parallel to that of

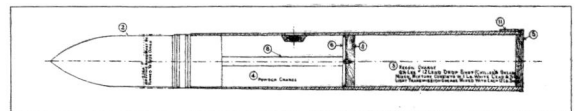

The cartridge case for the 6 pdr Davis RCL. Note that the rear element – the recoil charge with lead shot – is larger than the propellant charge. (Courtesy MoD Pattern Room)

Testing the Davis gun. The men seem more interested in observing the spectacular back-blast than on looking at the target! (*Courtesy Philip Jarrett*)

the barrel to clear the breech for extracting and replacing the cartridge.

To remedy this problem, a two-barrel gun and even a five-chamber revolver were considered. Even in the revolver, firing each shot in turn would have required separating both front and rear barrels from the cylinder, rotating the cylinder by hand to the next chamber, then retightening the gas seals. Neither design was built.

An unusual aspect of the Davis guns was that, owing to the lack of a conventional breech-block, the primer was in the side of the case, and it was ignited electrically rather than by percussion.

THE MAXIM POM-POM

The short-recoil Maxim gun was produced in large-calibre versions from early in its career. First was the belt-fed 37 mm 'pom-pom' of the late nineteenth century, so called because of the rhythmical noise it made on firing, and known in the UK by its projectile weight (450 g) as the One Pounder (or 1 Pr). Despite reports of its use (probably confusing it with

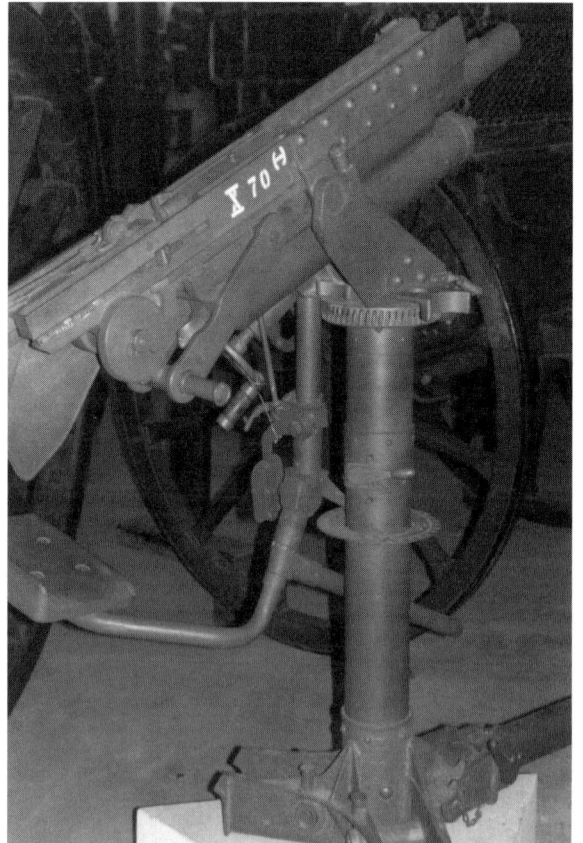

The 37 mm Sockelflak *cannon, shown on a ground AA mounting.*

the Vickers 1 pdr Mk III, described below) this gun was too heavy to fit into aircraft.

A lighter version of the pom-pom was built in Germany – the *Sockelflak*. This also fired its own ammunition, of 37 × 101SR calibre (450 g at 355 m/s) which was fed via ten-round clips inserted vertically over the breech. Although reportedly intended for aircraft (or at least airship) use, it was apparently only used in the AA role. It weighed 260 kg (with mounting), and fired at 120 rpm. The barrel was only 54 cm long.

LONG-RECOIL CANNON

The experience with large-calibre cannon clearly identified the need for weapons which could fire automatically without creating heavy recoil. One answer to this problem was the API blowback type described below; the other was the long-recoil mechanism described in Chapter 1.

One of the first of the long-recoil guns was the British COW gun, so-called because it was developed by the Coventry Ordnance Works. The first 1 pdr version, firing a rimless version of the usual 37 × 94 cartridge, was produced in 1913, but effort was soon switched to a 1½ pdr using a much larger (37 × 190) rimless case. The appearance was distinctive in that the recoil spring was wrapped around the barrel in the interest of compactness. Development work took a long time, and it was not until August 1917, following successful trials of the Mk III gun, that an order was placed for 90 of these weapons – the maximum that could be produced without affecting the output of other guns. The location of a 'shop' for making the COW gun was identified (somewhat improbably, a lace factory in Basford, Nottingham), and orders were increased to 250 for the Air Board, 50 for the Admiralty (cancelled in May 1918) and 50 for France. By August 1918 the orders had increased to 450 and the urgency of the order was stressed, but problems continued and only fourteen had been delivered. The end of the war saw the cancellation of the orders, with only those under construction being completed, and in all about 76 guns were delivered.

Vickers automatic 1-inch cannon. (Courtesy MoD Pattern Room)

Vickers also developed a long-recoil gun specifically intended for aircraft, the 1 inch, which fired a 25.4 × 87R cartridge (200 g at 470 m/s). The barrel group recoiled 19 cm between shots and the gun fired at 150 rpm. The weapon was 137 cm long, with a 76 cm barrel. The pintle mounting designed for it offered a maximum elevation of 40 degrees and could depress to a remarkable 90 degrees. Total weight of gun and mounting was 77 kg, the gun alone weighing 50 kg. Introduced in 1914, only one example entered British service (although it was made in Italy by Vickers-Terni who eventually sold some to the Swedish Navy), but it did inspire Revelli to design an improved weapon using rimless 25 × 87 ammunition, which was made by Fiat. This did get into service, but production had to be stopped when Vickers threatened to sue for breach of patent. In one respect, the Revelli-Fiat (or Fiat Revelli) M1917 was inferior to the Vickers; it used a small-capacity box magazine instead of a 25-round belt feed.

The 1.59 in Crayford gun (top) and 1½ pdr COW gun, showing the disparity in size. (Courtesy MoD Pattern Room)

Revelli-Fiat 25.4 mm cannon. (BuOrd USN)

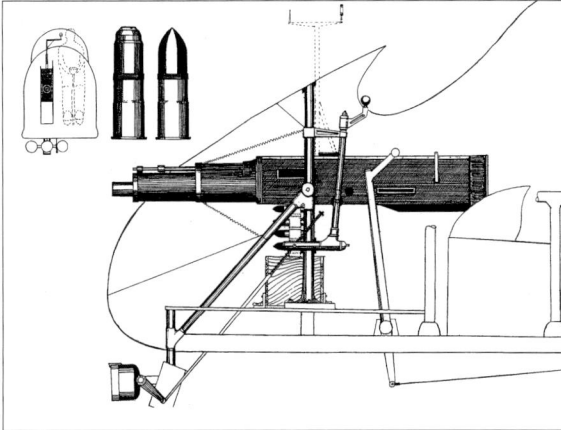

Vickers 1pdr Mk III with its 37 × 69R ammunition.
(Courtesy R.W. Clarke)

French experimental 'Puteaux' automatic cannon mounted in between the cylinder blocks of a Hispano-Suiza engine. (BuOrd USN)

The Vickers 1-inch design was scaled up to produce the 1 pdr Mk III, firing a shorter and less powerful cartridge (37 × 69R instead of 37 × 94R) than the usual 1 pdr Maxim with which it is often confused. It was accepted into service in 1915, but it appears that few were made. A special cone-type flexible mounting was devised for the gun. Some examples of a revised version, the Mk V, were built and tested just after the war in the R31 airship. No reliable figure for the rate of fire has been found, but it was probably in the region of 120 rpm.

The French were the major users of large-calibre aircraft cannon, but failed to get an automatic version into service before the end of the war. In 1918, two long-recoil AMC models were being developed at the Puteaux Arsenal – a low-velocity type using the usual 37 × 94R cartridge, and a high-velocity model designed around the COW gun's ammunition. The end of the war reduced the impetus for these developments, and it appears that neither saw service.

An automatic 75 mm gun was specified by France in 1917, and designs were prepared by COW, Armstrong and RGF. The COW design allowed for various loadings: a 5.4 kg shell at 400 m/s, 6 kg at 360 m/s, 6.2 kg at 350 m/s or 6.5 kg at 300 m/s. The total weight of the gun was estimated at 270 kg, with the recoiling parts weighing 190 kg, a recoil movement of 76 cm and a rate of fire of 30 rpm. Although an order was placed for four 75 mm COW guns (two of them for France), this was only a few days before the end of the war and none was built.

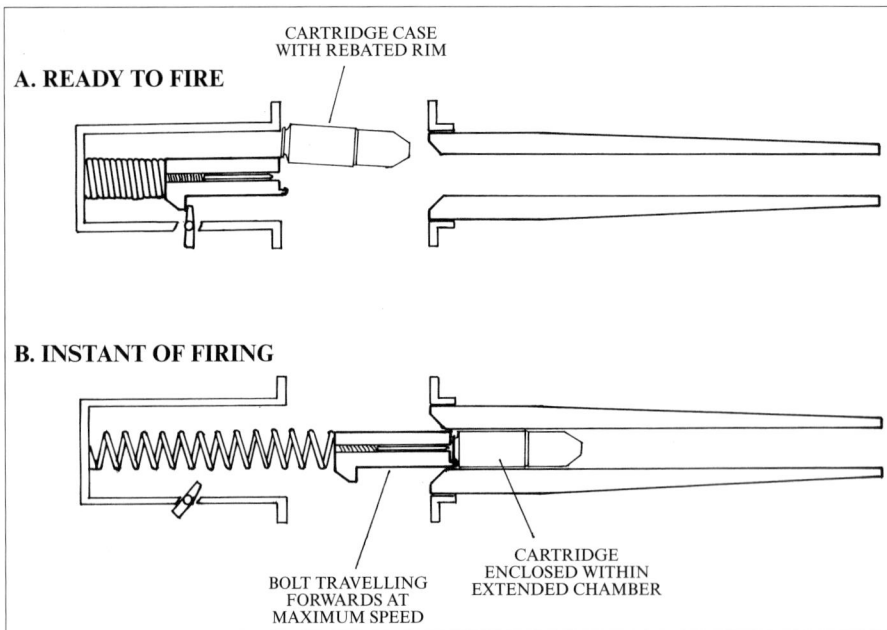

A. READY TO FIRE

CARTRIDGE CASE
WITH REBATED RIM

B. INSTANT OF FIRING

BOLT TRAVELLING
FORWARDS AT
MAXIMUM SPEED

CARTRIDGE
ENCLOSED WITHIN
EXTENDED CHAMBER

Advanced Primer Ignition Blowback (schematic).

API BLOWBACK GUNS

A different approach to automatic cannon design was taken with the German 2 cm Becker cannon. This was mechanically identical to the simple blowback except that the cartridge was fired just before it was fully chambered, while the bolt was still moving forwards at high speed. The initial rearward impulse of the cartridge case was therefore used up in stopping the forward movement of the bolt, before it could begin to drive the bolt backwards again. This delay gave sufficient time for the projectile to leave the barrel. Because the primer is fired before the cartridge is fully chambered, this operating principle is usually called advanced primer ignition, or API, blowback.

The API blowback is not only very simple, it has the added advantage of spreading the recoil energy over a long period of the firing cycle, as most of the initial recoil impulse is absorbed in stopping the forward movement of the bolt. Mountings for these weapons could therefore be simpler than with most other types of mechanism of equivalent power. The gun was also light, at 30 kg (plus 5 kg for a loaded 15-round box magazine; a 10-round magazine was also available). But there are some disadvantages: it works best with straight cases with parallel sides, because the case needs to slide to and fro in the chamber as the cartridge is being fired. As with other blowbacks, cartridges usually need to be lubricated with grease or oil to prevent the chamber pressure from sticking the case to the walls. The functioning of the gun is also very sensitive to the pressure generated by the cartridge, so it is affected by extreme temperatures and variable quality ammunition. One inherent feature of the APIB design is that it has to fire from an open bolt, so these weapons could never be used in synchronised mountings. The Becker was fitted with spade grips having two triggers – the right trigger for single shots, the left for full automatic fire.

All the cartridges for API blowbacks had rebated rims; this was important as it allowed the bolt, with extractor claw hooked over the rim, to fit within the lengthened chamber as it pushed the cartridge forward. It should be explained that in other weapons the shape of the chamber was designed to fit the cartridge precisely; in APIBs the fact that the cartridge was fired while it was still travelling forward, and needed to be supported in the initial stages of recoil, meant that the cylindrical chamber was significantly longer than the cartridge, which slid to and fro within it.

The concept for the Becker was reportedly developed by the Cönders brothers, but it was patented by Dr Rheinhold Becker of the *Stahlwerke Becker AG* in the Rhineland in September 1913. At first, the new weapon faced some resistance from the German armament authorities because of the lack of relevant experience of the company, but the German Army Air Service showed interest, and firing tests were

German 2 cm Becker with a 15-round box magazine.
(Courtesy MoD Pattern Room)

ordered in mid-1915. These tests were unsatisfactory, but the concept showed promise, so more technical assistance to Becker was provided by the nearby Spandau Arsenal in order to develop a satisfactory weapon. In June 1916 Becker received a production contract for 120 cannon, while Spandau continued developing the gun. This was followed-up by field trials of five cannon in August of that year, in which explosive tracer ammunition showed good results (it originally fired solid projectiles to avoid the prohibition on small explosive ammunition, but HE shells were soon developed). There were still ammunition feed problems which were not resolved until the introduction of the Type 2 Becker in November 1916. In 1917 it was agreed that Becker would build guns for air service, while Spandau and MAN-Nürnberg would make them for the Army, mainly for anti-tank use (the Type 3 built by Spandau was heavier – 42 vs 35 kg – and slower-firing – 250 vs 300 rpm – than the Type 2). By May 1918 the development of the gun was considered essentially complete, although work continued on the feed arrangements, with various drum and belt feeds being tested.

It is unclear how many Beckers were made. Some 362 were discovered by the Allies after the war, of which approximately one-third were supplied to the Army for anti-aircraft and anti-tank use. However, 428 aircraft Beckers were reportedly made by MAN alone (despite the earlier agreement). Becker's own production was very small until late in 1918; however, 111 cannon were delivered in September of that year.

In 1921 the patent for the Becker was acquired by the Swiss company SEMAG, which continued to market the weapon and developed its own, more powerful version, firing a 20 × 100RB cartridge instead of the original 20 × 70RB. In 1924 the rights to the guns were acquired by another Swiss company, Oerlikon, named after the suburb of Zurich in which the factory was based. They added a third weapon to the range, chambered for an even more powerful 20 × 110RB cartridge. By the late 1920s the three

*Two views of the 20 mm Oerlikon (SEMAG) Type L on
a flexible mounting with a 15-round drum magazine.*

(*Courtesy Harry Woodman*)

models were known as the Oerlikon F (20 × 70RB),
L (20 × 100RB) and S (20 × 110RB) and were offered in
various versions as aircraft, anti-aircraft and anti-tank guns,
but although these were effectively the only automatic cannon on the market at this time, sales were initially slow. All
three weapons were steadily improved through the 1930s,
with increases in rates of fire and muzzle velocity and
reductions in weight (during which their appearance was significantly altered), and they saw considerable use in the
Second World War, as described in the 1933–45 volume.

OTHER AUTOMATIC CANNON

In June 1915 the German War Ministry issued a specification for an airborne machine cannon with a calibre not to
exceed 3.7 cm, which should be able to fire ten rounds in
quick succession and weigh not more than 70 kg. It is known
that prototype guns to this specification were made by
Krupp, DWM (*Deutsche Waffen und Munitionsfabrik*) and
Rheinmetall (*Rheinische Metallwaren und Maschinenfabrik*),
but no further details of the weapons appear to have survived. It would seem that they were considered too heavy for
the aircraft in service at the time.

The Becker did of course already meet this specification,
as did another 20 mm weapon, the 2 cm Ehrhardt FlzK
(*Flugzeugkanone*, or aircraft cannon), which was made by
Rheinmetall. This fired a 20 × 70RB cartridge (similar to
the Becker's and often mistaken for it, but with a slightly fat-
ter case). It employed a scaled-up version of the Dreyse
short-recoil design, introduced in 1912 in an infantry
machine gun of that name, which used a pivoting-block lock
designed by Louis Schmeisser, a famous gun designer who

2cm Ehrhardt
FlzK aircraft
cannon.
(Courtesy MoD Pattern
Room)

ironically is best remembered in the popular name of a sub-machine gun with which he was not in fact involved. The Ehrhardt weighed 36 kg, was 150 cm long (with a 101 cm barrel) and fired at 250–300 rpm from a side-mounted box magazine. The locked-breech mechanism was considered superior to the Becker's by the APK (*Artillerie Prüfungs Kommission* = Artillery Test Commission), but it did produce more recoil and vibration, which led to many jams.

The Ehrhardt did make it into production, and at least 51 were built (one surviving example is stamped '51'), but it was too late to see service. After successful attempts to conceal its existence from the Allied Control Commission, it was developed post war by Solothurn, the Swiss subsidiary set up by Rheinmetall in 1929 in order to develop armaments away from the restrictions then in force in Germany. The results of these developments are described in the volume covering 1933–45.

In an advanced state of development at the end of the war was the German *Szakats*, a 19 mm gun which was intended to be produced in various versions for ground and air use. These all fired 19 × 114R cartridges, and used a form of retarded blowback mechanism with an additional piston and cylinder (liquid-filled in the later models) to check the violent recoil of the bolt.

One reference exists to a '3.5 revolver cannon' intended for installation in a Halberstadt CL.X, but no further details of this project are known.

There was considerable activity in developing cannon in Austria-Hungary. By the end of the war it reportedly had one 20 mm gun (given as the *Szanáts*, but this might have been the *Szakats*) and three different 25 mm cannon (the *Boykow-Czerney*, the *Szebeny* and one designed by the *Technischen Militärkomitee*) being developed, but details of how these weapons operated have not emerged.

THE FRENCH CANNON AEROPLANES

DESPITE THE FACT THAT EARLY AIRCRAFT HAD CONSIDERABLE difficulty in lifting themselves and their pilots into the air, experiments with fitting large-calibre cannon took place even before World War One. In 1910 the Frenchman Gabriel Voisin installed a 37 mm cannon in one of his aeroplanes for publicity purposes, but it never flew with this armament. The next year, ground tests of a 37 mm Hotchkiss mounted *in front of* the propeller of a Blériot 11 wrecked the aircraft. In 1913, a 37 mm gun was finally fired from a 'Voisin Canon,' a modified Voisin model 1913 with a 37 mm Hotchkiss cannon and a 200 hp engine.

Perhaps because of Voisin's experiments the French were the most enthusiastic and persistent users of airborne cannon. Various sub-types of the Voisin aircraft were available with manually loaded 37 mm cannon throughout the war. Both low-velocity (M1885) and high-velocity (M1902) versions were used, flexibly mounted in the front gun position of the pusher aircraft. The Breguet 5Ca2 was also originally fitted with a 37 mm cannon for bomber escort purposes, as

A 37 mm Hotchkiss M1885 in the nose of a Breguet Type 5. (Courtesy Harry Woodman)

A 37 mm M1902 on a Voisin. A note on the back of this photo records that the plane was brought down in January 1916. (Courtesy Philip Jarrett)

was the Caudron R.14, which appeared too late to see action.

Even larger guns were tried, including 47 mm Hotchkiss guns which were fitted to some of the last Voisins (for ground attack) and a Tellier flying-boat (for anti-submarine use; in British tests this gun managed to hole a submarine in Portsmouth harbour). Even a 75 mm gun, with reduced muzzle velocity compared with the artillery piece, was reportedly tested in a huge four-engined Voisin triplane in 1918. The ultimate cannon plane was still under construction at the end of the war, and never flew: the four-engined 'Henri Paul' was intended to be fitted with a 75 mm gun and several 37 mm for self-defence.

The original purpose of the French cannon was apparently to attack aircraft, and cannon-armed planes were used as bomber escorts. The first recorded engagement between a Voisin and a German plane was in May 1915, but without result. Some success was achieved in shooting down balloons during the Verdun battle, and in March 1916 a

Breguet 5Ca2 shot down an LVG with its cannon. Despite this success, the slow-firing cannon stood very little chance of hitting another aeroplane in the air, but the French persevered, drawing up in the spring of 1916 detailed specifications for cannon-carrying aircraft, designated Class D. The D1 types used the M1885 37 mm gun and were intended for air combat, while the D2 models had the M1902 version and were used for anti-balloon work and

A 47mm Hotchkiss in the nose of a Tellier flying-boat, for anti-submarine use. (Courtesy Harry Woodman)

ground attack. Cannon-armed aircraft were never very common; by 1 February 1916 there were just twenty-five at the front, and only about sixty by August 1917. One of the last of the pusher planes, the Breguet 12Ca2 of 1917, was equipped with a searchlight as well as a 37 mm gun and was stationed for defending Paris against Zeppelins.

Despite the problems of air-to-air shooting, the French fighter ace Guynemer was interested in the possibility of installing an engine-mounted cannon between the cylinder banks of the geared Hispano V8 aero engine, firing through the hollow propeller hub, and he inspired such an installation in the SPAD 12Ca1. There were two different types of 37 mm cannon available; some confusion as to their origins exists but it appears that one was a conventional SAMC design with a rifled barrel, the other was a modified M1885 smooth-bore firing canister shot, like a large shotgun. They are often referred to as 'Puteaux' guns, but this might just refer to the arsenal where they were made. A Vickers machine gun was also carried. The plane emerged in July 1917, and a number were built (although nothing like the 300 ordered), several pilots, including Guynemer, achieving some successes with it. These weapons were still manually loaded, however, and unpopular with most pilots because of their awkward loading and the propellant fumes which filled the cockpit on firing. Only eight were reported to be at the Front on 1 October 1918.

Forty SPAD 14 floatplanes, and some of the SPAD 24 land-plane version, were also ordered with a 37 mm cannon, of which a few may have reached service. Attempts were made to develop automatic-loading cannon, but these were too late for the war. Some French airships reportedly carried 47 mm and even 75 mm guns, but it is doubtful if they were ever used in action.

BRITISH AMBITIONS: RCLs AND AUTOMATICS

THE BRITISH ALSO PUT MUCH EFFORT INTO DEVELOPING cannon-armed aircraft, but with far fewer results, probably because they ambitiously aimed for fully automatic cannon at a time when these were too primitive to be reliable. Despite this, there was some interest in manually loaded guns, and the first installations were in specially designed pusher 'Gun-carrier' seaplanes from Short (S.81) and Sopwith (No. 127) equipped with a semi-automatic 1½ pdr (37 mm) Vickers Mark B gun (the Mark A being the fully automatic naval version). These were tested by the Admiralty with reasonable success, by firing them at a floating target in May 1914, although the effect of the recoil on the flying characteristics was reportedly noticeable. The British were also the main users of the Davis RCLs.

The British interest in cannon was principally for use in ground and naval attack rather than air fighting. They were also keen on upward-firing weapons to attack airships, although this proved ineffective. At the outbreak of the war Vickers had started work on a heavy fighter designed around the 1 pdr Vickers gun. The F.B.7 was a relatively conventional twin-engined biplane, with the gunner and gun in the nose. In August 1915 a dozen were ordered, but Vickers soon recognised that the type had no future and persuaded the War Office to cancel the contract. The concept was carried over in the smaller and lighter F.B.8, armed only with a Lewis gun, which it was hoped would possess superior performance to single-engined aircraft, but it did not and was abandoned.

The British equivalent to the light French 37 mm Hotchkiss was the 1.59 in (40 mm) Vickers Crayford which was developed in 1916. Interestingly, the initial order for 25 guns included ammunition consisting of 3,000 incendiary rounds and 2,000 of case-shot (i.e. like shotgun shells for close-range work), although interest in the latter ammunition soon disappeared. The order was increased to 100 guns and 250,000 rounds by the end of November 1916 for urgent home defence purposes, with higher-velocity AP shells being added to the order in February 1917. However, it seems that little use was made of these weapons, which despite being very light and handy were extremely slow loading. They were fitted to some F.E.2bs of Nos 100 and 102 Squadrons in April 1917 and tested on night operations. Experience was mixed: some liked them, and there is one report of stopping a train after firing thirty rounds at it, but other reports refer to unreliable ignition, leading to delayed 'hang-fires' owing to weak firing springs and defective primers. The Crayford was subsequently fitted to (or planned for) three different aircraft: the Parnell Zeppelin Scout of 1916, R.A.F. N.E.1 of late 1917 and the Vickers F.B.25 of early 1917. In all of these cases, the gun was intended for anti-Zeppelin use and could be fired upwards, but none of the aircraft entered production.

Some interesting experiments were inspired by the French. The Beardmore W.B.V had a geared Hispano-Suiza engine in the nose. It was intended to carry a 37 mm gun (probably an SAMC like the SPAD 12) firing through the propeller hub, but this was quickly discarded because pilots complained that the gun took up too much space in the cockpit, and were worried about the noxious fumes that escaped from the breech.

The problem of the heavy recoil of such cannon affecting the frail airframes of the early aircraft had already been addressed by the Davis recoilless cannon. These guns were tested in both the USA and Britain; in fact the Admiralty had expressed interest before the war began, and guns of various calibres were ordered during the war. In the USA, a gun was mounted in the front of the cockpit of a Curtiss

Twin JN aeroplane, aimed by means of a tracer-firing Lewis gun attached to the barrel.

The British carried out trials with the 2- and 6-pounder Davis guns in late 1916, and tested incendiary shells in these and the 12-pounder calibre. They were envisaged as being useful against airships (which were proving very difficult to destroy by other means) and an order was placed for 12-pounder incendiary shells to be tested against a 'Zeppelinette'. This was a target intended to represent an airship, and consisted of a 2 m cube of rubberised fabric containing hydrogen enclosed within a similar cube filled with engine exhaust gas (the British incorrectly believing this to be German practice).

The Davis guns were also considered useful for ground attack, with 'buildings, stores, ammunition dumps and trains' being identified as possible targets. The 2-pounder (40 mm) version was successfully fired from a Short 184 in April 1916, hitting a seaplane target which was being towed by a motor boat, but this installation could not be reloaded in flight.

Various anti-Zeppelin night-fighter aircraft were intended to use this weapon, probably the best-known examples being the large quadruplanes built by Pemberton-Billing. The P.B.29E of late 1915 was a twin-engined aircraft in which the fuselage was attached to the second wing, counting from below, and a streamlined gunner's nacelle filled the gap between the third and fourth wings – a 'fighting top' in the contemporary parlance. It was succeeded by the P.B.31E, which flew in early 1917. Its cockpit was faired into a towering structure that connected the fuselage between the second and third wings to gun positions on the upper wing carrying a Davis gun forward and a .303 in Lewis on a gun ring aft. The nose contained another gunner, with a Lewis. The purpose was to mount standing patrols against airships, and it was claimed that the P.B.31E could stay in the air for up to eighteen hours. But the ponderous aircraft could not have caught up with an intruder, and only the prototype was completed.

Also intended to be armed with the Davis gun was the Robey Peters R.R.F.25, designed to an Admiralty requirement. This was a large single-engined tractor biplane, with streamlined nacelles for two gunners attached to the upper wing, outboard of the propeller disk. The armament of the prototype consisted of a Lewis in the port nacelle and a Davis 2 pdr gun in the starboard nacelle, with ten rounds. Two prototypes were built in 1917, the second being intended to carry a Davis gun in each nacelle, but both aircraft crashed during testing.

The only service installations of the 2 pdr Davis gun appear to have been in a couple of D.H.4s at Dunkirk in 1917, and an R.E.8 in the Middle East in 1918 in which the gun was aimed forwards and downwards at a 45 degree angle for ground attack.

The Dutch designer Koolhoven created the Armstrong Whitworth F.K.5 and F.K.6. Both were sizeable single-engined triplanes, of which the central wing had a much greater span than the two other wings. Two small nacelles were attached to this central wing, outboard of the propeller, so that the gunners would sit in front of the wing. On the F.K.5 these were on top of the wing and on the larger F.K.6 they were attached to its underside. The F.K.6 may have been intended for Davis recoilless cannon, for in the spring of 1916 Armstrong Whitworth received wooden mock-ups of the 2-pdr and 6-pdr weapons. It is controversial whether the F.K.5 ever flew: pictures of the aircraft in a wrecked state suggest that it did so at least once. The F.K.6 was briefly tested.

The 6 pdr (57 mm) Davis gun was tested in the Short S.81 Gun-carrier in 1915 and subsequently fitted to a number of other aircraft for trial purposes: a B.E.2c in 1916 (it could be angled to fire 45 degrees up or down), a Short 310-B seaplane in April 1917 (aimed upwards for anti-Zeppelin use), a Felixstowe Porte Baby flying-boat, and a B.E.12 (in which the gun was mounted at an upward angle of 45 degrees for firing but could be lowered to the horizontal for loading). Trial installations of both 2 pdr and 6 pdr weapons were

Davis recoilless gun being loaded. (BuOrd, USN)

A Davis gun fitted to a Felixstowe flying-boat for anti-submarine use. The Lewis gun was used to sight the weapon. (*BuOrd, USN*)

A 1½ pdr COW gun on a Voisin. (*BuOrd USN*)

A 1½ pdr COW gun mounted in a D.H.4, late 1918.
(*Courtesy Harry Woodman*)

made in Handley-Page O/100s and O/400s, and several of these large bombers were fitted with the 6 pdr, for ground-attack and anti-submarine duties. It appears they were of little use, however, and were withdrawn before the end of the war.

There does not appear to be any record of the 12 pdr Davis gun being used in aircraft apart from initial tests. In 1915 the Admiralty issued a contract for a large seaplane, according to specifications drawn up by the Air Department for an anti-shipping aircraft. It was desired that the aircraft would be able to carry three alternative weapon loads: an 18 in Whitehead Mk VII torpedo and one Lewis; twenty-two 100 lb bombs and one Lewis; or a Davis 12 pdr recoilless cannon, firing 5.4 kg shells, and two Lewis machine guns. Extensive protection with armour plate was called for. To meet this specification Samuel Whites constructed the Wight A.D.1, a very large twin-boom seaplane. For some reason, perhaps because there were concerns about the blast and counterweight shot to the rear by the Davis gun, the design was then changed to accommodate a conventional 12 pdr Naval Landing Gun, with elevation ranging from -38 to +49 degrees. The first prototype turned out to be so overweight that it could barely fly; the second prototype was better streamlined and dispensed with some of the armour plate, but it never flew. The 12 pdr Davis gun never entered service, although there was a British scheme in 1916 for a Dyott 'Battleplane' to be fitted with one of these cannon, firing sideways while the aircraft circled the target. This was not built, but is remarkably reminiscent of the USAF's gunships of more than half a century later.

More interest was shown in automatic cannon, and two different types saw service – the 1½ pdr COW gun and the 1 pdr Vickers Mk III. The predecessor of the COW gun – the 1 pdr – was actually test-fired from an F.E.3 in 1913 (although the plane was suspended from a gantry rather than flying), and was also intended for the F.E.6 of 1914, but probably was never fired in the air.

The 1½ pdr version was much delayed by development and production problems. French aircraft were used for trials first, and only in October 1918 was a British machine available with a cockpit designed for the gun; it was fitted in the rear cockpit of three D.H.4 light bombers, angled upwards at 45 degrees for use against the giant R-plane bombers as well as Zeppelins. A hole was cut into the upper wing for the gun to fire through. Aiming was the job of the pilot, who instructed the gunner/loader when to fire. Various mounting, handling, sighting and buffer problems were resolved and over 1,000 rounds were fired, but the muzzle blast caused problems and the plane required light alloy plating to protect it, as well as some structural strengthening. In the event, just three D.H.4 aircraft fitted with this gun entered service in November, and only two of these reached the front, but they had no time to see action before the Armistice.

The gun was also tested in the Tellier flying-boat, a Voisin 8, two D.H.3As and a D.H.10 twin-engined bomber, and was intended for the three-seat F.E.4 of 1916. Two COW guns were proposed in August 1918 as defensive armament for the big Handley-Page V/1500 bomber.

The Vickers Mk III was in many ways the most promising of the First World War aircraft cannon, as it was light and compact, but its performance appeared to be disappointing as it saw little use. It was first installed in the Vickers F.B.7 of 1915, then in 1917 it was fitted together with searchlights in five F.E.2b aircraft for trials in the home-defence role. The gun was flexibly mounted in a widened front cockpit, with the gunner sitting next to the pilot. Two other F.E.2bs with this gun were sent to France and carried out night ground-attack missions during the summer of 1917 with some success, particularly against trains.

Although it was planned for the Curtis C and the Martinsyde F.1 and Vickers F.B.24 two-seat fighters of 1917, it appears that it only saw service in the F.E.2b. The use of the gun was not without problems: the recoil caused damage to the structure, and loose spent shell cases were sometimes blown back into the pusher propeller. The Mk III might have made a viable fighter weapon in a fixed installation, but the heavy mounting, plus the weight of the gunner, rather negated its compactness and light weight.

Another Vickers gun, the 1½ pdr Mk V NS (Naval Service), was experimentally fitted to airship R-31 for trials, but the war ended before the installation had been perfected.

In July 1918 a 'Statement of Guns for RAF' was drawn up which detailed all of the British cannon in service or on order, as follows:

GUN	IN SERVICE	ON ORDER	NOTES
1½ pdr COW Mk III	–	450	RAF, inc. 50 for France
1.59 in QF Vickers	150	–	Admiralty + RAF
2 pdr Davis	200	–	Admiralty + RAF
6 pdr Davis	60	25	Admiralty + RAF (cancelled October)
12 pdr Davis	40	–	Admiralty
6 pdr SA Vickers	–	25	Admiralty (to be cancelled)
2 pdr SA Vickers Mk III	1	–	Admiralty experimental
2 pdr SA Vickers Mk V	–	2	RAF trials expected
6 pdr EOC Non-recoil	–	2	Admiralty for trials
6 pdr COW Non-recoil	–	1	Admiralty for trials
6 pdr CSOF Non-recoil	–	1	Admiralty for trials
1 in Vickers	1	–	Admiralty experimental
1½ pdr EOC	–	1	Admiralty experimental

The list reveals many gun projects of which details no longer survive (and curiously omits the 1 pdr Vickers Mk III/V), but it does provide an interesting insight into the extent of British plans and experiments. In addition, COW guns in 47 mm and 75 mm calibre were reportedly developed for testing.

A 2 cm Becker (on the left) mounted along with an early model of the MG 14 Parabellum. (*Courtesy Philip Jarrett*)

GERMANY AND AUSTRIA-HUNGARY

THE MOST IMPORTANT GERMAN DEVELOPMENT SPECIFICALLY intended for aircraft use was undoubtedly the 2 cm (20 mm) Becker. An early version of the Becker was first tested in 1915 in a Gotha-Ursinus G.I, and at a June 1916 demonstration of the various 20 mm and 37 mm automatic cannon under development the Becker made the best impression. It was the only German cannon to see air service in the First World War.

There were a large number of projects and test installations of the Becker cannon, but very few of these saw any use. Although some applications were for air fighting purposes – it was fitted to some bombers and naval airships – it was primarily seen as a ground-attack weapon, particularly for use against tanks. There were therefore two basic types of installation: in the usual ring-type flexible mountings, for use by a gunner, and those fitted to fire downwards for ground attack. In addition, there were a few projects for using the Becker as a fixed, forward-firing gun in fighters.

At first, there were some problems with cramped flexible mountings because the rings were of too small a diameter; some early mountings used 90 cm diameter rings (an MG ring typically being 75 cm), but it was found that at least 100 cm diameter rings, and preferably larger, were needed to operate the gun effectively. The main users of such ring-mounted guns were the Friedrichshaven G.IIIa night-bomber and the armoured AEG G.IVk, also a twin-engined plane. The G.IIIa, several of which were delivered in September 1918, had a Becker in a nose mounting and used it to strafe ground targets when returning from bombing raids. A test was also made of a rear installation, and a ball turret for this aircraft was designed but not built. Five G.IVk were ordered in March 1918, following successful tests in a

A 2 cm Becker cannon in a specially modified nose of an AEG G.IVk. (Courtesy Harry Woodman)

G.IV. These were fitted with one Becker in a dorsal ring mounting (able to fire downwards through a 'Gotha tunnel') and another in an armoured turret in the lower part of the nose. In addition, two MG 14s were used for self defence. The planes were successfully tested in April, and four survived to be handed over in January 1918, but their service use is not known.

Unsuccessful or uncompleted projects using ring-mounted Beckers included the AEG J.I and C.IV, Dornier Gs.I flying-boat, Gotha WD 7 floatplane (two completed and tested) and the Hansa-Brandenburg W.19 floatplane (twenty ordered in June 1918, but never used). Hansa-Brandenburg also planned to use the Becker cannon in its W.23, installed to starboard with an LMG 08/15 to port, but it never saw service as its flying characteristics were unacceptable. A Becker was also proposed for arming the W.35 twin-engined flying-boat, but this was not built. The German naval air service was particularly interested in cannon in order to deal with the large and heavily armed Curtiss-type flying-boats which were a proving a nuisance over the North Sea.

The first downward-firing installation was a rather makeshift effort in an Albatros J.I ground-attack plane, in which the Becker was fitted to the left-hand side of the aircraft, outside the observer's cockpit, allowing a limited range of movement. This was tested in the air in December 1917, and eight examples of this model were delivered to the Front for combat evaluation in the spring of 1918. They were used successfully against rear-area transportation systems, but it was noted that fighter escort was essential. The installation was criticised for its limited field of fire and the difficulty of changing the big magazines against the slipstream (a large handle was accordingly added to the magazines). The ammunition also caused complaints because the trajectories of the tracer and HE shells were

different. One of these aircraft subsequently had the gun relocated to the floor of the observer's cockpit, which became the preferred location in single-engined ground-attack projects.

Other aircraft with downward-firing guns fitted in the observer's cockpit were the AEG J.II (twenty delivered in September 1918, use not known), Albatros J.II (not delivered), the LVG C.V (tested May–June 1918) and the AGO S.I *Schlachtflugzeug* (heavy ground attack – two completed October 1918, possibly never flown). The Albatros C.V was also tested with this installation, but with the curious twist that the pilot's controls were also located in the rear cockpit; it seems that the front observer was only expected to change the magazines. A (possibly fixed) downward-firing installation was also tested in the Gotha G.IV in mid-1918.

The Becker never saw service in fighters, although four projects involved it. The first was rather bizarre: it was fitted to an Albatros D.II fighter and tested in November and December 1916. The breech was in front of the pilot as usual, but because the gun could not be synchronised, it was angled up by 30 or 40 degrees to miss the propeller. The tests reportedly included combat evaluation, but this was presumably unfavourable as nothing more was heard of the installation. The only satisfactory configuration for installing this weapon in a single-engined fighter was the pusher layout, and this was adopted by the AGO C.I (planned in October 1918) and the Albatros D.VI. The D.VI actually flew in February 1918 but was damaged on landing. It was intended to carry an LMG 08 in its nose, as well as the cannon, but work on it was cancelled in June of that year. Finally, the Hansa D.I was a twin-engined fighter with a fixed Becker in the nose. It was still under construction at the end of the war.

Some of the experimental 37 mm German automatic cannon designed to the June 1915 specification were installed in aircraft. A Gotha-Ursinus G.I was tested with the 3.7 cm Rheinmetall cannon at the same time as the Becker trials in late 1915, and an AEG G.II carrying a Krupp or DWM cannon was shown to members of the *Reichstag* in April 1916. In 1917 a 3.7 cm DWM cannon was tested in two different Gotha WD 7 floatplanes, with air firing trials taking place between July and October, but the gun was rejected because of ammunition feed problems. No aerial tests of the 3.7 cm Krupp are reported, although four guns were made.

In complete contrast to the French, the Germans concentrated on automatic weapons, but did test one large-calibre manually loaded gun. A 13 cm *Ausstossrohr* ('launching tube') was mounted to fire downwards from the VGO.II R.9/15 bomber, and was tested on the ground and in the air during October 1916. This was apparently a recoilless weapon, but interest was then shown in a higher-velocity

An Austrian Albatros B.II with a 35 mm (?) cannon.
(Courtesy Philip Jarrett)

A 37 mm Obukhov on a Grigorovich M-9 flying-boat from the carrier Orlitsa, based in the Baltic. (Courtesy Harry Woodman/Y.J. Toivanen/A. Alexandrov)

Hansa-Brandenburg G.I bomber was used for various experiments in 1916, including a 50 mm gun and (separately) a 70 mm Skoda cannon weighing 200 kg, both being fitted in the nose, and a 37 mm Skoda was test-fired from a dorsal mounting early in 1917. A 37 mm weapon was also installed in a small flying-boat.

OTHER NATIONS' EFFORTS

THE MAJOR POWERS WERE NOT THE ONLY ONES TO EXPERIMENT with aircraft cannon: the Russians and the Italians also produced such installations, some of which saw service. The Russians fitted a 37 mm naval gun to an *Ilya Muromets* as early as 1914, mounted below the fuselage for ground attack, but tests showed that it was far too inaccurate, and so it was removed. Further tests in the following year of a 76 mm recoilless gun on the same type of aircraft were also fruitless, although that did not appear to discourage the development in 1916 of the unsuccessful *Morskoi Kreiser* (naval cruiser) floatplane, designed for a 75 mm gun of uncertain provenance. Apart from the 37 mm Obukhov gun mentioned earlier, which was fitted to at least one Grigorovich M-9 flying-boat (and presumably other aircraft as well), the only service use of cannon in Russia was of some Voisins armed with 37 mm Hotchkisses – probably the M1885.

The Italians produced and fielded one of the few fully automatic cannon – the 25 mm Revelli-Fiat. This was flexibly mounted in the nose of a Macchi L flying-boat, a dozen

and almost certainly conventional 10.5 cm weapon, which was ordered in November 1917. Lt. Dr Ernst Neuber designed an R-plane to carry this gun, firing downwards. It would have been a large but fairly conventional, eight-engined aircraft with a structure reinforced to absorb the 3,000 kg recoil force. Besides the cannon and 110 to 120 rounds of ammunition, eight machine guns would have been carried for self defence. This aircraft was never built.

The Austro-Hungarians were much more active in the development of large airborne cannon. They were responsible for fitting the 66 mm Skoda C95 L/18 Marine landing gun to the front cockpit of two large three-engined flying-boats designated G3 and G6. It was used to fire at Italian naval craft (apparently without result), and thereby earned the distinction of being probably the largest-calibre weapon to be fired in anger from an aircraft in the First World War.

Experiments and proposals were also made concerning weapons in 37 mm, 47 mm, 50 mm and 70 mm calibre. The

A 25 mm Fiat cannon mounted in the nose of a Macchi L. Note also the twin-barrelled Villar Perosa. (Courtesy Harry Woodman)

A Caproni Ca.3 with a bizarre mounting, reportedly for a Revelli-Fiat 25 mm 'cannoncino', although it more closely resembles the 1 in Vickers. (Courtesy Philip Jarrett)

First World War cannon cartridges: 7.92 × 57 for scale, 2 cm Becker (20 × 70RB), 25 mm Revelli-Fiat (25 × 87), Vickers 1 pdr Mk III (37 × 69R; with sensitive No. 131 fuze), Maxim 1 pdr pom-pom and French M1885 (37 × 94R), Vickers 1½ pdr (37 × 123R), French 'Tube canon' M1902 (37 × 201R), 1½ pdr COW gun (37 × 190), 1.59 in Vickers-Crayford (40 × 79R).

Savoia Pomilio S.P.2s, and a similar number of Caproni bombers, mainly Ca.3s but also Ca.4s and Ca.5s. However, a sensitive nose fuze caused problems with premature detonations of the HE shells. The Macchi was also reportedly tested with a 40 mm gun for anti-submarine purposes. The type is unknown, but it was most likely chambered for the 40 × 158R cartridge used in the Vickers 2 pdr AA gun, as this weapon was adopted by the Italian Navy.

POSTWAR DEVELOPMENTS

IN 1918 THE GERMANS WERE LEADING THE WAY WITH THE development of automatic aircraft cannon, with the Becker in limited service, the 20 mm Ehrhardt in production, and the 19 mm Szakats in advanced development. As we have seen, the direct line of development of the first two was continued in Switzerland, but at a much slower pace, and very little use of them was made until the mid-1930s.

One rare installation of the Oerlikon L (20 × 100RB)

was in the Savoia-Marchetti S.62bis flying-boats in the early 1930s, which carried one in the bows. A manufacturer's catalogue promoting this installation adds some interesting detail. The ring-type mounting weighed 55 kg and could traverse through 360 degrees while providing up to 90 degrees of elevation and depression (although depression was limited to 60 degrees in the S.62bis installation). The ammunition feed was via a 15-round drum which weighed 2 kg empty (each round weighed 220 g). Sights weighed another 2 kg and a sack to hold thirty fired cases weighed 1.2 kg (necessary because the S.62bis was a 'pusher', so it was important to prevent fired cases from flying back and striking the propeller). Although the gun had a cyclic rate of 350 rpm, the practical rate, allowing for magazine changes, was 125 rpm. The complete installation weight, including six loaded magazines, was 135 kg.

Once German rearmament commenced, automatic cannon again featured in their plans. Probably the earliest installation was in the Heinkel He 59 seaplane, which in its

The nose of a Savoia Marchetti SM.62bis showing the Oerlikon L mounting. (*Courtesy Harry Woodman*)

original version just fits within our 1933 time limit. This generally carried two MG 15s in nose and dorsal positions, but late in its life the nose gun was replaced for service in Spain by a 20 mm cannon mounted beside the gunner and used for attacking surface targets. This was probably a Solothurn weapon based on the Ehrhardt.

Various cannon were designed in the 1920s, but through lack of interest were not produced until later, if at all. Madsen started work on its 20 mm and 23 mm guns at this time, as did Hotchkiss on its 25 mm calibre. Lübbe, the prolific German designer, produced a 20 mm cannon in 1929 which reached test status, but this proceeded no further. Even the British tested 20 mm and 23 mm projectiles (but only fired from test barrels) before concluding that their extra destructiveness did not justify the substantial weight penalty of such weapons.

A British Admiralty study of 1921 referred to trials of 77 mm automatic guns in France and the USA, and noted that large-calibre guns had advantages over bombs in their striking velocity and in the ability to vary the range and angle of attack. This was despite the increased installation weight, the fact that the striking angle of the shells would not be vertical and the relatively small HE content of the shells (only 3–4 per cent of projectile weight, compared with 10 per cent for an AP bomb and up to 50–60 per cent for a blast bomb). The Admiralty considered that 3 in (76 mm) was the minimum useful calibre, with 4.7 in (120 mm) the maximum practicable. However, the 3 in was assumed to weigh 400 kg (over 1,100 kg including the mounting and 100 rounds of ammunition), while the equivalent weights for the 4.7 in were quoted as 2,200 and 4,300 kg respectively. It was noted that the muzzle blast from such weapons would be a major problem, and if they were to be fitted in flexible mountings this would put a limit on the permissible recoil length. A pusher or twin-engined aircraft would be needed to enable the gun to be mounted in the forward fuselage, and even the smaller weapon was considered too heavy for installation in a carrier-borne aircraft.

In practice, the only real British developments were the various efforts to find some productive use for the 1½ pdr COW guns which were mainly completed just after the war. Many of the trials were with large flying-boats in which the gun was intended primarily for anti-submarine work. The twin-engined Armstrong Whitworth Sinaia, the Short Cromarty and the experimental Vickers Valentia, all made in 1921, had provision for a 37 mm COW gun in the nose. In the late 1920s the Blackburn Iris and Perth, similar three-engined biplanes built in small numbers, were also available with a COW gun in their bow position instead of the usual Lewis, and in 1932 the Short Sarafand had a similar installation.

Some land-planes were proposed as mounts for the big

1½ pdr COW gun in Blackburn Perth flying-boat.
(BuOrd, USN)

cannon. The Bristol Bagshot and Westland Westbury were twin-engined, three-seat heavy fighters, designed to a 1924 specification for bomber-destroyers and based around the COW gun. The Bagshot was a high-wing monoplane, the Westbury a biplane, but both were armed with two flexibly mounted cannon in nose and dorsal positions. The muzzle blast was recognised to be severe enough to damage any normal structure, so strengthening had to be applied, and because of severe vibration on firing it was necessary to fit instruments and sensitive equipment on flexible mountings.

Perhaps the most remarkable were the two experimental COW gun fighters of 1931, designed to specification F.29/27 by Vickers and Westland. Not only did these single-seat, single-engined planes have a 37 mm COW gun as their sole armament, but it was angled upwards at 45–55 degrees for attacking bombers from below. The installation was based on the theory of the 'no allowance angle', at which the body lift from the projectile would compensate for gravity drop over an important part of the trajectory. The gun breeches were within reach of the pilot, who needed to keep the beast

An American Baldwin 37 mm cannon mounted in the nose of a Boeing GA-1. The four objects under the nose pointing downwards may be Lewis guns; the GA-1 is known to have carried eight. *(BuOrd USN)*

Despite all of this work, which including testing in various countries (including the USA, in an F.5L flying-boat), the only significance the COW gun achieved was to be used as the starting point for the Vickers 40 mm Class S design, after Vickers had taken over the Coventry Ordnance Works. The remaining COW guns saw out their days on AA mountings as airfield defence weapons (some mounted on lorries) in the Second World War. They were not finally declared obsolete until 1948.

Work on the Davis recoilless guns continued for a while. Following a series of experiments with all three calibres of weapon, the British concluded in April 1919 that 'no type of machine can be found which would enable a useful zone of fire to be obtained owing to the restrictions imposed by the rear charge', and the RAF took the decision to abandon all Davis guns. The USA also continued experiments with these weapons and were still testing them in 1921. The recoilless principle was then taken up by Kurchevski in Russia. His DRP-76 did see some service use and he went on to develop self-loading RCLs, including the APK-45. However, this was considered too slow-firing, and conventional cannon were adopted instead. A reported test of a 102 mm gun in an ANT-29/DIP was also unsuccessful.

The Americans acquired and studied with interest an example of the French automatic 37 mm cannon being developed at the Puteaux Arsenal. It was used as the basis for the Baldwin gun, which was tested during 1919–21 in the experimental GA-1 and GA-2 armoured ground-attack planes, but never accepted. Its main claim to fame is that John Browning was so unimpressed by his examination of the weapon that he decided he could do better, and he produced the basic design of the long-recoil cannon which was later developed in several versions to see extensive service in the Second World War.

fed with ammunition (the Vickers used 5-round clips of cartridges, the Westland a 42-round rotary dispenser from which rounds had to be fed singly by hand), and so they were mounted on the right-hand side of the cockpit. Both aircraft were unusual for their time: the Westland was a monoplane, while the biplane Vickers used a pusher layout. The RAF subsequently lost interest in this concept.

Chapter 4

Absorbing the Lessons: Aviation to 1932

Soon after the guns of the First World War fell silent at 11.00 a.m. on 11 November 1918, the vast military and naval forces accumulated by the warring powers started to be dismantled. Fighting did not cease everywhere, of course: the aftermath of the Russian Revolution of 1917 continued in the form of a civil war (with foreign interventions), with further fighting between Russia and Poland lasting until 1921. However, the strong European feeling of revulsion for war which resulted from four years of unprecedented slaughter soon led to armed forces being reduced to a fraction of their former size.

Air forces suffered particularly badly. These new organisations were mainly a constituent part of their nations' armies and navies (the British Royal Air Force, formed on 1 April 1918, being a rare independent exception), and with budgets being slashed dramatically, the better-established elements of the services used their greater reservoir of influence to defend themselves. The RAF's independence afforded it no benefit; the Army and the Royal Navy owed it no favours, and efforts were made to disband it altogether. These efforts very nearly succeeded: in November 1918 the RAF had almost 150 operational squadrons with 3,300 aeroplanes and 103 airships, but its decline was so drastic that it was soon down to one-tenth of that number, mostly abroad. Between April 1920 and September 1922, the air defence of Great Britain was in the hands of just *one squadron* of fighters.

In such an anti-militaristic, cost-saving atmosphere, the development of war machines almost ground to a complete halt. The aircraft in, or just entering, service at the end of the war remained the mainstay of air forces for many years. Even when they wore out, their replacements tended to be cautious and conservative designs, benefiting from gradual increases in engine power which permitted greater weights but only incremental improvements in performance. The revolution that saw the traditional biplane layout, with its fabric covering, bracing struts and wires and fixed undercarriage, replaced by sleek monoplanes, only began to have a

significant impact in the mid-1930s.

It need not have been like this. After a slow start, Germany developed in the First World War an increasing technological lead over other nations. They fielded the first synchronised gun installations, the first fighters with twin guns, the first of the classic two-seater tractor aeroplanes with a rear-cockpit gun layout, the first strategic bombing campaign, and by far the best airships. The Junkers D.I fighter of 1918 was remarkable: a very clean, all-metal low-wing monoplane, its configuration was about fifteen years ahead of its time. The same could be said for the little Junkers F 13 civil transport of 1919, which remained in production for thirteen years. The big, four-engined Zeppelin-Staaken E.4/20, which first flew in 1920, was less fortunate. This very advanced, all-metal, four-engined, monoplane civil transport was considered to have too much military potential and was scrapped by the Allied Control Commission, for under the terms of the Treaty of Versailles Germany was permitted no air force – or aircraft guns.

In 1918 it was again the Germans who were leading the way with a different approach to armament. The 2 cm Becker cannon had entered limited service and the 2 cm Ehrhardt was in production, with the 19 mm Szakatz in advanced development. No other nation had, or was developing, comparable weapons, and cannon were rarely fitted to aircraft until the mid-1930s. Even rifle-calibre guns were going through a revolution, with the twin-barrel Gast and the (Austrian) twin-barrel engine-driven Gebauer in advanced development. None of this had any post-war impact, except for the very gradual development of the Becker and Ehrhardt designs in Switzerland, away from the Control Commission's watchful eye.

Fighter guns in other post-war nations remained the usual pair of synchronised rifle-calibre machine guns mounted in the cowling. The guns themselves changed very little for several years. The USA standardised on the .30 in Browning which was just about to enter service at the end of the war, the French developed the Darne (later adapted to a new, rimless, 7.5 × 54 cartridge), but the British retained the Vickers and Lewis guns (albeit in improved form) until the late 1930s. Defensive armament actually deteriorated: one gun per mounting (cheaper, lighter and easier to handle) became usual instead of the twin mountings which were general at the end of the war.

This does not mean to say that nothing was learned from the First World War, or that no changes took place in the fifteen years that followed. On the contrary, service staff (with no serious wars to fight) concentrated endlessly on analysing and appraising the past conflict, seeking to draw conclusions that might guide the future development of strategy and tactics, and the military equipment that these would require. Sometimes these analyses showed considerable insight amounting almost to prescience; sometimes the ideas were completely mistaken. There were even some wars during the 'inter-war' period which involved air combat, for example the Peru–Colombia conflict of 1932–33 and the Bolivia–Paraguay 'Gran Chaco' war of 1932–35, in which the belligerent nations used a variety of American and European aircraft, but it appears that little was learned from these. Instead, many of the advances in aeroplane design which occurred in the 1930s were inspired by civil rather than military developments.

LESSONS OF THE FIRST WORLD WAR
DESPITE THE POPULAR EMPHASIS ON THE MORE GLAMOROUS

fighters and bombers, the key function of aeroplanes throughout the war was reconnaissance. This was vital in ensuring that commanders were well informed, and its existence turned the course of some of the early battles of movement, for example the Marne and Tannenberg in 1914. Later on, aerial reconnaissance became particularly important in the static conditions of the trench warfare which dominated the Western Front, as it was usually the only way of finding out what was happening on the enemy's side of the line. This kind of reconnaissance affected strategy, as it became virtually impossible to mass the force needed for a major attack without that becoming known to enemy aircraft. The removal of the element of surprise in attack may even have had the effect of prolonging the war, as it was much easier to defend effectively against a known attack.

Airships were originally preferred for naval reconnaissance because of their great range and endurance, plus their ability to fly slowly enough to keep station with the fleet without falling out of the sky. They remained of interest well into the inter-war years; in 1931 and 1933 the USN commissioned two huge helium-filled dirigibles (*Akron* and *Macon*) which acted as flying aircraft-carriers, each carrying four small fighter-reconnaissance biplanes in an internal hangar (Curtiss F9C Sparrowhawk, armed with two synchronised .30 in). However, both dirigibles were lost at sea in accidents by 1935 and the experiment was not repeated. The only airships that remained in military service were the non-rigid

Inter-war MG cartridges: 6.5 mm Swedish (6.5 × 55), 7.5 mm French (7.5 × 54), 7.5 mm Swiss (7.5 × 55), 7.62 mm Russian (7.62 ×54R), American .30-06 (7.62 × 63), 7.65 mm Swiss (7.65 × 22), 7.65 mm Belgian (7.65 × 53), 7.7 mm Breda (7.7 × 56R; also British .303 in and IJN 7.7 mm), 7.7 mm IJA Type 92 (7.7 × 58SR), German 7.9 mm (7.92 × 57), 11.35 mm Madsen (11.35 × 62).

'blimps', used by the USN, initially for anti-submarine work and later as airborne early warning and control craft until the 1960s. None of these craft carried a gun armament heavier than machine guns.

The more bellicose wartime activities can be divided into air fighting, ground attack, and tactical and strategic bombing. There were clearly overlaps between these; fighters were used for ground attack, and the distinction between ground attack, tactical and strategic bombing sometimes depended more on the particular mission than the aircraft used.

By the end of the war the fighter had evolved into a pattern that remained little changed until the mid-1930s. The emphasis was on manoeuvrability and rate of climb rather than speed. With little serious warfare going on (or anticipated in the foreseeable future), the priority was flying rather than fighting qualities. In contrast, the ground-attack role and the aircraft and armament selected for it were much more controversial, for several reasons.

First, there was no agreement about the optimum type of ground-attack aircraft, and several different schools of thought emerged. The first two represented a continuation of the wartime dispute about the merits of specialised two-seat armoured aeroplanes (previously favoured by Germany) and those of modified fighters (as preferred by the UK). The former was vulnerable to enemy fighters unless protected by escorts, the latter to ground fire unless well armoured (in which case they were less good as fighters). The other two approaches were represented by light single-engined bombers, faster than specialised ground-attack aircraft but essentially unarmoured, and (later on) by dive-bombers. It was also very common to retain the wartime concept of combining the reconnaissance role with that of ground attack, in the 'army co-operation' type of aeroplane.

An even bigger issue was whether the air force should be engaged in ground attack at all. Pilots had learned the hard way that while trench strafing could be spectacularly effective against inexperienced infantry, it could also be extremely costly against tougher opposition. Losses towards the end of the war had been heavy, with, for example, No. 80 Squadron of the RAF losing an average of 75 per cent of its pilots *each month* in ground-attack missions over the last ten months of the war. Even more significant in some air forces (particularly the RAF) was the concern that the ground-attack mission was politically dangerous, in that it subordinated the air force to the army's demands. Officers in various air forces came to believe that the best chance for sustaining an independent existence was to adopt roles that enabled aircraft to operate by themselves, to achieve results which the two older services could not. This was the key reason for the wholehearted adoption of the concept of strategic bombing and the preference for long-range bombers able to take the war to the enemy.

Modified Scarff ring installation mounting twin Lewis guns. Note the elastic-cord elevation adjustment compensation device. 1920.

THE STRATEGIC BOMBING PHILOSOPHY

THE FIRST WORLD WAR HAD SEEN VERY LITTLE WHICH could be called strategic bombing. This may be defined as attacking the enemy infrastructure far away from the scene of the ground fighting; factories, rail junctions, ports and even whole cities were the targets. The immediate aim was to cripple the enemy's ability to sustain its army in the field, but the ultimate hope of the strategic bombing enthusiasts (despite the lack of evidence from the war) was that the horror of being bombed would compel civilian populations to demand peace without armies or navies needing to be engaged at all.

Germany had taken an early lead with strategic bombing, using first airships and later the G- and R-class bombers. However, it was the British who showed most interest in the aggressive use of air power. As early as June 1917, General Henderson of the British Air Board was urging the American Mission, led by Col. Bolling:

> Over and above the army machines and the fighters, there must be on hand a maximum number of airplanes that a country is able to produce to use against the enemy in bombarding him out of his position and cutting off his communications and destroying his sources of supply.

Furthermore, the British practised what they preached. In June 1918 a strategic bombing arm called the 'Independent Force' was established, although it was still in embryonic form by the time of the Armistice. By August 1918 the percentages of aircraft in the three categories of Fighter, Observation and Bomber in the RAF were 55/23/22 respectively. In contrast, the German ratios were 42/50/8 and the averages for the USA, Italy and France were all very similar at 42/48/10. The Allied plans for July 1919, had the war continued, showed the growing interest in bombers, with the

RAF, still in the lead, planning to change its emphasis to 36/10/54 and the three other Allies to averages of 24/48/28. The ideal of the bombing enthusiasts was to acquire as many fighters as were needed to ensure dominance of your airspace, to acquire as many observation aircraft as were needed to support the army, then to devote all other available aviation resources to bombers, capable of operating at night.

The most extreme among the enthusiasts for strategic bombing was the Italian soldier and writer, Giulio Douhet. He commanded one of his country's first army air units and gave much thought to the future of air power. By 1915, when Italy entered the First World War, he had already conceived of the strategic bombing of cities directed against the morale of an enemy population, rather than the destruction of military communications and sources of supply envisaged by most other bomber advocates. In 1921 he published *The Command of the Air*, in which his theories were expounded, and supplemented this with further writings until his death in 1930. His views had considerable influence among inter-war military aviation enthusiasts of many nations, not only for their apparent merits in suggesting a quick and decisive form of waging war which would avoid the long-drawn-out agony of trench warfare from which Europe was still recovering, but also for the inter-service political reasons previously mentioned.

Douhet provided the rationale for an entirely independent – and important – air force with a role quite separate from that of the army and navy. This was music to the ears of the military aviation establishments, which in most cases were subordinate to the army and/or navy (the Italian *Regia Aeronautica* joined the RAF in achieving independent status in 1923). Even the RAF felt itself under constant threat and seized eagerly on an independent role as a potential war-winner. This led the RAF to ignore, as far as it possibly could, any notion of providing support to the Army or Navy, with unfortunate results in the Second World War. It also led to a serious neglect of the needs of the Fleet Air Arm. In contrast, the US Army and Navy retained control of their air arms, albeit Congress in 1920 established the US Army Air Service (USAAS) as equivalent to the Infantry, Cavalry and other arms (this became the USAAC – US Army Air Corps – in 1926).

By the end of his life, Douhet had consolidated his ideas into a series of principles, the first and key one being:

The purpose of aerial warfare is the conquest of the command of the air. Having the command of the air, aerial forces should direct their offensives against surface objectives with the intention of crushing the material and moral resistance of the enemy.

In order to achieve this, Douhet proposed a fleet of large, general-purpose 'battleplanes', armed to defend themselves and to sweep aside enemy opposition as well as for bombing, many of which could be converted from civilian transports as soon as war threatened. He regarded all other types of military aircraft (or air defences) as a waste of resources, with the exception of a high-speed armed reconnaissance type. Everything was to be concentrated on the offensive: the aim was to destroy the enemy's will to fight as quickly as possible, and Douhet envisaged that wars would be very brief. His final principle was:

An Independent Air Force formed with all the resources a nation has at its disposal for its aerial forces, made up of a mass of battleplanes and (some) reconnaissance planes, acting decisively and exclusively on the offensive, will soon wrest command of the air from an enemy air force constituted, organised and performing in a different way.

The experience of the Second World War was of course to prove him wrong on many counts (although the advent of nuclear weapons ironically made his ideas relevant again), but his importance lies in the influence his ideas had at the time. It was popularly and firmly believed that 'the bomber will always get through', and there was a general expectation that the next major European war would commence with an immense aerial bombardment which would devastate cities within days. This contributed to the fear of war which made the European democracies reluctant to confront the cancerous growth of dictatorships until circumstances forced them to.

These attitudes had a significant effect on aircraft and armament policy. The independently minded air forces wanted bombers, the bigger the better, well armed with defensive machine guns. Speed was not thought to be important. Fighters remained in service partly, one suspects, because they were popular with pilots and partly because politicians liked them since they were more obviously defensive and also, of course, less expensive.

The RAF did make one compromise to the demands of ground fighting in the form of a series of 'army co-operation' aircraft, but their job was less to co-operate with the Army than to replace it. Britain's resources were severely stretched by the desire to police the more turbulent areas of the Empire, such as the Middle East, Africa and the extensive and mountainous terrain of the North-West Frontier between India and Afghanistan. The RAF demonstrated that a small force of aircraft could undertake the role of colonial policing or, as it was called at the time, 'Air Control'. This involved punitive air raids against rebellious or unruly populations, and was advocated by the RAF as a cheap and effective way to maintain order in the Empire. At the Cairo conference of 1921, Sir Hugh Trenchard advocated eight squadrons of aircraft to replace thirty-nine Army battalions and sixteen batteries of artillery, a plan that was approved despite the hostility of the Army and the Navy. The policy of air control meant that almost all the strength of the RAF was based in the colonies and in Ireland, with at one time just one squadron left in England.

In general, the targets of air control operations were property, in the form of houses or livestock; before the raid the people where warned with leaflets or by aircraft equipped with loudspeakers, and instructed to remove themselves to a safe place. Humanitarian concerns did not always prevail, and on several occasions the population was bombed or machine gunned. Opposition was minimal and consisted of tribesmen taking shots against the attacking aircraft with obsolete rifles. Crews forced down by damage or mechanical problems were, evidently, at great risk.

Spain and France made similar use of aeroplanes in their own colonial excursions in Morocco against the Rif forces of al-Karim. In 1924 the Spanish tried a Douhet-style, five-month strategic campaign against villages, markets, livestock and crops, including the use of poison gas, but achieved so little that emphasis shifted back towards the tactical use of air power. French Morocco was drawn into the conflict in 1925, and the French made very effective use of air power for reconnaissance, observation and liaison, as well as in direct attacks. Most notably, their aeroplanes worked very closely with mobile forces, including tanks and armoured cars.

The USA seemed to be least receptive to the bombing philosophy. Of the total of 3,633 aircraft accepted from manufacturers in the eleven years between 1920 and 1930, 22 per cent were pursuit planes (fighters), 72 per cent were for observation and just 6 per cent were bombers. However, the USMC started experimenting with dive-bombing during the 1920s, following its introduction by the British during the First World War. As a tactic, it seemed far preferable to the dangerous low-altitude strafing attacks. The workhorse of the Marines was the D.H.4, equipped with suitable bomb racks. In 1927 the USA sent the Marines to intervene in an internal conflict in Nicaragua. At first the USMC did not get involved in the fighting, but this changed when the rebel officer Augusto Sandino refuzed to accept the negotiated cease-fire and withdrew to the mountains. Again, air support proved its value in difficult terrain in which ground troops could move only very slowly, when dive-bombing attacks saved a beleaguered Marine outpost.

The US Navy also showed interest. Dive-bombing held promise as an accurate method to attack ships, especially as ships at this time carried very few AA guns that would present a real danger to a dive-bomber. It was found that machine gun bullets could penetrate the decks and bulkheads of destroyers. Machine guns and light bombs could also cause serious damage to equipment on deck and would cause casualties to crew in unprotected positions. On the other hand, heavy bombs were required to seriously damage large ships of war. Hence the Navy defined two categories.

The light dive-bombers were derived from the initial experiments with fighter aircraft such as the Boeing FB, Curtiss F6C and Vought VE-7. These led to the development of the Curtiss F8C-2, -4, and -5, which were primarily dive-bombers despite their fighter designations. They were three-seat aircraft, armed with two fixed and one flexible .30 in Browning guns, and able to carry a 500 lb (227 kg) bomb. The line extended to the BF2C of 1934, a single-seat fighter and dive-bomber (hence its dual BF designation) armed with two fixed .30 in guns. The 'heavy' dive-bombers of the USN did not have a secondary role as fighters, and were able to carry 1,000 lb (454 kg) bombs. Martin built the BM, from which Great Lakes later developed the BG. These aircraft were armed with one fixed and one flexible .30 in gun. The category evolved into dual-role scout (i.e. reconnaissance) and dive-bomber aircraft.

After evaluation the combination of the fighter and dive-bombing role was seen as less desirable, so the Vought F3U and Curtiss F12C multi-role fighter type were redesigned as the Vought SBU and Curtiss SBC dive-bombers. In the process, the fixed armament was reduced from two machine guns to one, combined with one flexible gun.

FIGHTERS

AS ALREADY INDICATED, FIGHTER DEVELOPMENT WAS generally slow and cautious. Once the wartime designs needed replacing, the RAF acquired a series of basically similar biplanes in small numbers, starting with the Gloster Grebe of 1923, followed in 1924 by the Armstrong Whitworth Siskin (notable for having the RAF's first all-metal structure), the 1926 Gloster Gamecock, the 1925 Hawker Woodcock and the 1929 Bristol Bulldog.

The original Siskin, flown in 1919, had two guns mounted in the open in front of the pilot – the same as the World War Two pattern. Complete redesign produced the Siskin II of 1922, in which the Vickers Mk II guns were moved to lower positions on the engine cowling, entirely exposed to the air stream. A similar mounting was made on the Siskin V for export, but on the Siskin III for the RAF the guns were again moved to directly in front of the pilot, and enclosed in the bulging front fuselage decking, only the barrels being visible. The breech ends and cocking handles of the guns protruded into the cockpit above the instrument board.

The not very successful Hawker Woodcock of 1925 was the RAF's first dedicated night-fighter. The two synchronised Vickers machine guns were not installed in their traditional location above the engine, as the muzzle flash would have blinded the pilot. Instead they were attached externally to the fuselage sides. Not even a gesture towards streamlining the gun installation was made.

On most later RAF fighters, which were usually described as 'day- and night-fighters', the guns were installed on the sides of the fuselage and buried within its contours. Gloster used such an installation on its long series of fighters, from the Grebe of 1923 over the Gamecock and Gauntlet to the Gladiator of 1935; the latter carried two more guns on the lower wing. The breeches of the Vickers guns had to be within reach of the pilot to clear jams, and on Gloster fighters they were at the same level as his seat. Bristol followed a similar practice with the Bulldog of 1929, but put its guns rather higher, at the level of the shoulders of the pilot, which must have made them easier to reach in flight. The gun barrels fitted in a trough that extended forward, to a point between the cylinders of the radial engine.

Some British designs achieved sales despite not being accepted by the RAF, as there was a small but worthwhile market in countries that did not have a mature aviation industry. One oddity was the Fairey Pintail of 1920, which was designed to meet a requirement for a two-seat fighter for operation with a wheeled or float undercarriage. To clear the field of fire for the rear gunner, there was no upright tail fin; instead there was a small ventral fin and the rudder was attached to the fuselage and the ventral fin. The type was not adopted by the RAF (although Japan bought three Pintail IV fighters), and Fairey did not use this type of tail design again. Several other designs were adopted by Japan, the Danecock went to Denmark, and in 1930 the Vickers Type 143 Bolivian Scout was sold, unsurprisingly, to Bolivia. This had the effect of spreading the traditional British armament around the world, with Vickers and Lewis guns being used in many different countries and the associated .303 in cartridge (7.7 × 56R) being widely adopted.

An interesting experiment was the Boulton Paul Bittern night-fighter of 1928, a twin-engined, single-seat monoplane. The first prototype had a fixed Vickers in each side of the fuselage, but the second prototype had instead a Lewis mounted on a revolving barbette on each side, so that they could fire forwards or upwards. The ring-and-bead gunsight was mounted on a frame which elevated together with the guns.

There were other experiments with the use of upward-firing armament, described in the RAF as 'no-allowance shooting'. In 1934 a pair of Vickers guns firing upwards at 60 degrees were installed in one Bristol Bulldog fighter, and a pair of Lewis guns in another. Results were good, with a hit rate of 90 per cent at a target 1,000 ft (300 m) above the fighter; nevertheless, the system was not adopted.

After the war air-cooled radial engines, usually without any cowling, had become the most popular power sources for aircraft, because they were light and reliable. But the

development of liquid-cooled engines had not ended. Early versions, like the German six-cylinder in-lines, the Rolls-Royce and Liberty V-12s and the unusual post-war Napier Lion W-12 (with three rows of four cylinders connected to the same crankshaft), were made with separate cylinders, but the wartime Hispano-Suiza engine started a new trend with its one-piece cast-aluminium cylinder blocks. This led to a generation of new aircraft engines, most of them of V-12 or inverted V-12 configuration, with cast light-alloy crankcases and cylinder blocks, the latter with steel sleeves for the cylinders. These engines were compact, efficient, could be installed in low-drag cowlings, and in geared versions they potentially allowed the installation of engine guns mounted between the cylinder blocks to fire through a hollow propeller hub.

The first of the new engines was the Curtiss D-12, and Curtiss unsurprisingly designed a fighter around it, the PW-8 of 1924, which soon evolved into the P-1 Hawk. A development with a more powerful V-1650 Conqueror engine became the P-6. All these were armed with twin synchronised .30 in Browning guns, installed on top of the cowling between the cylinder banks, except for the P-6E, which had its guns moved to the side of the fuselage, below the cylinder banks. The experimental XP-6H was armed with six guns, one Browning being installed in each wing just outside the propeller disk. The last P-6E off the production line was converted into the XP-23, much modified and armed with one .50 in and two .30 in guns. These experiments did not result in production orders.

The first British aircraft to profit from the new breed of engines was the controversial Fairey Fox. The designers of this streamlined single-engined biplane bomber ignored Air Ministry specifications and, perhaps even worse, installed an American engine, the D-12. To reduce drag Fairey developed a 'high-speed mounting' for the Lewis gun in the rear cockpit. It took the form of a hinged semicircular arm, which allowed the gun to be stowed in a plywood box that was incorporated in the upper decking of the aft fuselage. This also had the benefit that the rear cockpit had a smaller opening than required by a Scarff ring, and therefore was less draughty. The gun was provided with six ammunition drums and could also be moved to a bracket on the floor of the rear cockpit, firing downwards through a trapdoor in the lower fuselage. This was considered quite useful to defend the aircraft when it flew at high altitude. The pilot had a fixed Vickers Class E gun with 300 rounds.

Fairey's outright heresy had produced an aircraft that could easily outpace contemporary fighters. But only 28 were ordered, some of them powered by the Rolls-Royce Kestrel, the British adaptation of D-12 technology. When the annoyed Air Ministry issued a revised requirement for a fast bomber, Fairey was not even sent a copy until it protested.

The contract went to the Hawker Hart, also powered by the Kestrel and armed with a fixed Vickers Mk II or Mk III and a Lewis on a Hawker gun ring in the rear cockpit (the Swiss version was fitted with their 7.5 mm Fl. Mg 29 guns). The Hart was an excellent aircraft, and like the Fox before it was faster than contemporary RAF fighters. The short-term solution to that problem was to develop a fighter version from it. The Hart Fighter, soon renamed the Demon, initially had one synchronised gun, but two were fitted to production Demons. The fuselage was slimmer and the gunner's position in the rear cockpit was redesigned, the gun ring being tilted forwards to improve the field of fire.

Trials soon showed that the gunner could not efficiently operate his gun in the powerful 300+ km/h slipstream. Experiments with air current deflectors did not produce satisfactory results. A better solution was the powered 'lobster-back' turret, so named because of the segmented metal shielding that protected the gunner's back from the airflow; its front and top were open. This hydraulically operated turret was designed by Frazer-Nash and Gratton-Thompson, under the joint tradename of Nash & Thompson, but many turrets were built by Parnall. Aircraft equipped with this turret were known as 'Turret Demons' and several dozen were retrofitted, a process which involved cutting the plane in half to install the turret. The turret included adjustable seating, heating for both gun and gunner, an oxygen supply, an illuminated reflector gunsight, a telephone to the pilot and, as a last resort, room for a parachute. The Aeroplane and Experimental Establishment (A&EE) at Martlesham Heath preferred a rival solution demonstrated on the experimental Bristol Type 120, which consisted of a Scarff ring surmounted by a transparent cupola which rotated with the gun ring. Despite this, it was the Nash & Thompson turret that saw squadron service with the RAF.

In the early 1930s a very original fighter design was submitted by Westland and Geoffrey T. R. Hill, a designer who aimed to create stable tailless aircraft. The Pterodactyl V mounted the traditional pair of synchronised Vickers guns, but because it was a tailless tractor design it was also ideally

A Lewis gun mounted in the Frazer Nash 'lobster-back' turret fitted to a Hawker Demon fighter. (Courtesy Philip Jarrett)

suited for a tail turret with a wide field of fire. A very compact electrically operated turret was designed for it, mounting twin Lewis guns installed on their sides. The turret was operated by a continuously running electric motor, coupled to the turret drives by infinitely variable friction clutches. Both rotation and elevation were controlled by a single control stick. The performance of the aircraft was disappointing, and it is unclear whether the turret was ever installed in the airframe.

The long-term solution was to fit the Kestrel engine in a streamlined biplane fighter design. This emerged in 1931 as the Hawker Fury. Twin synchronised Vickers Mk II or Mk IIID guns were installed in the top decking. Because the pilot sat relatively far aft, their barrels rested not on top of the engine but on top of the fuel tank, which featured two deep troughs for the guns. Gun stoppage problems, especially at high altitude, were frequent: that the guns were not kept warm by the engine may have been a factor. Both the Fury and the Hart were also produced with radial engines for export, but this did not affect the armament.

The RAF remained faithful to the Vickers and Lewis combination throughout the inter-war period, but for Latvia Beardmore designed a two-seat fighter armed with its own guns. On the Beardmore W.B.26 of 1925 the pilot fired two fixed, synchronised Beardmore-Farquhar machine guns. The observer was to have one or two similar weapons, and his position was carefully designed to give an optimum field of fire. The Latvians rejected the underpowered aircraft after brief testing.

A need for increased armament was recognised, because the increasing speed of bombers reduced firing times, and a specification for a multi-gun fighter was issued, F.10/27. Saunders-Roe offered the A.10, which had four synchronised Vickers guns, all in the cowling. The Gloster SS.19 had two synchronised Vickers guns and four Lewis guns, one on each wing. Firing trials with this aircraft demonstrated the value of multi-gun armament. Also of future significance was another prototype, the Vickers Vireo of 1928, a low-wing monoplane naval fighter which had its two Vickers guns mounted in the wings outside the propeller disk, with a mechanical linkage to enable the pilot to operate the charging mechanism. However, the Vickers was too unreliable to be mounted out of reach of the pilot: a better gun was necessary.

Other experiments concerned various tests with heavy machine guns, including the US Browning .5 in M1921 (12.7 × 99), the Vickers .5 in Class B (12.7 × 81) and the BSA .5 in M1924 (12.7 × 81). Specification F.20/27 was also intended to call for an armament of four .30 in guns, but because of an administrative mix-up it was released in a version calling for only two guns, although with the option of replacing .30 in by .50 in guns. The British felt that the HMGs

The BSA M1924 .5 in MG, here shown on a tripod for ground use. *(Courtesy MoD Pattern Room)*

did not inflict significantly greater damage on (unarmoured) airframes to be worth the extra weight, recoil, cost and complexity, and lower firing rates, compared to RCMGs. The .5 in gun's typical recoil blow of 2,250 kg, compared with 800 kg for an RCMG, also caused mounting problems. The range advantage of the bigger gun was not felt to be worthwhile because the maximum effective range of an aircraft gun, limited by aiming problems, was well within RCMG capabilities anyway. With ball or AP bullets, the large-calibre weapon would simply punch a slightly bigger hole, although it was acknowledged that if armour became generally fitted to aeroplanes that could alter the balance of advantages. The possibility of loading HMGs with explosive shells was regarded with interest, but felt to be too dangerous to use in a synchronised weapon, and there was also some concern about infringing the Declaration of St Petersburg, which was still officially in force (despite its widespread flouting during the war). Similar tests were carried out in the USA, with .50 in Browning guns being fitted to various aircraft, and although the reports were sceptical about the advantages of the HMG it was not entirely discarded and remained in limited use, although none was in service even by 1928.

The British conducted experiments with 20 mm and 23 mm calibres as already mentioned, but interest switched in the late 1920s to a high-velocity, high-RoF 7 mm gun, with a twin-barrel version for observers. This did not result in an acceptable weapon.

The other major inter-war exporters were the French, who maintained a highly productive aircraft industry and sometimes displayed a rather more adventurous attitude to aircraft design. The Dewoitine company produced a series of parasol-winged monoplanes from the D.1 of 1922 to the D.27 of 1930 which sold well abroad but saw little use in France. The D.1 was sold to Yugoslavia and made in Italy as the Ansaldo A.C.2. The D.9 was also Italian built as the A.C.3, while the D.21 sold to several countries. All of these had the usual twin synchronised guns (Vickers at first,

7.7 mm Darne later) but the D.9 was also available with two additional Darnes in the wings. The Swiss acquired several versions and equipped them with their own 7.5 mm guns: the D-1, D-9 and D-19 with the MG 11, the D.26 and D.27 with the Fl. Mg 29.

Dewoitine were not the only French company that favoured parasol-wing monoplanes: the 1923 Gourdou-Leseurre GL-21 and GL-22, with one or two synchronised Vickers, were built in small numbers for export to Finland, Czechoslovakia, Estonia and Latvia, and the successor GL-32 of 1927, with two 7.7 mm, saw French service. The 1929 Wibault Wib.72 of similar configuration was also made by Vickers as the Type 121 for export to Chile, while the 1932 Morane-Saulnier M.S.225 parasol was the last of this type to sell in significant numbers, curiously quoted as being fitted with Vickers rather than Darne guns.

The famous firm of Nieuport, now twinned with Delage, continued to produce a range of traditional biplanes, culminating in the 1928 Nieuport-Delage Ni-D 42C sesquiplane, which unusually was fitted with two wing-mounted 7.7 mm guns as well as one synchronised one. This was developed into the Ni-D 52, which was sold to Spain, and the Ni-D 62, both of them being fitted with twin Vickers synchronised guns.

The French also made some use of two-seat fighters, notably the 1920 Breguet 17, a scaled-down Breguet 14 bomber, which had twin synchronised Vickers plus a twin Lewis flexible mounting and a single down/rearward-firing Lewis for the gunner.

The Italians, having mainly relied on foreign designs in the war and for a while afterwards, began to develop a family of biplanes produced by Fiat, starting in 1924 with the C.R.1 and continuing with the 1927 C.R.20 (built in considerable numbers) and the 1932 C.R.30. The last of these saw the usual Vickers guns replaced by Breda-SAFAT in the same 7.7 mm calibre, although the service adoption of this weapon did not take place until after the period covered by this volume. An interesting pointer to the future was that the prototype had an early version of the 12.7 mm Breda-SAFAT, but this installation did not make it into production.

Many of the smaller European countries developed their own fighters. The most successful was the Dutch Fokker company, whose owner switched production of his designs from Germany to his native Netherlands at the end of the war. The series of Fokker sesquiplanes started in 1924 with D.XI and finished in 1932 with the D.XVII. These initially used the Hispano-Suiza, but the D.XII, D.XIII, D.XVI and D.XVIII represented developments of the same basic biplane design with different engines, although the D.XIV was an experimental monoplane fighter.

Initially these had the usual twin synchronised Vickers, but the armament varied to suit the customer. The D.XI fighter aircraft ordered for the clandestine German air force usually had the old LMG 08/15, a few being equipped with the MG 08/18. The D.XIII was created following the Ruhr crisis of 1922, when France and Belgium occupied the Ruhr in an attempt to force further restitution payments, as agreed in the Versailles treaties, out of the bankrupt Germany. With an eye on possible armed resistance, the *Reichswehr* ordered 100 Fokker D.XIII fighters in the Netherlands. The USAAS versions of the Fokkers (purchased for evaluation purposes) were fitted in the USA with .30 in and .50 in Brownings. The later D.XVI and D.XVII standardised on a pair of FN Browning 7.92 mm M36s.

German military aviation was slowly recovering since the relaxation of the terms of the Treaty of Versailles in 1926, and Germany established a flying training school at Lipetsk in the USSR. However, funds were short given the economic conditions of the late 1920s, so the Germany military had to abandon its plans to develop new bombers. In 1930 a new fighter was introduced, the Arado Ar 64, but this was a highly conventional biplane design armed with twin synchronised 7.92 mm machine guns; and the same was true for its replacements, the Ar 65 and He 51. Other types tested in Lipetsk were the Albatros L 76 and the slightly different L 77. Both were two-seat biplane fighters, armed with two fixed synchronised guns and a single flexible one, although as we have seen one of them was tested with a 20 mm cannon of unknown type in the dorsal position.

The requirements set out in 1932 for new German aircraft still provided for little innovation in armament: the planned single-seat fighters would have two fixed guns, the two-seat fighters two fixed guns and two flexible ones, the light bombers and reconnaissance aircraft one fixed and one flexible gun. However, as alternative armament for the fighter a 20 mm engine cannon with 200 rounds was considered. This was important, because it influenced the design of a new generation of engines and allowed the installation of engine guns on the German fighters during World War Two.

In 1925 Czechoslovakia adopted the Avia BH-21 biplane (two synchronised Vickers), in 1931 Sweden chose the Svenska J 6A *Jaktfalk*, and in 1932 Poland fielded two native designs, both high-wing monoplanes: the PWS 10, which was not entirely successful, and the PZL P.7, the first of a range of fighters from this company. Both had the usual paired synchronised guns, initially Vickers in 7.92 × 57, but soon replaced by Brownings in the same calibre.

Meanwhile, by far the most interesting developments were occurring in the Soviet Union. At first, the disruption caused by the establishment of the USSR meant that foreign designs were acquired, including, between 1922 and 1924, 100 Martinsyde F-4s, 30 Ansaldo A-1 Ballilas and 200 Fokker D.XIs. In 1923 the prototype Polikarpov-designed IL-400 flew. This was an advanced low-wing monoplane fighter (I for *Istrebitel* (fighter), L for the US Liberty engine which was

made as the M-5), but although several were produced these saw no service use. In 1925 the Grigorovich-designed I-2 biplane, later fitted with two 7.62 mm PV-1s mounted on the fuselage sides, became the first Russian-designed fighter to enter service.

In 1928 the pace quickened with the Sukhoi-designed I-4 all-metal sesquiplane and the Polikarpov-designed I-3 composite construction biplane, both with two synchronised guns. Soviet officialdom could be impatient with delay, and in 1930 the I-5 was produced by a design team, including Grigorovich and Polikarpov, while they were interned in a hangar of a Moscow plant to encourage them to get on with the job! This was a composite-construction biplane, initially with two PV-1 guns, but later versions had four. Slow deliveries of this aircraft led in 1932 to the licence-construction of Heinkel HD37c biplanes as I-7.

By 1932 the Soviets had decided on two complementary fighter types – *manevrennye istrebiteli* = manoeuvrable fighters (biplanes), and *skorostnye istrebiteli* = high-speed fighters (monoplanes). This meant that they kept biplanes in service for longer than most nations, but it also stimulated the development of fast monoplanes at a time when few other nations were interested. Two-seat fighters, such as the DI-6, were also produced.

The Soviets were imaginative in their use of fighters. They developed the concept of 'parasite fighters' in the early 1930s: a TB-1 monoplane bomber carried two I-4s above its wings in order to extend their range and provide some self-protection. This combination flew in December 1931 and the fighters were successfully released. The whole combination was known as *Samolet-Zveno* = aircraft-aircraft link, or Z-1, and experiments continued for some years.

The USA, having slammed its burgeoning military aircraft industry to a virtual halt at the end of the war just as it was getting under way, began to develop its own designs. The Army's aircraft included the 1920 Thomas Morse/Boeing MB-3A, 1925 Boeing Model 15 (PW-9), 1926 Curtiss P-1 and 1929 Boeing P-12 and Curtiss P-6. All of these were conventional biplanes with twin synchronised .30 in Browning guns (although experiments with the .50 in Browning were conducted), but the unsuccessful 1932 Berliner-Joyce P-16 added a rear gunner with a flexibly mounted gun.

The Imperial Japanese Army (IJA) acquired a range of foreign designs for production in Japan, in order both to obtain the latest technology and to help establish its own aircraft industry. In 1919 the Nieuport 24.C1, built by Nakajima, was adopted as the Army Type Ko-3 (one synchronised Vickers), followed in 1923 by the Army Type Ko-4 (Nakajima Nieuport 29.C1) with two Vickers – the Army's first mass-produced fighter, in production until 1932. In 1931 the Nakajima Army Type 91 parasol-wing fighter was adopted, followed in 1932 by the German-designed

Kawasaki Army Type 92, both of these featuring twin synchronised Vickers guns.

SINGLE-ENGINED BOMBER/ RECONNAISSANCE AIRCRAFT

SINGLE-ENGINED TWO-SEATERS FORMED THE MOST COMMON type of military aircraft produced in the inter-war years. They were cheaper than multi-engined types yet more versatile and useful than fighters, with their suitability for reconnaissance, light bombing and liaison duties. There were subdivisions of this type, with some concerned solely with reconnaissance, and others, often of lower performance, tasked with general army co-operation duties, including the colonial policing role. More specialised functions included torpedo-bombing, ground attack and, towards the end of this period, dive-bombing. For the most part, they were tractor-engined biplanes with the classic front pilot/ rear gunner layout first introduced in the German C class in 1916.

The RAF ended the war with large numbers of D.H.4 and D.H.9A aeroplanes in this class, so it was 1924 before a replacement emerged in the form of the unsuccessful Fairy Fawn. This was followed in 1926 by the Fairey Fox and in 1930 by the Hawker Hart, as already described. Also entering service in 1930 was the Fairey Gordon, a development of the IIIF naval reconnaissance bomber with a radial engine and a distinctly less spectacular performance than the Hart. All of these planes had the usual synchronised Vickers gun plus a Lewis for the rear gunner.

The army co-operation role involved certain equipment differences, including message pick-up hooks and long exhausts to prevent glare from affecting the pilot in low-level night flying. In other respects, many of the aircraft were

A carefully posed picture showing the reloading of an inter-war British plane with ammunition for the Vickers and Lewis guns. (Courtesy Philip Jarrett)

virtually identical to the light bombers. The 1924 Fairey IIID general-purpose aircraft (also available as a seaplane) was followed in 1927 by the Armstrong Whitworth Atlas, the first aircraft expressly designed for the support of ground troops to be used by the RAF, particularly in the Middle East. It was supplemented in 1928 by the Westland Wapiti (which used D.H.9 wings as an economy measure), and in 1932 it was replaced by the Hawker Audax, based on the Hart bomber. This was followed by the Hawker Hardy (a 'tropicalised' version of the Hart) and the Vickers Vincent, a development of the Vildebeest, both in 1934. All had the standard Vickers plus Lewis gun armament. The G.4/31 competition for a 'general purpose' aircraft nevertheless produced some interesting armament installations, including the rotating transparent cupola installed in the Bristol 120, as mentioned before. Westland equipped its P.V.7 with the 'Westland Patented Shielding Device', in fact a segmented canopy that could be folded back to operate the gun. And Vickers equipped its Type 253 (the winner of the competition, though not built in production) with a windmill-driven rear gun mounting. The windmill below the fuselage drove one half of a friction clutch, and the gunner could engage the clutch using a dial to rotate his gun mount. The ingenious mount also adjusted the gunner's seat with the elevation of the gun, and provided him with oxygen and electricity for his heated flying suit – for the gunner remained completely exposed to the elements. As far as the doctrine of army co-operation missions was concerned, such types had an adverse effect because the RAF was left totally unprepared for the demands of European warfare. In 1936 the second prototype of the new Westland Lysander army co-operation aircraft was sent for service testing – on the North-West Frontier of India!

RAF land-based torpedo-bombers also had the same general configuration and the same Vickers plus Lewis gun armament. The Hawker Horsley was introduced in 1927, and was replaced in 1932 by the Vickers Vildebeest (which looked about as attractive as the beast it was named after), which was still in service in 1939.

The RAF also received a 'heavy' single-engined biplane bomber, the Avro Aldershot, which entered service in 1924. Its defensive armament consisted of a fixed Vickers for the pilot, offset to port on the fuselage top decking, a single Lewis on a Scarff ring for the gunner, and a ventral Lewis gun that could be operated by the bombardier. To give the gunner the best possible field of view, the tailplane was raised to the level of his eyes, so it was well above the fuselage. Only fifteen of these aircraft were built and little is known about them, but records indicate that they were (intended to be) equipped with electric gun heaters and self-sealing fuel tanks – well ahead of their time!

France produced the Amiot 120, a single-engined biplane.

The production version was the Amiot 122, of which 80 entered service from 1929 onwards. The type had originally been designed as a two-seat night-bomber (Category *Bn2*) armed with two guns, but was reworked into a three-seat high-altitude bomber (or *Bp3*). Armament was increased to a single fixed Vickers gun (optionally two), two Darne guns on a dorsal ring mount, and one or two Darnes firing through a ventral window.

Despite the slowness (185 km/h) of the Amiot 122, the air current impeded the dorsal gunner if he wanted to train his guns forward. The prototype featured a flap at the underside of the upper wing that could be lowered by the gunner to deflect the air current, but the drag was unacceptable. After a very short career the type was struck off as obsolete.

The Fokker C.I reconnaissance aircraft was actually developed and entered production (although not service) in Germany, but from 1919 was built in the Netherlands both for the Dutch air force and for export. One difference from the German-built versions was that it was equipped with the usual 7.7 mm Vickers/Lewis combination. By 1924 this had developed into the C.IV, with armament increased to one or two synchronised Vickers and a twin flexible Lewis mounting. The following year saw the C.V-series reconnaissance bomber with a similar armament, but this time with a change to 7.9 mm calibre (probably FN-built Brownings). This was a very successful aircraft used, among others, by the Swiss, who fitted their usual 7.5 mm Fl. Mg 29 guns. Apart from Switzerland, the C.V was licence-built in Denmark, Finland, Hungary, Italy and Sweden.

Other European countries produced their own versions of the type. The 1919 Swiss Häfeli DH-3 reconnaissance plane used one flexible and one synchronised MG 11 (Maxim chambered for the Swiss 7.5 × 55 cartridge). It was replaced by the DH-5 in 1922, in which the armament was steadily developed. Initially the 7.65 mm *Flieger Doppelpistole* was use as a flexible gun, with 20–40 magazines carried. This was

A Swiss MG-94 in a Häfeli DH-3. Note the spool for winding the cloth ammunition belt. (*Courtesy Verlag Stocker-Schmid, Dietikon-Zürich*)

favoured as it was light and easy to handle even in the slipstream, and it seems that the barrels were set to diverge slightly to increase the dispersion and thereby the hit probability. However, the effective range was less than 150 m and the gun proved unreliable, so both this and the MG 11 were replaced by twin installations of the 7.5 mm Fl. Mg 29.

In 1920 the Czech Letov S-1 and S-2 reconnaissance aircraft were equipped with three 7.7 mm guns, while the same country's Aero A.11 reconnaissance/bomber had only one flexible gun. In Italy, Fiat had success with the BR series starting in 1922, a development of the S.I.A series by the same designer (Rosatelli) and equipped with the usual synchronised and flexible gun combination. The Breguet 19 light bomber and reconnaissance aircraft of 1923 had one Vickers and twin Lewis, as did the Breguet 27 observation plane of 1930 and the highly successful Potez 25 observation and general-purpose aircraft built in huge numbers from 1925. Poland produced the little parasol-wing Lublin R-X observation plane of 1929, with a single flexible 7.7 mm rear gun (rather unusually, a pan-fed Vickers using the Lewis magazine), although twin-gun mountings were sometimes fitted in the succeeding R-XIII of 1932. Even Romania got in on the act with the SET 7 of 1930, a two-seat tactical reconnaissance/liaison plane with two 7.7 mm (synchronised and flexible) guns.

The newly formed Soviet Union's aircraft industry was helped by the diversification activities of German companies no longer allowed to build military aircraft in Germany. Junkers set up a Moscow factory which between 1923 and 1925 made some Ju 21 high-wing monoplane reconnaissance aircraft, equipped with a fixed 7.62 mm PV-1 and a flexible DA gun, and a few low-wing Ju 20 monoplanes. This inspired Soviet interest in all-metal construction, and the plant was taken over by the USSR in 1926 to use for their own projects.

An early success was the Polikarpov R-1 (R = *Rasvedchik* or reconnaissance), a 1923 development of the D.H.4 and D.H.9 already in service. By 1931 2,800 R-1s had been produced, equipped with one fixed synchronised PV-1 gun and single or twin flexible 7.62 mm DA mountings. A more radical attempt was the Tupolev-designed ANT-3, an all-metal sesquiplane (with the same armament as the R-1) which was adopted as the R-3, but only 101 were made. The definitive inter-war aircraft in this class, however, was the Polikarpov R-5 biplane of 1931, of which nearly 5,000 were built. The usual armament was a fixed PV-1 and flexible DA-1 or DA-2 combination, but the specialised ground-attack R-5Sh of 1933 (and the improved R-SSS) was equipped with four or eight obliquely mounted down-firing PV-1s on the wings, plus two rear guns, and was fitted with added armour.

In the late 1920s and early 1930s Letov built on its success with the S-28, S-228, S-328 and S-528 series of reconnaissance biplanes, of which the S-328 of 1933 was the most

A truck-and-track type flexible mount for a single .30 in machine-gun. When the handle is pulled away from the box, a cam releases a locking mechanism, allowing the post mount to be repositioned on the semicircular track. 1932.

successful. In Czechoslovakian service it was armed with *Ceska-Zbrojovka* ZB30 machine guns, two fixed ones in the upper wing and two flexible ones for the observer. Their service life stretched well into the second half of World War Two.

In the USA this class of aircraft was dominated by Curtiss and Douglas designs. In 1925 they were in direct competition with the Curtiss O-1 and Douglas O-2 observation planes, both of which had the usual one synchronised, one flexible combination; the fixed gun was a Browning in both cases, but for the flexible mounting Curtiss chose a .30 in Lewis gun instead of the Douglas's Browning. One O-2 was experimentally fitted with six forward-firing .30 in Brownings, together with armour protection for the engine, cooling system and cockpit. In 1931 the Douglas O-31/43/46 range of gull- or parasol-wing observation planes were unusual in having the fixed gun mounted, unsynchronised, in the right wing. More warlike was the Curtiss A-3 ground-attack plane of 1927, which had four fixed .30 in guns combined with a twin flexible mounting. The A for

Attack designation indicated the USAAC's interest at this time in specialised aircraft for this role.

Japan continued to make use of foreign designs or designers while developing its own design skills. The 1922 Army Type Otsu 1 reconnaissance plane was the Salmson 2-A.2 biplane, fitted optionally with a single 7.7 mm synchronised, and single or twin 7.7 mm flexibly mounted, guns. In 1928 the similarly armed Kawasaki KDA2 entered service as the Army Type 88, followed in 1932 by the Mitsubishi 2MR8 parasol design, adopted as the Army Type 92 and featuring twin 7.7 mm guns in both fixed and flexible mountings. Light bombers were represented by the British-designed Mitsubishi 2MB1 of 1927 (Army Type 87), with single or twin fixed and flexible 7.7 mm, plus provision for one flexible ventral gun to deal with attacks from below. Next came the 1930 Type 88 Light Bomber of 1930 (the same plane as the Kawasaki KDA2, but fitted with bomb racks), followed in 1933 by the Kawasaki Type 93 with two or three 7.7 mm guns.

MULTI-ENGINED BOMBERS

MOST OF THE HEAVY BOMBERS OF THIS PERIOD CONFORMED to a standard configuration: biplanes with twin tractor engines between the wings and two open gun positions with ring mountings, in the nose and in the fuselage behind the wings. The main variation, apart from the gun type selected by different nations, was whether single or twin installations were used. Occasionally the dorsal gun position could also be fitted with another flexibly mounted gun, pointing downwards to deal with attacks from below. Despite this general conformity, some of the aircraft that were built were spectacularly different.

The Armstrong Whitworth Sinaia of 1921 was designed as a twin-engined day-bomber, and good defensive armament was required. For this purpose the engine nacelles were lengthened, and the aft end of each nacelle was swept upwards to create a raised firing position for a gunner with a Scarff ring. As already mentioned, the originally planned machine gun in the nose was replaced by a mount for a 37 mm COW gun during the construction of the prototype. Only one prototype was completed, and it was soon abandoned when structural weakness was discovered.

Despite this, the RAF remained generally true to its conservative policies in this area with a succession of entirely conventional twin-engined bombers, all equipped with Lewis guns. The first was the 1923 Vickers Virginia, a 'stretched Vimy', which was fitted with a number of experimental installations, including 'fighting tops' – nacelles on the upper wing. These each carried a single gunner and two Lewis guns, one firing forwards and one aft. They increased the weight of this bomber by 468.5 kg, or 11 per cent of the empty weight of the aircraft. They were later replaced by smaller, more streamlined nacelles with one gun only, attached to the wing's trailing-edge and firing aft. Initially access was by a central ladder, which required the gunners to crawl over the upper wing to the stations; later ladders were placed under each nacelle. Despite prolonged testing, they were never adopted for production aircraft.

A reluctant Air Ministry was persuaded by Vickers to try an alternative – a gunner's position in the extreme tail with one or two Lewis guns. This position took the form of a round pulpit aft of the biplane tail, equipped with two Lewis Mk III guns on a Scarff ring. It was standardised on the Mk IX and Mk X (which also distinguished itself from earlier models by its all-metal construction), although the tail position was subject to considerable fuselage flexing in flight. The gunner benefited from an electrically heated flying suit and a small windscreen, but his position was an extremely isolated one.

The Virginia was followed by the Handley-Page H.P.24 Hyderabad of 1925, which featured a ventral gun, as did the 1928 Boulton & Paul Sidestrand, the 1929 Handley-Page H.P.36 Hinaidi (a re-engined development of the Hyderabad) and the 1933 Handley-Page H.P.50 Heyford. The Heyford looked odd because the fuselage was attached to the upper wing, leaving the lower wing dangling underneath, but it was of some interest because its ventral gun was mounted in a retractable 'dustbin' to improve the gunner's field of fire.

The Sidestrand was a twin-engined biplane bomber, armed with a gunner position for a Lewis in the nose. The rear gunner operated Lewis guns in dorsal and ventral mountings. Despite this modest armament, the RAF contemplated sending these agile bombers out to fly their missions alone, the logic being that single aircraft were less easily detected than a formation and the Sidestrand could look after itself!

Development of the Overstrand, initially known as the Sidestrand Mk IV, began in 1932 following a request from the Air Ministry to give the gunner protection from the slipstream, in any firing position and without reducing his field of fire. The turret was designed under the leadership of H.A. Hughes; a mock-up was ready in January 1933. Production turrets were wider than the prototype and omitted a fabric seal with a zipper in the vertical slot for the gun.

The Overstrand turret was cylindrical with a hemispherical top and bottom. The rotation, at a speed of 72 degrees per second, was pneumatically powered. Air pressure sufficient for 20 revolutions was stored in bottles which were recharged by an engine-driven compressor. The turret could rotate fully if the gun was raised enough to clear the fuselage. The height of the gunner's seat was hydraulically linked to the elevation and depression of the Lewis gun. On test, the Overstrand turret increased the hits scored against towed targets from 15 per cent for an open mounting to no less than 55 per cent.

The rear gunner still had a Lewis on a No. 7 Scarff ring, but was provided with a windshield. Although the Overstrand equipped only a single squadron, it was influential because it was the first RAF bomber with a gun turret.

The Overstrand turret was not related to the Boulton Paul turrets of World War Two, which were based on the French electrohydraulic SAMM turrets, designed by de Boysson. In 1937 Overstrand K8175 was used to test these turrets, first the AB 7 with four rifle-calibre machine guns and later the AB 15 with a 20 mm HS.404 cannon. A pneumatic turret for two Lewis guns was also developed for a monoplane bomber to Specification B.3/34; but Boulton Paul would build no more bombers, and the pneumatic turrets were superseded by the electro-hydraulic system.

The RAF used some 'bomber-transports' such as the Vickers Vernon, Victoria and Valentia (not to be confused with the eponymous experimental flying-boat of 1921), based on the bombers but with more capacious fuselages, which were equipped to perform bombing duties in the colonial policing role. There was not normally any gun armament as no aerial opposition was expected, but the Valentia of 1933 was fitted with Lewis guns in a variety of improvised positions in response to the Italian invasion of Abyssinia, which threatened British interests in the area.

From 1922 onwards the French Air Force and Navy received the military versions of the Farman 60 Goliath, an ugly twin-engined biplane. There were two gunnery positions on this aircraft, a dorsal one and one in the nose, both with twin Lewis guns. As on many bombers of the period, the nose gun mount was stepped down to allow the pilot to look forwards over the head of the gunner.

The standard French night-bomber between 1928 and 1939 was the Lioré et Olivier LeO 20, a hideously ugly, twin-engined, three-seat biplane with a very modest performance. The armament of the LeO 20 consisted of a single Lewis for the nose gunner, two for the dorsal gunner, and one ventral gun in a retractable 'dustbin'. The family include the four-engined LeO 203 and 206 and the LeO H-25 which could also be operated as a seaplane. Later aircraft in this series had Darne or MAC 1934 machine guns.

More interesting was the 1928 Blériot 127/2 monoplane twin, which was fitted with six Lewis guns in twin mountings in the nose and at the rear of each engine nacelle. Turbulence over the tail, caused by the nacelle gunnery positions,

A flexibly mounted DA in the nose of an ANT-7. (Courtesy Philip Jarrett)

contributed to the handling problems that resulted in it being grounded after a series of crashes. Blériot followed up with the 137, all-metal with a cleaner wing, and two dorsal gunners located in large bulges, protruding half a metre from the sides of the fuselage. This proved to be even worse for airflow over the tail, and the type was grounded as well; although, for some obscure contractual reason, eight production aircraft were ordered nevertheless!

The prize for the most spectacular European bomber of the period must surely go to the Caproni Ca.90 of 1929, a six-engined (in push-pull configuration) biplane fitted with seven guns, including one in the middle of the upper wing, but only one of these giants was built.

In the USSR, the renamed 'Red Muromets' four-engined biplanes continued to serve up to 1921, but subsequently some interesting new bombers were designed, supplemented by foreign purchases such as the trimotor Junkers R-42 (known as the TB-2) and the Farman F.62 Goliath twin, both bought in 1926 to maintain numbers until Soviet-designed bombers could take their place.

The American bomber efforts of this period were relatively modest. The Martin MB-2 of 1919 was followed in 1932 by the Keystone B-4A–B-6A range. Both were twin-engined biplanes, with three to five guns. Rather more interesting was the Douglas B-7 of 1932, a high-mid gull-wing monoplane with retractable undercarriage, but only two MGs in nose and dorsal positions.

The Imperial Japanese Army initially used Farman F.50 and F.60 heavy bombers as the Type Tei 1 and Tei 2 respectively, but in 1927 the Army Type 87 Heavy Bomber entered service. It was a twin-engined parasol-wing metal monoplane, designed by Kawasaki with aid from Dornier. It was armed with two flexibly mounted 7.7 mm (Lewis) guns in nose and dorsal positions, with one in a ventral mounting.

CARRIER AIRCRAFT

THE END OF THE FIRST WORLD WAR HAD SEEN THE introduction of the concept of the aircraft-carrier as it still exists today: an essentially flat-topped vessel on which aeroplanes could land and take off. The advent of large carriers equipped with substantial numbers of high-performance fighters and bombers transformed the nature of naval warfare and was its most significant development in the inter-war period. Many of the aircraft deployed on carriers merely represented adaptations of land-planes, with arrestor hooks, folding wings and possibly a strengthened undercarriage to cope with the more violent landings. This particularly applied to fighters, which were basically similar to their land-based equivalents. Bombers tended to be different, however. They were inevitably smaller (single engines being universal), and some were more specialised; both

Training a Fleet Air Arm gunner with a camera gun.

(*Courtesy Philip Jarrett*)

torpedo planes and dive-bombers were designed specifically for carriers and were usually different from their land-based equivalents.

The British Fleet Air Arm was a part of the Royal Air Force throughout this period. Its fighters bore a close resemblance to the RAF types, starting with the 1922 Gloster Mars Mk X Nightjar and continuing with the agile 1923 Fairey Flycatcher, the 1932 Hawker Nimrod (much sleeker and faster, in part owing to its in-line engine) and the two-seat Hawker Osprey of the same year, a navalised Hart used as a multi-purpose spotter/reconnaissance/fighter plane. All had the usual twin Vickers, except the Osprey which had one Vickers and one Lewis for the rear gunner. In line with RAF practice of the period, the Flycatcher's machine guns were simply attached externally to the sides of the fuselage. Apparently they were easily removed, for many pictures show the aircraft without them.

The more specialised designs were initially bulky and ugly, with speed sacrificed for load-carrying ability. In 1922 the Avro Bison 3/4-seat reconnaissance plane entered service (equipped with the usual Vickers-Lewis pair) accompanied in the same year by the similarly armed Blackburn Blackburn, and the gunless Blackburn Dart single-seat torpedo-bomber. In 1924 the Parnall Panther reconnaissance plane, with one Lewis gun, entered service and was also sold to the Japanese Navy. By 1928, with the introduction of the relatively sleek Fairey IIIF 2/3-seat reconnaissance plane, the aesthetics at least were improving. This was equipped with the Vickers-Lewis combination with Fairey's own 'high-speed' mounting, as was the Fairey Seal development of 1933. The Dart torpedo-bomber was replaced in 1929 by the two-seat Blackburn Ripon, this time with the Vickers plus Lewis armament, the same company's Baffin in 1934, and the last of the Blackburn torpedo-bomber biplane line, the Shark of 1935. The Fairey Seal reconnaissance aircraft replaced the IIIF in 1933. All of these retained the Vickers plus Lewis combination.

Only the French among other European countries developed carrier forces, and they were much more limited than the British. In its search for a shipboard torpedo-bomber, the French Navy first acquired a small series of Levasseur PL2s, single-engined biplanes which were never embarked and apparently did not carry any defensive armament. In 1927 these were replaced by the PL4, which could not carry a torpedo but became the first French carrier-borne aircraft. The observer had a single machine gun to defend the aircraft. On the PL7, which entered service in 1930 and was capable of carrying a torpedo, the observer had two 7.5 mm Darne guns. When war approached in the late 1930s, the French Navy decided to re-equip its units with the American Vought V-156F dive-bomber. The Wibault Wib.74 parasol-wing fighter, a version of the air force's Wib.72, entered service around 1930.

The US Navy took to aircraft-carriers with great enthusiasm and developed a wide range of aircraft for them. These commenced with the Naval Aircraft Factory TS-1 fighter of 1922, available in carrier or floatplane versions, but for much of the rest of this period Boeing or Curtiss supplied the Navy's fighters. These included the 1925 Boeing Model 15, adopted as the FB-1 (also used by the Air Service), the 1927 Curtiss F6C (a version of the Army's P-1), the 1928 Boeing F2B-1 (which interestingly sometimes had one of its two guns in the much more powerful .50 in calibre), the 1928 Boeing F3B-1 and the 1929 Boeing F4B-1 (equivalent to the USAAC's P-12), both being developments of the F2B-1, but with twin .30 in. These were joined in 1932 by the Curtiss F11C Goshawk single-seat fighter/dive-bomber with two guns, one which could be of .50 in calibre.

The combination of one .50 in gun with one .30in had obvious ballistic disadvantages, although it limited the weight. The M1921 Browning .50 in gun could be fed only from the left side, and because guns were typically fed from inboard and dumped empty cases from a port in the fuselage side, the .50 in weapon was usually installed as the right-hand gun. This difficulty was removed with the M2 became available, as this version could be converted to feed from either side.

More specialised USN aircraft included the 1920s Martin SC-1/SC-2 (adopted as the T3M and T4M) three-seat torpedo-bombers available with wheels or floats and fitted with one flexibly mounted .30 in, and the 1930 Curtiss O2C Helldiver 2-seat dive-bomber (with one synchronised and one or two flexibly mounted guns). The USN and USMC were the most enthusiastic advocates of dive-bombing at this time, inspiring later developments in Germany and Japan.

The Japanese also developed a great interest in naval aviation, again with foreign design help, in this case mainly British. The 1922 Mitsubishi 2MR (Navy Type 10 Reconnaissance) with twin synchronised and twin flexible guns, 1923 Mitsubishi 1MF1 (Navy Type 10 fighter) with twin synchronised guns, the 1924 Mitsubishi B1M (Navy Type 13 Carrier Attack Aircraft, which also became the Army Type 87 light bomber) with twin, flexibly mounted guns plus (in a later variant) twin synchronised guns, were all designed by the prolific Herbert Smith, an Englishman working in Japan. Similarly the 1930 Nakajima A1N1 (Navy Type 3 Fighter) was designed as the Gloster Gambet, and the 1932 Mitsubishi B2M (Navy Type torpedo-bomber), with both synchronised and flexible guns, was a Blackburn design. The 1931 Nakajima A2N1 (Navy Type 90 carrier fighter) with two synchronised guns appears to have had an indigenous design. Unsurprisingly, the guns used were the usual Vickers and Lewis types.

All navies were much more conservative with their carrier aircraft designs than were the corresponding air forces. They were particularly concerned with low wing loadings to retain low landing and take-off speeds, so biplanes remained standard until close to (and in some cases beyond) the start of the Second World War. This does not mean that there were no technical developments. The USN in particular adopted enclosed cockpits and retractable undercarriages for the last generation of biplanes. A fixed undercarriage contributed a large part of the drag of a conventional biplane, so when Grumman delivered in 1933 the FF-1 two-seat fighter with retractable undercarriage, it demonstrated a high performance despite having a tubby fuselage to accommodate the gear.

The FF-1 was armed with two fixed Browning .30 in guns in the top fuselage decking, in front of the cockpit, and a flexible one for the observer, whose seat swivelled and pivoted with the gun support. A number of Canadian-built aircraft later saw combat in the Spanish Civil War, but in the USN the FF was quickly replaced by the single-seat F2F, armed with two .30 in Browning guns. The final aircraft in the series was the improved F3F single-seat fighter, armed with a .30 in to port and a .50 in to starboard. The new features of the F3F included long blast tubes, extending forward from the guns to the engine cowling. The ducts for the spent casings were prolonged to an ejection port below the lower wing, presumably to avoid damage to the tail surfaces.

The Curtiss BF2C-1 (a modified Goshawk) single-seat dive-bomber, with two .30 in guns, also featured a retractable undercarriage (rather less successfully), as did the two-seat Curtis SBC-3/4 Helldiver, with one .30 in fixed and one flexible guns.

Vought contributed a series of biplane observation aircraft, suitable for catapult launching. From the two-seat UO of 1923 a single-seat fighter version was evolved, the FU of 1926, armed with the standard two cowl guns. Next in line was the O2U Corsair, which was finally developed in the O3U. Characteristic of the Corsair was that the fixed, forward-firing Browning gun was installed in the right section of the upper wing, outside the propeller disk, thus saving the weight of the synchronisation gear. The observer had a Scarff ring with one or two Lewis guns at first, but the O3U-2 introduced a post-mount for the gun, presumably to reduce drag.

The O2U was also exported, and Vought again produced a single-seat fighter version, the V-80, which had two machine guns in the upper wing as well as two cowl guns. Only a handful were completed. Vought also designed two-seat fighters for the Navy: the F2U, armed with two fixed machine guns in the upper wing centre section and a flexible gun in the rear cockpit, and the F3U, which had its fixed armament again located on the fuselage. The Navy bought neither.

The British Fleet Air Arm (FAA) was less adventurous, although this was at least in part because of the low priority given to carrier aircraft, both before and after 1937 – the year when the FAA transferred from the RAF to the Royal Navy. Its best fighters until the start of the war remained biplanes with fixed undercarriage. The last of these was the Sea Gladiator of 1938, which boasted four .303 in Brownings instead of the usual two (the extra pair being in the lower wings). This was faster than the contemporary Blackburn Skua fighter/dive-bomber (the only monoplane in FAA service at that time), just as fast as the later Fairey Fulmar two-seat monoplane fighter, and had a far better climb rate than either. However, that says more about the poor quality of the monoplanes than it does about the Sea Gladiator.

The Imperial Japanese Navy also retained the traditional design and armament formula with the Nakajima Type 95 carrier fighter of 1935 and the Yokosho Type 92 attack aircraft, otherwise known as the B3Y1.

FLYING-BOATS AND SEAPLANES

The development of aircraft-carriers did not mean that the former types of aeroplane operating over water were abandoned. Large flying-boats retained their place for long-range reconnaissance independent of naval vessels, and some floatplanes were also used by themselves. Furthermore, cruisers and battleships retained their own small catapult-launched floatplanes or flying-boats, mainly for reconnaissance and gunfire spotting purposes.

The RAF used a range of large flying-boats during this period. The Felixstowe F.5, a development of the wartime F.2A/F.3, mounted four Lewis guns in two positions (one in the bow, three amidships), and entered service just after the war. It was the RAF's standard flying-boat (and was even adopted by the USN and built by Curtiss, somewhat ironically, since the Felixstowe range started as modified Curtiss designs) until it was replaced in 1927 by the Supermarine

Southampton, a twin-engined biplane which mounted three Lewis guns in bow and two dorsal positions. The dorsal positions were diagonally installed and set so close to the edge of the hull that their fire could converge on an aircraft attacking from behind. From the late 1920s this was supplemented by the Blackburn Iris and Perth, similar three-engined biplanes built in small numbers. They normally carried a Lewis gun in the bow position (although they could be fitted with the 37 mm COW gun instead). The Iris had in addition a ring-mounted dorsal Lewis, plus provision for two more fired from sliding hatches in the hull, while the Perth added a ring-mounted Lewis in the tail, a layout followed by the monoplane variant of 1930, the Sydney.

The Short Singapore Mk I of 1926 shared the armament arrangement of the Southampton. On the experimental Singapore Mk II of 1930, which had four engines arranged in tandem pairs instead of two, a tail gun position was added, as was a rearward-sliding bow gun mounting to allow access to the bow for mooring. This became a common feature of British flying-boats. The final service version became the Singapore Mk III of 1934, with gunnery positions in the nose and the extreme tail, and a single dorsal position, which was located rather low in the fuselage and had a limited field of fire. All three had single Lewis guns.

Short contributed the three-engined Short Rangoon of 1931. This was the military version of the Calcutta, with a similar armament to the Southampton. A larger development of the Calcutta was built in France as the Breguet Bizerte. These had a quite different armament installation, with guns in four lateral windows (two behind the cockpit and two aft of the wings) and a tail gun position. With the exception of the first two, which carried Lewis guns, they were armed with five 7.5 mm Darnes.

An upgraded development of the Southampton was the Scapa of 1932. Its final (and much modified) development was the Supermarine Stranraer of 1935, which had a single

The offset gun positions of a Short Rangoon flying-boat, surprisingly fitted with an old Mk I Lewis and 47-round drum magazine. (Courtesy Philip Jarrett)

dorsal gunner, a tail gunner and a nose gunner. These aircraft remained in service until 1940.

In the smaller category of floatplanes, the Fairey IIID of 1920 (also available as a land-plane) saw extensive use. It was a conventional single-engined two-seat biplane, with one flexibly mounted Lewis. It was succeeded by the same company's Seal in 1932, which featured their 'high-speed' ring mounting for the Lewis, as well as a Vickers for the pilot.

The Italians remained very interested in flying-boats and built a considerable variety of them, commencing in 1919 with the SIAI S.13 pusher biplane, which had a flexibly mounted 7.7 mm in the nose. Macchi produced two different types in the 1920s: the M.18 three-seat biplane with a single pusher engine (developed from the wartime M.8) which had one 7.7 mm Vickers in a ring mounting in the nose, and the larger M.24/25 series which had two engines in a push-pull nacelle installation, with two 7.7 mm Vickers in bow and dorsal positions. Savoia-Marchetti was also active in developing flying-boats, producing in 1926 both the S.59 single-engined reconnaissance plane (one Lewis gun in the nose), plus its S.62 successor in 1927 (with four MGs) and the S.62bis development in 1930 (which, as we have seen, carried a 20 mm Oerlikon L in the bows), and also the remarkable SM.55 twin-hull design, with two engines in a push-pull arrangement, and four Lewis guns mounted in the hulls. Finally, in 1931 Macchi revived the idea of the flying-boat fighter in 1931 with the single-seat M.41/M.71 pusher biplane, with twin Vickers guns. Amid all this flying-boat activity, Piaggio produced in 1928 the P.6 floatplane, fitted with one flexibly mounted MG, which was carried by capital ships and cruisers.

By comparison with the Italian activity the French were relatively quiet, the two most notable developments both being in 1930: the Gourdou-Leseurre 810–813 family of twin-float, single-engined 2/3-seat monoplanes which equipped cruisers of the French fleet (one synchronised Vickers, one twin Lewis), and the CAMS 55 twin-engined (push-pull) flying-boat with twin Lewis guns in each of bow and dorsal positions.

In other European countries, the Dutch firm of Fokker produced in 1927 the T.IV twin-engined torpedo/bomber/reconnaissance twin-float monoplane, with a single 7.9 mm in nose, dorsal and ventral positions. Germany was not slow to develop new naval aircraft, introducing in 1933 two Heinkel biplane floatplanes – the single-engined He 60, which equipped warships, and the twin-engined He 59. The He 59 generally carried two MG 15s in nose and dorsal positions. The Dornier Wal was also produced in military versions, featuring open gun positions in the bow and aft fuselage.

There had been much Russian use of naval aircraft in the First World War, particularly the Grigorovich series of flying-boats. The M-5 to M-15 all carried a flexibly mounted MG. From 1923 onwards the acquisition of new aeroplanes increased considerably. In that year, fifty Savoia-Marchetti SM-16bis aircraft were imported and forty Junkers J20 monoplane floatplanes were purchased, equipped with a flexible bow gun. Also in 1923, production of the Grigorovich M-24 pusher biplane flying-boat commenced, again with a flexibly mounted bow gun. Three years later the mix of foreign and domestic acquisitions continued, with the Dornier Wal being imported and the Polikarpov MR-1, a floatplane version of the R-1, entering service.

The American firm of Curtiss continued its development of flying-boats into the post-war years, with the large NC-4 four-engined biplane of 1919. This had three tractor and one pusher engines, but only two defensive MGs. Douglas concentrated on floatplanes, notably the DT-2 torpedo-plane of 1922, a two-seat biplane which also came fitted with wheels, and five years later the T2D twin-engined torpedo land-plane or floatplane, which was fitted with two flexibly mounted 7.62 mm MGs. The needs of cruisers and battleships for a catapult-launched plane was met by the Vought O2U-1 Corsair of 1927. This had a central float, although there was also a wheeled version. Two or three MGs were carried.

The Imperial Japanese Navy unsurprisingly placed great emphasis on sea-capable aeroplanes, and developed both large flying-boats and warship-based seaplanes. In 1921 the Felixstowe F.5 flying-boat was adopted (manufactured by Hirosho), fitted with two flexible 7.7 mm guns. This was followed by the short-lived Type 15 of 1929 (Hirosho H1H1/3) with a similar armament, and its replacement in the following year, the Type 89 (Hirosho H2H1), which doubled the armament with a twin flexible nose mounting and two single dorsal guns. Finally, the Type 90-2 (Kawanishi H3K1, designed with assistance from Short) was a large three-engined flying-boat well armed with twin 7.7 mm guns in nose, two dorsal and tail positions, but only five were built.

The requirement for reconnaissance seaplanes was met by a variety of types. The 1927 Type 15 (Nakajima E2N) and 1928 Type 2 (Aichi version of Heinkel HD 25) both had one flexible MG. The 1931 Navy Type 90-3 (Yokosho E5Y1) boasted two synchronised, one dorsal and one ventral guns, whereas the two additions in 1932 – the Type 90-1 (Aichi E3A1) and Type 90-2-2/3 (Nakajima E4N2/3) – each had the more usual one synchronised and one flexible guns.

CONCLUSION

THE PERIOD BETWEEN 1919 AND 1933 WAS ONE OF QUIET transition in the development of military aviation. The vast majority of the aeroplanes which entered service were simple, single-engined types with one or two seats and two or three

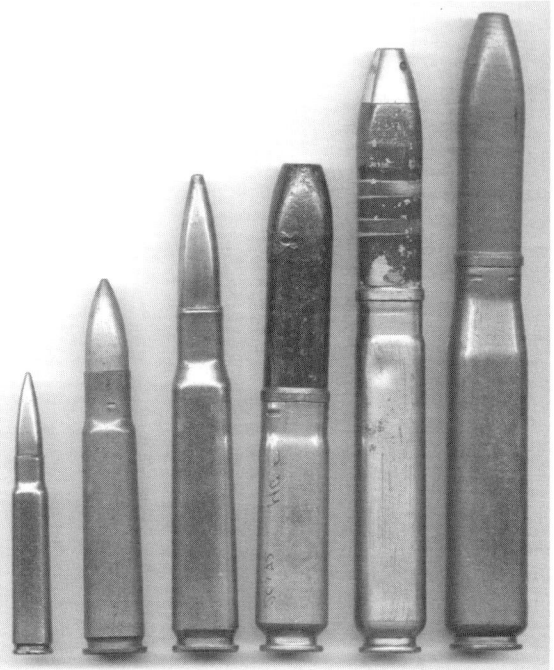

Increasing firepower (from left to right): 7.92 × 57 for scale, 12.7 × 81SR (Vickers V/565, Breda-SAFAT and Scotti), 12.7 × 99 (.50 Browning), 20 × 72RB (Oerlikon F), 20 × 100RB (Oerlikon L – this one is the nearly identical Japanese 20 × 101RB), 20 × 110RB (Oerlikon S).

rifle-calibre machine guns. The expensive multi-engined types were only acquired in small numbers. There were developments in aircraft structures, with metal replacing wood, but the vast majority of aircraft were still clad in fabric. Only in the Soviet Union was the German wartime development of metal-skinned aeroplanes continued in a range of heavy bombers which at the time were well ahead of anything being built elsewhere. This early lead was not maintained, however.

Aircraft guns also developed very gradually, with the use of the Vickers gun in synchronised mountings and the Lewis in flexible ones initially almost universal outside the USA and USSR. By the early 1930s new rifle-calibre designs were emerging, from France, Italy, Germany and later the USSR. The American Browning was also achieving export sales, helped by its manufacture under licence, in various calibres, by FN of Belgium. The first heavy machine guns were beginning to be fitted in Italy and the USA, and the three types of 20 mm Oerlikon cannon were also making a tentative appearance. The next dozen years were to see huge strides made both in aircraft guns and in the aircraft which carried them.

Appendix 1

INSTALLATION TABLE

THE PURPOSE OF THIS TABLE IS TO GIVE A REASONABLY complete listing of operational aircraft types with permanently or optionally installed gun armament. In addition, a few types that did not proceed past beyond the prototype or service test stage, but had interesting gun installations, are also listed.

Readers should not have excessive faith in the standard of accuracy or completeness that is possible in a general overview such as this. Research on the armament of World War One aircraft is still ongoing. And during the Great War the replacement of guns, especially flexible guns, by non-standard or captured weapons was not uncommon.

The table consists of records as below:

of designations or names, describing the subtype(s) of the basic type that had the armament installation described in the record. As a change in armament installation was not always considered sufficient by officials to be reflected in the designation, this may be somewhat confusing.

- The **Func** field gives the role of the subtype. The letter system used here is broadly based on the American tri-service designation system, with some codes from the older US Navy system mixed in and a few conventional additions. The meaning of most of the codes may be (more or less) familiar to readers. Readers should be aware, however, that there is no universal agreement on function descriptions.

Type Name	Subtype Name	Func	Gun Type	n × c	am	f	Location
Codename	Year Status	Built	Gun Type	n × c	am		Location
			Gun Type	n × c	am	f	Location
	Comments on a subtype.						
	Subtype Name	Func	Gun Type	n × c	am		Location
	Year Status	Built	Gun Type	n × c	am	f	Location
	Comments on a subtype.						
Comments on a type.							

The meanings of the fields are as follows:
- The **Type Name** is the designation or name, or a series of designations or names, of the basic type of aircraft, preceded by that of the manufacturer. The relation between the designation of a type of aircraft and its variations (subtypes) depends on the country, and may often be unclear. In many cases aircraft design was evolutionary, and sometimes an arbitrary convention (often influenced by budgetary or political considerations) dictated when a design was considered a new type.
- The **Subtype Name** is the designation or name, or a series

A	Attack
B	Bomber
C	Transport
F	Fighter
FB	Fighter-bomber
FR	Reconnaissance fighter
G	Glider
NF	Night-fighter
O	Observation and Army Co-operation
P	Patrol
PB	Flying-boat

R Reconnaissance
SAR Search and Rescue
SB Dive-bomber
T Trainer
TB Torpedo-bomber
Y Autogyro

- The **Year** is the year of service entry for operational aircraft; the year of first flight for all others.
- The **Status** field indicates whether an aircraft remained a prototype, was only experimentally evaluated, or was subjected to a limited-scale service test. If none of these is specified, the type has become operational.
- The number of aircraft **Built** may vary slightly from source to source, as sometimes prototypes and experimental models are included and sometimes not; or may

vary wildly when the facts are unknown and authors are guessing. Readers are advised to treat large, round figures as indicative only.
- The **Gun Type** is the type of gun installed, as far as is known. The exact model is often unknown, and for some gun designations it is not clear what they refer to (see main text). The gun type is followed by:
  - The number of guns installed in a particular installation.
  - The calibre of the gun, in mm.
  - The ammunition capacity in rounds per gun. Left blank when this is unknown.
  - The letter f for fixed installations.
  - A short description of the installation.

AUSTRIA-HUNGARY

Aviatik B.II	**B.II** 1915	O				
	Some were retrofitted with machine guns for the observer.					
Aviatik B.III	**B.III** 1916	O	Schwarzlose	1 × 8		Rear cockpit
Aviatik C.I	**C.I** 1917	O	Schwarzlose Schwarzlose	1 × 8 1 × 8	 f	Rear cockpit Top of upper wing, angled 15 degrees up
	Because of a shortage of synchronisation systems, the gun on the upper wing was standard armament, but a few had a synchronised gun. A number were converted to single-seat reconnaissance fighters with one or two synchronised guns.					
Aviatik D.I	**D.I** 1917	F	Schwarzlose	1 × 8	f	Top of upper wing, aimed 15 degrees up
	D.I 1917	F	Schwarzlose	2 × 8	300 f	Sides of the engine cowling, during 1918 moved to top of cowling
	Total production 677.					
Aviatik D.II	**D.II** 1917 Service Test	F 19	Schwarzlose	2 × 8	f	Engine cowling
Lloyd C.I	**C.I** 1914	O 400	Schwarzlose	1 × 8		Rear cockpit
Lloyd C.II	**C.II** 1915	O/T	Schwarzlose	1 × 8		Rear cockpit
	Many were operated without armament.					
Lloyd C.III	**C.III** 1916	O	Schwarzlose	1 × 8		Rear cockpit
	Early aircraft had three pintle mounts for the gun, later semi-circular gun rings were installed.					
Lloyd C.IV	**C.IV** 1916	O 37	Schwarzlose	1 × 8		Rear cockpit

Lloyd C.V	**C.V**	O	Schwarzlose	1 × 8		Rear cockpit
	1917	96	Schwarzlose	1 × 8		Type II VK canister on upper wing, optional
Lohner B.VII	**B.VII**	R				
	1915	65				

Initially unarmed, but some were retrofitted with machine guns in the rear cockpit during 1916. Nine were brought to series 17.8 standard with a machine gun ring in the rear cockpit.

Lohner C.I	**C.I**	O	Schwarzlose	1 × 8		Rear cockpit, optional
	1916	40				

Most were unarmed. A few were used for home defence duties with an 8 mm Schwarzlose in a Type II VK canister on top of the upper wing.

Oeffag C.I	**C.I**	O	Schwarzlose	1 × 8		Rear cockpit
	1915	25				
Oeffag C.II	**C.II**	O	Schwarzlose	1 × 8		Rear cockpit
	1916	64				
Phönix C.I	**C.I**	O	Schwarzlose	1 × 8	f	Synchronised
	1918	140	Schwarzlose	1 × 8		Rear cockpit
Phönix D.I	**D.I**	F	Schwarzlose	2 × 8	f	
	1917	140				
Phönix D.II	**D.II, IIa**	F	Schwarzlose	2 × 8	f	
	1918	96				
Phönix D.III	**D.III**	F	Schwarzlose	2 × 8	f	
	1918	140				
Ufag C.I	**C.I**	O	Schwarzlose	1 × 8	f	Late models had two fixed guns
	1918		Schwarzlose	1 × 8		Rear cockpit
WKF D.I	**D.I**	F	Schwarzlose	2 × 8	f	Top of engine cowling
	1918	26				
CZECHOSLOVAKIA						
Aero A.11	**A.11**	O	Vickers	1 ×	f	
	1923	440	Lewis	1 ×		Rear cockpit
Aero A.12	**A.12**	R	Vickers	1 ×	f	
	1923		Lewis	2 ×		Rear cockpit
Aero A.18	**A.18**	F	Vickers	2 × 7.92	f	Engine cowling
	1923	20				
Aero A.30, A.230	**A.30, A.230**	R	Vickers	1 ×	f	
	1927	79	Lewis	2 ×		Rear cockpit
Aero A.32	**A.32**	O	Vickers	2 ×	f	
	1928	116	Lewis	2 ×		Rear cockpit
Avia B.34	**B.34**	F	model 28	2 × 7.7	f	Side of the fuselage
	1932	12				
Avia B.534	**B.534 I**	F	model 28	2 × 7.7	f	On lower wing
	1933	46	model 28	2 × 7.7	f	In fuselage

Alternatively, the 7.92 mm model 30 gun was installed.

	B.534 II, III, IV	F	model 30	4 × 7.92	300 f	Fuselage
	1936	419				
	Bk.534	F	model 30	2 × 7.92	f	
	1938	35	Oerlikon FF S	1 × 20	f	Engine cannon
	The engine cannon was unreliable and later replaced by a third model 30.					
Avia BH-3	**BH-3**	F	Vickers	2 × 7.7	f	
	1921	10				
Avia BH-17	**BH-17**	F	Vickers	2 × 7.7	f	
	1924	24				
Avia BH-21	**BH-21**	F	Vickers	2 × 7.7	f	
	1925	184				
Avia BH-26	**BH-26**	NF	Vickers	2 × 7.7	f	Fuselage sides
	1927		Lewis	2 × 7.7		Skoda mount in rear cockpit
Avia BH-33	**BH-33**	F	Vickers	2 × 7.7	f	
	1927					
	BH-33E	F	Vickers	2 × 7.7	f	
	1929					
	BH-33L	F	model 28	2 × 7.7	f	Engine cowling
	1929					
Letov S-1, S-2	**S-1, S-2**	O				
	1919	72				
	Three 7.7 mm machine guns. The S-1 and S-2 were also known as the SH-1 and SM-1.					
Letov S-4	**S-4**	F	Vickers	2 × 7.7	f	
	1922					
	Fewer than 20 built.					
Letov S-16	**S-16**	B	Vickers	1 × 7.7	f	
	1926	150	Lewis	1 × 7.7		Rear cockpit
Letov S-20	**S-20**	F	Vickers	2 × 7.7	400 f	
	1925	115				
Letov S-31	**S-31**	F/T	Vickers	2 × 7.7	f	
	1931	32				
	Aircraft retired from Czech service and exported to Spain were armed with two Vickers on the lower wing. Some also had a third, synchronised gun.					

DENMARK

Nielsen & Winther Aa	**Aa**	F	Madsen	1 × 8	f	On upper wing
	1917	6				
Royal Aircraft Factory IO, IIO	**IO**	T	Madsen	2 × 8		Optional
	1926	15				
	IIO	T				
	1932	7				

FINLAND

VL Sääski	**Sääski II, IIA**	T		1 × 7.7		Rear cockpit
	1928	33				
VL Kotka	**Kotka II**	R	Vickers	1 ×	f	Fuselage
	1931	6	L-33/36	1 ×		Rear cockpit, also Lewis

VL Tuisku	**Tuisku I, II** 1935	T 29		1 ×		Rear cockpit
FRANCE						
Amiot 122	**122** 1928	B 55		1 × 7.5 1 × 7.5 1 × 7.5	f	One or two Dorsal, one or two Ventral, one or two
AR.1, A.R.2	**A.R.1, A.R.2** 1917	O 1,435	Vickers Lewis	1 × 7.7 1 × 7.7	f	Starboard side of the fuselage Rear cockpit, one or two
Blériot-SPAD S.51	**S.51-2** 1925 **S.51-4** 1928	F 50 F 10	Vickers Darne Vickers	2 × 7.7 2 × 2 ×	f f f	Upper wing Upper wing Fuselage
Blériot-SPAD S.61	**S.61** 1925	F 380	Vickers	2 × 7.7	f	
Blériot-SPAD S.81	**S.81** 1924	F 80	Vickers	2 × 7.7	f	
Borel-Odier B.O.2	**B.O.2** 1917	TB 92	Lewis	2 × 7.7		Two flexible mounts
Breguet 5, 6, 12	**5** 1916	F 200	Hotchkiss	1 × 37		Flexible mount in the nose
	The gun was not installed if the aircraft was equipped for bombing.					
	6 1916	F 50	Hotchkiss	1 × 37		Nose
	The gun was removed if the aircraft was converted for bombing missions.					
	12 1916	B	Hotchkiss	1 × 37		Nose
	The 12 was a 5 or 6 modified for night-bombing missions, but could carry a Hotchkiss cannon.					
Breguet 14	**14** 1917	R/B 2,200	Vickers Lewis	1 × 7.7 2 × 7.7	f	Left side of fuselage T.O.3 or T.O.4 ring mount in rear
Breguet 16	**16** 1917	B 200	Vickers Lewis	1 × 7.7 2 × 7.7	f	Left side of the fuselage Rear cockpit
Breguet 17	**17** 1917	F 10	Vickers Lewis Lewis	2 × 7.7 1 × 7.7 2 × 7.7	f	Ventral gun, fired by rear gunner Rear cockpit
	The Breguet 17 was a fighter derivative of the Breguet 14.					
Breguet 19	**19** 1923	B 3,285	Vickers Lewis	1 × 7.7 2 × 7.7	f	Rear cockpit
Breguet 270, 271, 273	**270, 271, 273** 1931	R/B 151	Vickers Lewis	1 × 7.7 2 × 7.7	f	Rear cockpit
Breguet AG 4	**AG 4** Prototype	F	Hotchkiss 2	1 ×		Rear cockpit

125

Breguet-Michelin BLM, BUM, BUC, BLC	**BLM, BUM** 1915	B 100	Hotchkiss	1×8		Nose, also Lewis	
	BUC, BLC 1915	B	Hotchkiss	1×37		Flexible mount in nose	
	Pusher biplanes, with a gun on a flexible mount in nose. The second letter of the designation indicated the engine type, the third the installation of a machine gun or cannon.						
Breguet-Michelin BM 4	**BM4** 1916	B 200	Hotchkiss	1×8		Flexible mount in nose	
	Pusher biplane.						
CAMS 37	**37** 1927	PB 110	Vickers Vickers	1×7.7 1×7.7		Dorsal Bow	
CAMS 55	**55** 1930	PB 112	Lewis Lewis	2×7.7 2×7.7		Dorsal Bow	
Caudron G.3	**G.3** 1913	O 2,450					
	From 1915 onwards, some G.3s were modified to make the carriage of a machine gun possible.						
Caudron G.4 1915	**G.4**	B 1,358	Hotchkiss	1×8	f	Fixed on the top wing, firing upwards, installed on some aircraft	
			Hotchkiss	1×8		Gunner in the nose of the central nacelle	
	Lewis guns were also used, instead of the Hotchkiss.						
Caudron G.6	**G.6** 1916	B 512	Lewis Lewis	2×7.7 2×7.7		Aft fuselage Nose	
Caudron R.4	**R.4** 1916	R 249	Lewis Lewis	2×7.7 2×7.7		Dorsal Nose	
Caudron R.11	**R.11** 1918	F 370	Lewis Lewis Lewis	2×7.7 1×7.7 2×7.7		Dorsal Nose, firing downwards Nose	
Coutant	**Coutant** 1917	PB		1×7.7			
Deperdussin TT	**TT** 1914	O					
	Two were modified with a high stand which allowed the observer, who was seated in front of the pilot, to fire over the propeller with a machine gun.						
Dewoitine D.1	**D.1** 1925	F 118	Vickers	2×7.7	f	Cowling	
Dewoitine D.9	**D.9** 1927	F 10	Darne Vickers	2×7.7 2×7.7	f f	Wings Fuselage	
Dewoitine D.19	**D.19** 1926	F 3	Vickers	2×7.7	f	Fuselage	
Dewoitine D.21	**D.21** 1928	F 100	Vickers	2×7.7	f	Fuselage	
	The 40 built for Argentina had Madsen guns.						

Aircraft	Type			Gun	Armament		Location
Dewoitine D.25	**D.25**	F		Madsen	2 × 7.9	f	Fuselage
	1928	4		Madsen	2 × 7.9		Rear cockpit
	These aircraft were built for Argentina.						
Dewoitine D.27	**D.27**	F			2 × 7.7	f	Fuselage
	1928	72		Oerlikon F	2 × 20	f	Pods under upper wing
	Built in Switzerland.						
Donnet-Denhaut D.D.2	**D.D.2**	P			1 ×		Flexible gun in bow
	1917	400					
Donnet-Denhaut D.D.8	**D.D.8**	P			1 × 7.7		Aft fuselage
	1917	500			1 × 7.7		Bow
	No armament was carried by machines operating over open seas; the gun was fitted only when operating over the Channel.						
Donnet-Denhaut D.D.9	**D.D.9**	F		Lewis	2 × 7.7		Aft of the wing
	1918	100		Lewis	2 × 7.7		Flexible guns in nose
Donnet-Denhaut D.D.10	**D.D.10**	P			1 × 75		Optional
	1918	30		Lewis	2 × 7.7		Gunner aft of the wings
				Lewis	2 × 7.7		Flexible guns in nose
Farman F.40	**F.40**	O		Lewis	1 × 7.7		Flexible Étéve mount in nose, usually with a Lewis
	1915						
Farman F.50	**F.50**	B			1 ×		Dorsal gunner
	1918				1 ×		Nose gunner
FBA Type B	**Type B**	P			1 × 37		Three fitted with a cannon, the rest were unarmed
	1915	80					
	Type B	P		Lewis	1 × 7.7		A single Lewis was carried by aircraft in British service
	1915						
FBA Type C	**Type C**	P			1 × 7.7		
	1916	78					
FBA Type H	**Type H**	P			1 ×		Nose
	1916	982					
FBA Type S	**Type S**	P			1 × 7.7		Flexible gun in nose
	1917						
Georges Levy 40HB 2	**40 HB 2**	PB		Lewis	1 × 7.7		
	1918	100					
Gourdou-Leseurre 2C1	**2C1**	F		Vickers	2 × 7.7	f	
	1923	20					
Gourdou-Leseurre GL-2	**GL-2**	F		Vickers	2 × 7.7	f	Engine cowling
	1918	20					
Gourdou-Lesseurre GL-21	**GL-21**	F		Vickers	2 × 7.7	f	Fuselage
	1923	30					
Gourdou-Lesseurre GL-22	**GL-22**	F		Vickers	2 × 7.7	f	Fuselage
	1920	20					
Gourdou-Lesseurre GL-23	**GL-23**	F		Vickers	2 × 7.7	f	Fuselage
	1926	9					

Gourdou-Lesseurre GL-810	**GL-810Hy, 811Hy, 812Hy, 813Hy** 1931	R 86	Vickers Lewis	1 × 7.7 2 × 7.7	f	Rear cockpit
Hanriot H.D.1	**H.D.1** 1916	F 1,000	Vickers	1 × 7.7	f	Port side of the fuselage
	Field modifications in Belgian service included the fitting of an 11 mm gun or two 7.7 mm guns.					
Hanriot H.D.2	**H.D.2** 1917	F 17	Vickers	2 × 7.7	f	Above the engine cowling
Hanriot-Dupont H.D.3	**H.D.3** 1918	F 75	Vickers Lewis	2 × 7.7 2 × 7.7	f	Fixed Rear cockpit
Henry Farman H.F.20	**H.F.20** 1914	O				
	Many armed with one machine gun, operated by the gunner seated in the nose of the nacelle. In unarmed aircraft the pilot sat in front.					
Henry Farman H.F.22	**H.F.22** 1914	O		1 ×		Front of nacelle
Henry Farman H.F.27	**H.F.27** 1915	O	Lewis	1 × 7.7		Front of nacelle
Henry Farman H.F.30	**H.F.30**	O		1 ×		Front of nacelle
Latécoère Laté 290	**Laté 290** 1933	R 40		2 ×		Dorsal turret
Letord 1, 2, 4, 5	**1, 2, 4, 5** 1917	R	Lewis	1 × 7.7		Gunner in rear cockpit, one or two guns
			Lewis	1 × 7.7		Gunner in nose, one or two guns
	Total production possibly between 250 and 300.					
Levasseur PL 5	**PL 5** 1926	F 20	Vickers Lewis	2 × 7.7 2 × 7.7	f	Rear cockpit
Levasseur PL 7	**PL 7**	TB 40		2 × 7.7		Rear cockpit
Levasseur PL 10, 101	**PL. 10, 101** 1930	R 59		1 × 7.7 2 × 7.7	f	Rear cockpit
Levy-Besson 1918	**1918** 1918	PB		2 × 7.7 1 × 75		Optional
	Probably carried two machine guns in addition to its optional 75 mm cannon.					
Levy-Besson 450hp	**450hp** 1917	PB 12	Lewis	1 × 7.7		Bow gunner
Levy-Besson Alerte	**Alerte** 1917	PB 100		1 ×		Optional
Levy-Biche / Levasseur LB 2	**LB 2** 1928	F 20	Vickers	2 × 7.7	f	
Lioré et Olivier LeO 7	**LeO 7/2, /3** 1922	O/F 32		× ×		Rear cockpit Nose gunner

Lioré et Olivier LeO 20	**LeO 20**	B		2 ×		Retractable ventral turret
	1927	318		2 ×		Dorsal
				2 ×		Nose
	LeO 206	B		1 ×		Ventral fairing
	1932	37		2 ×		Dorsal
				2 ×		Nose
Lioré et Olivier LeO H-13	**H-136**	PB		×		Dorsal
		12		×		Bow
Lioré et Olivier LeO H-254, 256, 257, 258, 259	**LeO H-257bis**	RB	Darne	1 × 7.5		Ventral
	1935	60	Darne	1 × 7.5		Dorsal
			Darne	1 × 7.5		Nose
	Alternatively, 7.7 mm Lewis guns were used.					
Loire-Gourdou-Leseurre LGL-32	**LGL-32**	F	Vickers	2 × 7.7	f	Engine cowling
	1927	443				
Maurice Farman M.F.7	**M.F.7**	O				
	1913					
	Some were equipped with a machine gun mount in the nose.					
Maurice Farman M.F.11	M.F.11	O	Colt	1 ×		Gunner in front of the nacelle
	1914					
Morane Saulnier AC	**AC**	F	Vickers	1 × 7.7	f	
	1916	30				
Morane-Saulnier AI	**AI**	F	Vickers	2 × 7.7	400 f	
	1918					
	One (with 500 rounds) or two (with 400 rounds per gun) synchronised guns were fitted.					
Morane-Saulnier BB	**BB**	O	Lewis	1 × 7.7	f	Fixed on top of upper wing, firing upwards
	1916	80				
			Lewis	1 × 7.7		Rear cockpit
Morane-Saulnier G	**G**	F	Hotchkiss	1 × 8	f	
	1915 Experimental					
	The armed version of the G had fixed guns and bullet deflectors on the propeller. This was probably only experimental.					
Morane-Saulnier I	**I**	F	Vickers	1 × 7.7	f	Originally it was designed to carry a Lewis. Mounted centrally
	1916	24				
Morane-Saulnier L, LA	**L**	O	Lewis	1 × 7.7		Rear cockpit, optional
	1914	1,030				
	Includes 430 built in Russia.					
	LA	O	Lewis	1 × 7.7		Rear cockpit
	1915					
Morane-Saulnier N	**N**	F	Hotchkiss	1 × 8	f	Engine cowling, unsynchronised
	1915	44				
	Bullet deflectors were fitted on the propeller. Usually a Hotchkiss gun was fitted, fed by 25-round clips. Lewis and Vickers guns were also used.					
Morane-Saulnier P	**P**	O	Vickers	1 × 7.7	f	Synchronised gun installed on top of the upper wing
	1917	565				
			Vickers	1 × 7.7		Rear cockpit

Morane-Saulnier T	**T** 1917	R 90		1 × 1 ×		Nose Dorsal
Morane-Saulnier V	**V** 1916	F 12	Vickers	1 × 7.7	f	Top of the engine cowling
Nieuport 10	**10** 1915	F				

Several armament options were experimented with, including an Étéve gun mount in the rear cockpit; a machine-gun fixed on the upper wing, firing upwards and controlled by the observer; and a fixed, forward-firing machine-gun on the upper wing of machines modified to single-seat fighters.

Nieuport 11	**11** 1916	F	Hotchkiss	1 × 8	f	Fixed in top of the upper wing

Some were fitted with single or twin Lewis guns.

Nieuport 12	**12** 1916	F	Lewis	1 × 7.7		Étéve mount in rear cockpit

Some had a second gun fixed on top of the upper wing. Total production of the Nieuport 10 and 12 was 7,200.

Nieuport 14	**14** 1916	O	Lewis	1 × 7.7		Rear cockpit
Nieuport 16	**16** 1916	F	Lewis	1 × 7.7	f	On top of upper wing

Some were equipped with a synchronised gun on the engine cowling.

Nieuport 17	**17** 1916	F	Lewis	1 × 7.7	f	On top of the upper wing, one or two
	17 1916	F	Vickers	1 × 7.7	f	On top of the engine cowling

The Nieuport 17 was fitted with a Vickers on top of the engine cowling, or a Lewis on the upper wing, or both. Some machines had two Lewis guns on the upper wing.

Nieuport 20	**20** 1916	O 21	Vickers Lewis	1 × 7.7 1 × 7.7	f	On top of the engine cowling Rear cockpit
Nieuport 21	**21** 1917	F	Vickers	1 × 7.7	f	On top of the engine cowling
Nieuport 23	**23** 1917	F	Lewis	2 × 7.7	f	Optional, one or two Lewises installed on top of the upper wing
			Vickers	1 × 7.7	f	On top of engine cowling. Not installed on aircraft in RFC service
Nieuport 24	**24** 1917	F	Lewis	1 × 7.7	f	Optional, gun on top of upper wing
			Vickers	1 × 7.7	f	On top of engine cowling. Not installed on aircraft in RFC service

*Built in Japan as the **Nakajima Ko-3**.*

Nieuport 25	**25** 1917	F	Vickers	1 × 7.7	f	

Nieuport 27	**27** 1917	F	Lewis	1 × 7.7	f	Optional gun on top of upper wing
			Vickers	1 × 7.7	f	On top of engine cowling. Not on aircraft in RFC service
	Built in Japan as the **Nakajima Ko-3.**					
Nieuport 28	**28** 1917	F 310	Vickers Vickers	1 × 7.7 1 × 7.7	f f	On top of engine cowling Port side of fuselage
Nieuport-Delage NiD-29	**NiD-29** 1921	F 1,130	Vickers	2 × 7.7	f	Fuselage top decking
	Built in Japan as the **Nakajima Ko-4.**					
Nieuport-Delage NiD-42	**NiD-42** 1925	F 30	Darne Vickers	2 × 7.7 2 × 7.7	f f	Wings, optional Fuselage
Nieuport-Delage NiD-52	**NiD-52** 1929	F 135		2 × 7.7	f	Engine cowling
Nieuport-Delage NiD-62	**NiD-62** 1928	F 350	Vickers	2 × 7.7	f	Engine cowling
	NiD-622 1930	F 130	Vickers	2 × 7.7	f	Engine cowling
	NiD-626 1932	F 12	Vickers	2 × 7.7	f	Engine cowling
	Built for export to Peru.					
	NiD-629 1933	F 50	Vickers	2 × 7.7	f	Engine cowling
Nieuport-Delage NiD-72	**NiD-72** 1929	F 8	Vickers	2 × 7.7	f	Engine cowling
Nieuport-Delage NiD-123	**NiD-123** 1935 *Built for export to Peru.*	F 6	Vickers	2 × 7.7	f	
Paul Schmitt	**Paul Schmitt** Floatplane 1916	R	Vickers Lewis Lewis	1 × 7.7 1 × 7.7 1 × 7.7	f	 Ventral gun, operated from rear cockpit Rear cockpit
Paul Schmitt 7	**7** 1917	B 150	Lewis	2 × 7.7		Rear cockpit
Ponnier M.1	**M.1** 1916	F 20	Lewis	1 × 7.7	f	On top of upper wing
Potez 25	**25** 1925	O 4,000	Vickers Lewis	1 × 7.7 2 × 7.7	f	 Rear cockpit
Potez 27	**27** 1924	O 205	Vickers Lewis	1 × 7.7 2 × 7.7	f	 Rear cockpit
Potez 33	**33** 1931	T/O 54	Vickers	1 × 7.7		
Potez 39	**39** 1932	O 244	Vickers Lewis	2 × 7.7 2 × 7.7	f	 Rear cockpit
Potez 452	**452** 1930	O 16	Darne	1 × 7.5		

Salmson 2	**2**	R	Vickers	1 × 7.7		f	On top of the engine cowling
	1917	3,200	Lewis	2 × 7.7			Rear cockpit
Salmson-Moineau	**S.M.1**	R	APX	1 × 37			Dorsal gunner
S.M.1	155		APX	1 × 37			Nose gunner
	Cannon appear to have been removed or replaced by Lewis machine guns on at least some service aircraft. APX = *Atelier de Puteaux.*						
SEA 4	**4**	F/R	Vickers	1 × 7.7		f	
	1918	115	Vickers	2 × 7.7			T.O.3 ring mount in rear cockpit
SPAD 7	**7**	F	Vickers	1 × 7.7		f	Above engine cowling
	1916	3,700					
SPAD 11	**11**	O	Vickers	1 × 7.7		f	
	1917	1,000	Lewis	1 × 7.7			Rear cockpit
SPAD 12	**12**	F	SAMC	1 × 37	12	f	Firing through the propeller hub
	1917		Vickers	1 × 7.7		f	Above the engine cowling
	Fewer than 300 built.						
SPAD 13	**13**	F	Vickers	2 × 7.7		f	Above the engine cowling.
	1917						
	In US service, Marlin instead of Vickers guns were fitted. Total production somewhere around 8,000.						
SPAD 14	**14**	F	SAMC	1 × 37	12	f	Firing through the propeller hub
	1918	40	Vickers	1 × 7.7		f	On top of the engine cowling
SPAD 16	**16**	O	Vickers	1 × 7.7		f	On top of the engine cowling
	1918	1,000	Lewis	1 × 7.7			Rear cockpit; one or two guns
SPAD 17	**17**	F/R	Vickers	2 × 7.7		f	Above engine
1918	Service Test	20					cowling
	Only one gun was carried if a camera was fitted.						
SPAD 20	**20**	F	Vickers	2 × 7.7		f	Above engine cowling
	1918	95	Lewis	1 × 7.7			T.O.3 ring mount in rear cockpit; later two guns were fitted
SPAD SA.1	**SA.1**	F	Lewis	1 × 7.7			Pulpit
	1915	10					
	The gunner was seated in a pulpit attached in front of the propeller.						
SPAD SA.2	**SA.2**	F	Lewis	1 × 7.7			Pulpit
	1915	99					
	The gunner was seated in a pulpit attached in front of the propeller.						
SPAD SA.4	**SA.4**	F	Lewis	1 × 7.7			Pulpit
	1916	11					
	The gunner was seated in a pulpit attached in front of the propeller.						
Tellier T.3	**T.3**	PB		1 ×			Bow
	1916						
	Total production of the T.3 and T.6 was about 245, plus 20 T.3s built in Russia.						
Tellier T.4	**T.4**	PB		1 ×			Bow
	1918						
Tellier T.5	**T.5**	PB	Hotchkiss	1 × 47			Bow
	1918	10					

Tellier T.6	**T.6** 1918	PB	Hotchkiss	1 × 47	30	Bow
Villiers II	**II** 1927	F 30	Vickers Lewis	2 × 7.7 2 × 7.7	f	 Rear cockpit
Voisin 3	**3** 1914	O/B				
	A number were modified with machine guns. The gunner sat behind the pilot, and fired forward over his head.					
Voisin 4	**4** 1915	F/A		1 × 37		Gunner in front of the nacelle
Voisin 7	**7**	O 100		1 ×		Nose
Voisin 8	**8 LBP** 1916	A	Hotchkiss	1 × 37		Nose
	8 LAP 1916	B		1 ×		Nose
	The attack version was armed with a 37 mm or sometimes 47 mm cannon. The LAP bomber version was not. Total production of both was around 1,100.					
Voisin 10	**10 LAR** 1917	B		1 ×		Nose
	10 LBR 1917	A/B	Hotchkiss	1 × 37		Nose
	Usually used as a bomber, but a cannon was fitted in production aircraft intended for ground support. Total production of the LAR bomber and the LBR was around 900.					
Voisin L	**L** 1914	O 70				
	At least six were equipped with Hotchkiss machine guns. The gunner sat behind the pilot, and fired forward over the latter's head.					
Wibault WiB 7	**WiB 7, 72, 73, 74** 1928	F 140	Vickers	2 × 7.7	f	Fuselage
	The prototypes also had 7.7 mm Darne 1919 guns in the wings.					
GERMANY						
AEG C.I	**C.I** 1915	R	Parabellum	1 × 7.92		Rear cockpit
AEG C.II	**C.II** 1915	R	Parabellum	1 × 7.92		Rear cockpit
AEG C.IV	**C.IV** 1916	O 400	LMG 08/15 Parabellum	1 × 7.92 1 × 7.92	f	 Rear cockpit
AEG G.II	**G.II**	B	Parabellum Parabellum	1 × 7.92 1 × 7.92		Dorsal Nose
AEG G.III	**G.III**	B	Parabellum Parabellum	1 × 7.92 1 × 7.92		Dorsal Nose

AEG G.IV	**G.IV** 1916	B	Parabellum Parabellum	1 × 7.92 1 × 7.92		Rear cockpit Nose
	G.IVk 1918	B 5	Becker Becker Parabellum	1 × 20 1 × 20 2 × 7.92		Dorsal, able to fire downwards Armoured nose turret
	Total production of the AEG G-series was over 540.					
AEG J.I	**J.I** 1917	A	LMG 08/15	2 × 7.92	f	Firing downwards, rear cockpit floor
			Parabellum	1 × 7.92		Rear cockpit
	Total production of the J.I and J.II together was about 600.					
AEG J.II	**J.II** 1918	A	LMG 08/15	2 × 7.92	f	Firing downwards, rear cockpit floor
			Parabellum	1 × 7.92		Rear cockpit
AGO C.I, C.II	**C.I, C.II** 1915	O	Parabellum	1 × 7.92		Nose
AGO C.IV	**C.IV** 1917	O 70	LMG 08/15 Parabellum	1 × 7.92 1 × 7.92	f	Nose Rear cockpit
Albatros C.I	**C.I** 1915	O	Parabellum	1 × 7.92		Rear cockpit
Albatros C.III	**C.III** 1916	O	LMG 08/15	1 × 7.92	f	Starboard side of the engine, late production aircraft
			Parabellum	1 × 7.92		Rear cockpit
Albatros C.V	**C.V** 1916	O 424	LMG 08/15 Parabellum	1 × 7.92 1 × 7.92	f	 Rear cockpit
Albatros C.VIII	**C.VIII** 1916	O	LMG 08/15 Parabellum	1 × 7.92 1 × 7.92	f	 Rear cockpit
Albatros C.X	**C.X** 1917	O	LMG 08/15 Parabellum	1 × 7.92 1 × 7.92	f	 Rear cockpit
Albatros C.XII	**C.XII** 1917	O	LMG 08/15 Parabellum	1 × 7.92 1 × 7.92	f	 Rear cockpit
Albatros D.I	**D.I** 1916	F 50	LMG 08/15	2 × 7.92	f	On top of engine cowling
Albatros D.II	**D.II** 1916	F	LMG 08/15	2 × 7.92	f	On top of engine cowling
	D.II 1917	F 16	Schwarzlose	2 × 8	f	Sides of fuselage, one or two
	As built in Austria-Hungary.					
Albatros D.III	**D.III** 1917	F 1,470	LMG 08/15	2 × 7.92	f	On top of engine cowling
	D.III 1917	F	Schwarzlose	2 × 8	f	Sides of fuselage, from mid-1918 on top of engine cowling
	As built in Austria-Hungary.					
Albatros D.V	**D.V, D.Va** 1917	F 2,500	LMG 08/15	2 × 7.92	f	On top of engine cowling

Albatros D.VI	**D.VI**	F	Becker	1×20	f	Nose
	1918 Prototype	1	LMG 08/15	1×7.92	f	Nose
	Pusher biplane, flown only once.					
Albatros J.I	**J.I**	A	LMG 08/15	2×7.92	f	Firing 45 degrees down
	1917		Parabellum	1×7.92		Rear cockpit
Albatros W 4	**W 4**	F	LMG 08/15	1×7.92	f	Cowling, one or two guns
	1916	128				
Arado Ar 64	**Ar 64d, e**	F		2×7.92	f	Engine cowling
	1932	20				
Aviatik C.I	**C.I, C.III**	O	Parabellum	1×7.92		
	1915					
	Early installations were made of two guns, mounted on each side of the front (observer's) cockpit.					
Brandenburg C.I	**C.I**	O	Schwarzlose	1×8		Rear cockpit
	1916	1,258	Schwarzlose	1×8	f	Type II VK gun canister on upper wing, optional
	Built for Austria-Hungary. The fixed gun was standard on the last production series.					
Brandenburg CC	**CC**	F	LMG 08/15	1×7.92	f	Bow
	1917	36				
	For Germany. The last ones had two guns.					
	CC	F	Schwarzlose	1×8	f	Bow
	1916	37				
	For Austria-Hungary.					
Brandenburg D.I	**D.I**	F	Schwarzlose	1×8	f	On top of upper wing in Type II VK canister
	1916					
	A few had a synchronised gun installed.					
Brandenburg G.I	**G.I**	B	Schwarzlose	1×8		Nose gunner
	1916	12	Schwarzlose	1×8		Dorsal gunner
	Built for Austria-Hungary. The aircraft was a failure and flew only one operational mission. One was modified to have a 70 mm Skoda cannon and a Schwarzlose M7/12 in the nose.					
Brandenburg KDW	**KDW**	F	LMG 08/15	1×7.92	f	Starboard side of the nose
	1916	58				
	On the last 20 a second gun was added.					
Brandenburg W 12	**W 12**	F	LMG 08/15	1×7.92	f	Nose
	1917	146	Parabellum	1×7.92		Rear cockpit
	One batch of 30 had two nose guns.					
Brandenburg W 18	**W 18**	F	Schwarzlose	2×8	f	Bow
	1917	47				
Brandenburg W 19	**W 19**	F	LMG 08/15	2×7.92	f	Nose
	1917	53	Parabellum	1×7.92	f	Rear cockpit
	One was tested with a 20 mm Becker.					
Brandenburg W 23	**W 23**	F	Becker	1×20	f	Starboard side of bow
	1918 Prototype	3	LMG 08/15	1×7.92	f	Port side of bow
Brandenburg W 29	**W 29**	F	LMG 08/15	2×7.92	f	Nose
	1917	150	Parabellum	1×7.92		Rear cockpit
	One nose gun if a radio was carried.					

Brandenburg W 33	**W 33**	F	LMG 08/15	2 × 7.92	f	
	1918	161	Parabellum	1 × 7.92		Rear cockpit
	One LMG 08/15 was omitted if a radio was fitted. One was experimentally fitted with a 20 mm Becker in the rear cockpit.					
Daimler D.I	**D.I**	F	LMG 08/15	2 × 7.92	f	Top of engine cowling
	1918	20				
DFW B.I	**B.I**	O/T				
	1914					
	A gun could be installed on top of the upper wing.					
DFW C.I	**C.I**	O				
	1915	130				
	A gun could be installed on top of the upper wing.					
DFW C.II	**C.II**	O	Parabellum	1 × 7.92		Rear cockpit
	1915					
DFW C.IV	**C.IV**	O	LMG 08/15	1 × 7.92	f	
	1916		Parabellum	1 × 7.92		Rear cockpit
DFW C.V	**C.V**	O	LMG 08/15	1 × 7.92	f	
	1916		Parabellum	1 × 7.92		Rear cockpit
DFW R.I	**R.I**	B	Parabellum	1 × 7.92		Dorsal
	1917	1	Parabellum	1 × 7.92		Ventral
			Parabellum	1 × 7.92		Nose
DFW R.II	**R.II**	B	Parabellum	1 × 7.92		Dorsal
	1917	2	Parabellum	1 × 7.92		Ventral
			Parabellum	1 × 7.92		Nose
Euler D.I	**D.I**	F/T		1 × 7.92	f	
	1916					
Euler D.II	**D.II**	F/T		1 × 7.92	f	
	1917					
Fokker C.I	**C.I**	O		1 ×	f	
	1919	250		1 ×		Rear cockpit
	Did not enter service during WWI, but was produced post war in the Netherlands.					
Fokker D.I	**D.I**	F	LMG 08/15	1 × 7.92	f	
	1916	120				
	B.II	F/T	LMG 15nA	1 × 7.92	f	In front of pilot
	1916	1	Schwarzlose	1 × 8	f	On top of upper wing
	Designation in Austrian service. Only the first one was armed, the 22 others were used as unarmed trainers.					
Fokker D.II	**D.II**	F	LMG 08/15	1 × 7.92	f	
	1916	181				
	*62 more D.IIs were built for Austria, under the designation **B.III**. Most of these were unarmed, but a few had a Schwarzlose on the upper wing.*					
Fokker D.III	**D.III**	F	LMG 08/15	2 × 7.92	f	One or two fitted
	1916	210				
Fokker D.IV	**D.IV**	F/T	LMG 08/15	2 × 7.92	f	Top of cowling
	1916	44				
	Version of the D.I with twin-gun armament. Saw no combat service.					

	D.II 1916	F/T 42	Schwarzlose	2×8	f	Synchronised
	The type was known as the D.II in Austria-Hungary. Most were used as trainers.					
Fokker D.V	**D.V** 1916	F 300	LMG 08/15	1×7.92	f	
	Used as a trainer.					
Fokker D.VI	**D.VI** 1917	F 60	LMG 08/15	2×7.92	f	
	In Austrian service, 15 were armed with a Schwarzlose on the upper wing, angled 15 degrees up.					
Fokker D.VII	**D.VII** 1918	F 2,626	LMG 08/15	2×7.92	f	On top of engine cowling
	Aircraft built in Austria-Hungary could have Schwarlose M16 guns instead. A few were completed and saw post-war service with the Gebauer engine gun installation.					
Fokker Dr.I	**Dr.I** 1917	F 318	LMG 08/15	2×7.92 100	f	On top of engine cowling
Fokker E.I	**E.I** 1914	F 54	LMG 08	1×7.92	f	On top of engine cowling
	Known as the A.III in Austria-Hungary. A few of these reportedly had a synchronised Schwarzlose M7/12.					
Fokker E.II	**E.II** 1915	F	LMG 08/15	1×7.92	f	On top of engine cowling
		23				
Fokker E.III	**E.III** 1915	F	LMG 08/15	2×7.92	f	On top of engine cowling. One or two guns fitted
	Between 120 and 150 built.					
Fokker E.IV	**E.IV** 1915	F 49	LMG 08/15	2×7.92	f	On top of engine cowling
	A few were fitted with three guns, but this was not effective. Early machines also had their guns tilted up 15 degrees in an attempt to simplify aiming.					
Fokker E.V, D.VIII	**E.V** 1918	F 289	LMG 08/15	2×7.92	f	On top of engine cowling
	Designation was changed to D.VIII in October 1918.					
Friedrichshafen FF 33	**FF 33F** 1914	O	Parabellum	1×7.92		Rear cockpit
	FF 33L 1915	F	LMG 08/15 Parabellum	1×7.92 1×7.92	f	Rear cockpit
Friedrichshafen FF 49	**FF 49C** 1917	F 240	LMG 08/15 Parabellum	1×7.92 1×7.92	f	Rear cockpit
Friedrichshafen G.III	**G.III** 1917	B	Parabellum Parabellum	1×7.92 1×7.92		Rear cockpit Nose gunner
	A version with a different tail assembly was known as the G.IIIa. Some of these were equipped with a 2 cm Becker cannon in the nose for ground strafing.					
Friedrichshafen G.IV	**G.IV** 1918	B	Parabellum Parabellum	1×7.92 1×7.92		Nose Rear cockpit
Gotha G.II	**G.II** 1916	B	Parabellum Parabellum	1×7.92 1×7.92		Nose Dorsal

Gotha G.III	**G.III**	B	Parabellum	1 × 7.92		Rear cockpit
	1916		Parabellum	1 × 7.92		Nose gunner
	Some G.IIIs had a tunnel in the aft fuselage that allowed the rear gunner to fire downwards.					
Gotha G.IV	**G.IV**	B	Parabellum	1 × 7.92		Rear cockpit
	1917		Parabellum	1 × 7.92		Nose
	The rear gunner could fire downwards through a tunnel in the fuselage.					
Gotha G.V	**G.V**	B	Parabellum	1 × 7.92		Nose
	1917		Parabellum	1 × 7.92		Dorsal
Gotha WD 14	**WD 14**	TB	Parabellum	1 × 7.92		Rear cockpit
	1916	67	Parabellum	1 × 7.92		Nose gunner
Halberstadt C.V	**C.V**	R	LMG 08/15	1 × 7.92	f	Port side of forward fuselage
	1918		Parabellum	1 × 7.92		Rear cockpit
Halberstadt CL.II	**CL.II**	F/A	LMG 08/15	1 × 7.92	f	One or two guns
	1917	900	Parabellum	1 × 7.92		Rear cockpit
Halberstadt CL.IV	**CL.IV**	F/A	LMG 08/15	1 × 7.92	f	One or two guns
	1918		Parabellum	1 × 7.92		Rear cockpit
Halberstadt CLS.I	**CLS.I**	F/A	LMG 08/15	2 × 7.92	f	
	1918 Prototype	4	Becker	1 × 20		Rear cockpit
Halberstadt D.II, D.III	**D.II, D.III**	F	LMG 08/15	1 × 7.92	f	Port side of forward fuselage
	1916	110				
	Only the engine distinguished the D.III from the D.II.					
Halberstadt D.V	**D.V**	F	LMG 08/15	1 × 7.92	f	Port side of fuselage; the last
	1916	87				production aircraft had two guns
Hannover CL.II	**CL.II**	F/A	LMG 08/15	1 × 7.92	f	
	1917	639	Parabellum	1 × 7.92		Rear cockpit
Hannover CL.III	**CL.III, IIIa**	F/A	LMG 08/15	1 × 7.92	f	
	1918	653	Parabellum	1 × 7.92		Rear cockpit
	Tail as CL.II.					
Hannover CL.V	**CL.V**	F	LMG 08/15	2 × 7.92	f	On top of engine cowling
	1918	108	Parabellum	1 × 7.92		Rear cockpit
	*Also built in Norway (14 completed) as **F.F.7 Hauk**.*					
Heinkel HD 37	**HD 37**	F		2 × 7.7	f	
	1932	134				
Heinkel HD 42	**HD 42C-2**	O		1 × 7.92		Rear cockpit
	1931					
	Most versions of this aircraft were unarmed.					
Heinkel HE 8	**HE 8**	R		1 ×		Rear cockpit
	1928	22				
	Known as the H.M.II in Danish service.					
Heinkel He 45	**He 45C**	O/A		1 × 7.92	f	
	1931	512		1 × 7.92		Rear cockpit
Heinkel He 46	**He 46C**	O		1 × 7.92		Rear cockpit
	1931	480				

Heinkel He 50	**He 50A**	SB		1×7.92	f	
	1931			1×7.92		Rear cockpit
	*For dive-bombing operations, the aircraft was flown by the pilot alone, and the rear gun was removed. Exported as the He 66, and known in Soviet service as the **I-7**.*					
Junkers CL.I	**CL.I**	F/A	LMG 08/15	2×7.92	f	
	1918	63	Parabellum	1×7.92		Rear cockpit
Junkers D.I	**D.I**	F/A	LMG 08/15	2×7.92	f	On top of engine cowling
	1918	40				
Junkers H 21	**H 21**	O	Vickers	$1 \times$	f	
	1922	100	DA	$1 \times$		
	Built in the USSR.					
Junkers J.I	**J.I**	A	LMG 08/15	2×7.92	f	
	1917		Parabellum	1×7.92		Rear cockpit
Junkers K53, R53	**K53**	F	Vickers	2×7.7	f	
	1926	20	Lewis	2×7.7		Rear cockpit
Kondor D.I	**D.I**	F	LMG 08/15	2×7.92	f	
	1918	10				
LFG Roland C.II	**C.II**	R	LMG 08/15	1×7.92	f	Fixed gun retrofitted on some aircraft
	1915		Parabellum	1×7.92		Rear cockpit
LFG Roland D.I	**D.I**	F	LMG 08/15	2×7.92	f	
	1916					
LFG Roland D.II	**D.II, IIa**	F	LMG 08/15	2×7.92	f	Cowling
	1917	320				
LFG Roland D.III	**D.III**	F	LMG 08/15	2×7.92	f	Cowling
	1917					
LFG Roland D.VI	**D.VIa, b**	F	LMG 08/15	2×7.92	f	
	1918	350				
LVG C.I	**C.I**	R	Parabellum	1×7.92		Rear cockpit
	1915					
	This was the first German aircraft on which a ring mount was fitted for the gun.					
LVG C.II	**C.II**	R	LMG 08/15	1×7.92	f	Added later
	1915		Parabellum	1×7.92		Rear cockpit
LVG C.IV	**C.IV**	R	LMG 08/15	1×7.92	f	
			Parabellum	1×7.92		Rear cockpit
LVG C.V, C.VI	**C.V, C.VI**	R	LMG 08/15	1×7.92	f	
	1917	1,160	Parabellum	1×7.92		Rear cockpit
Pfalz A.I, A.II	**A.I, A.II**	O/T				
	1914	60				
	Copy of the Morane-Saulnier L. Most were unarmed, but some had a 7.92 mm gun in the rear cockpit.					
Pfalz D.III	**D.III, D.IIIa**	F	LMG 08/15	2×7.92	f	Top of fuselage
	1917	600				

Pfalz D.VIII	**D.VIII** 1918	F 40	LMG 08/15	2 × 7.92	f	Top of fuselage
Pfalz D.XII	**D.XII** 1918	F 200	LMG 08/15	2 × 7.92	f	Top of fuselage
Pfalz E.I	**E.I** 1915	F	LMG 08/15	1 × 7.92	f	Top of fuselage
Pfalz E.II	**E.II** 1915	F	LMG 08/15	1 × 7.92	f	
Pfalz E.III	**E.III** 1916	F	LMG 08/15	1 × 7.92	f	Top of fuselage
Pfalz E.IV	**E.IV** 1916	F 24	LMG 08/15	2 × 7.92	f	Top of fuselage
Pfalz E.V	**E.V** 1916 Service Test	F 20	LMG 08/15	2 × 7.92	f	Top of fuselage
Rumpler C.I	**C.I** 1915	O	LMG 08/15 Parabellum	1 × 7.92 1 × 7.92	f	Fitted to late production aircraft Rear cockpit
Rumpler C.IV	**C.IV** 1917	R	LMG 08/15 Parabellum	1 × 7.92 1 × 7.92	f	Rear cockpit
Rumpler C.V	**C.V**	R	LMG 08/15 Parabellum	1 × 7.92 1 × 7.92	f	Rear cockpit
Rumpler C.VII	**C.VII** 1917 **C.VII Rubild** 1917	R R	LMG 08/15 Parabellum Parabellum	1 × 7.92 1 × 7.92 1 × 7.92	f	Rear cockpit Rear cockpit
Rumpler D.I	**D.I** 1918 Service Test	F	LMG 08/15	2 × 7.92	f	
Rumpler G.I	**G.I** 1915	B 58	Parabellum	1 × 7.92		Nose
Rumpler G.II	**G.II** 1916	B	Parabellum Parabellum	1 × 7.92 1 × 7.92		Nose Dorsal
Rumpler G.III	**G.III** 1917	B	Parabellum Parabellum	1 × 7.92 1 × 7.92		Nose Dorsal
Siemens-Schuckert D.I	**D.I** 1916	F 95	LMG 08/15	1 × 7.92	f	Top of fuselage
	This was a close copy of the Nieuport 11.					
Siemens-Schuckert D.III	**D.III** 1918	F 80	LMG 08/15	2 × 7.92	f	On top of engine cowling
Siemens-Schuckert D.IV	**D.IV** 1918	F 140	LMG 08/15	2 × 7.92	f	On top of engine cowling
Siemens-Schuckert E.I, E.III	**E.I, E.III** 1916	F 26	LMG 08/15	1 × 7.92	f	Top of fuselage

Zeppelin-Staaken R.VI	**R.VI** 1917	B 18	Parabellum Parabellum Parabellum	1 × 7.92 2 × 7.92 1 × 7.92		Ventral Dorsal Nose
	Reportedly up to 7 guns could be installed. The Parabellums were routinely replaced by three captured Lewis guns.					
Zeppelin-Staaken R.XIV	**R.XIV**	B 3	Lewis Lewis Lewis	2 × 7.7 2 × 7.7 2 × 7.7		Upper wing positions Dorsal Ventral
	A mix of Parabellum and Lewis guns was used.					
Zeppelin-Staaken R.XV	**R.XV** 1918	B 3	Parabellum	6 × 7.92		
ITALY						
Ansaldo A 120 Ady	**A.120** 1925	0 77		2 × 1 ×	f	Rear cockpit
Ansaldo A.1 *Balilla*	**A.1** 1918	F 168	Vickers	2 × 7.7	f	
Ansaldo A 300	**A.300-4** 1922	RB 700		2 × 1 ×	f	Rear cockpit
Ansaldo A.C.2	**A.C.2** 1925	F 112	Vickers	2 × 7.7	f	
	Derived from the Dewoitine D.1.					
Ansaldo A.C.3	**A.C.3** 1926	F/A 150	Darne Darne	2 × 7.7 2 × 7.7	f f	Wings Fuselage
	Wing guns sometimes replaced by a fixed upward-firing gun on the wing centre section. Derived from the Dewoitine D.9.					
Ansaldo Idro-S.V.A.	**Idro-S.V.A.** 1918	F 50	Vickers	2 × 7.7	f	
Ansaldo S.V.A.2	**S.V.A.2** 1917	F/T 65	Vickers	2 × 7.7	f	
Ansaldo S.V.A.3	**S.V.A.3** 1917	FR	Vickers	2 × 7.7	f	
	A few were fitted with an additional, fixed upward-firing gun.					
Ansaldo S.V.A.4	**S.V.A.4** 1918	FR	Vickers	2 × 7.7	f	
	Starboard gun sometimes removed.					
Ansaldo S.V.A.5	**S.V.A.5** 1918	RB	Vickers	2 × 7.7	f	
	Total S.V.A. production was 1,248, most of them S.V.A.5s.					
Ansaldo S.V.A.10	**S.V.A.10** 1918	RB	Vickers Lewis	1 × 7.7 1 × 7.7	f	Rear cockpit
CANT 25	**25M** 1931	F 19	Vickers	2 × 7.7	f	Bow
Caproni Ca.1 (300 hp bomber)	**Ca.1** 1916	B 162	Fiat-Revelli Fiat-Revelli	1 × 6.5 1 × 6.5		Nose Tall mount behind upper wing

Caproni Ca.2	**Ca.2**	B	Fiat-Revelli	1 × 6.5		Nose
(350 hp bomber)	1916	9	Fiat-Revelli	1 × 6.5		Tall mount behind upper wing
Caproni Ca.3	**Ca.3**	B		1 × 7.7		Tall mount behind upper wing
	1917	299		1 × 7.7		Nose
	At least one fitted with a 25 mm cannon.					
Caproni Ca.4	**Ca.4**	B		2 × 7.7		Gunners in front of tail booms
	1918	42		1 × 7.7		Nose
Caproni Ca.5	**Ca.5**	B		1 × 7.7		Tall mount behind upper wing
	1918	674		1 × 7.7		Nose
Caproni Ca.31, 32,	**Ca.36**	B	Fiat-Revelli	1 × 6.5		Nose
33, 36	1918	153	Fiat-Revelli	1 × 6.5		Tall mount behind upper wing
Caproni Ca.73	**Ca.73**	B		1 × 7.7		Ventral
	1926			1 × 7.7		Dorsal
				1 × 7.7		Nose
	The Ca.73 quarter G, also known as the Ca.89, had a retractable ventral 'dustbin' turret and a manually operated dorsal turret.					
Fiat B.R., B.R.1,	**B.R., B.R.1,**	B	Darne	1 × 7.7	f	
B.R.2, B.R.3, B.R.4	**B.R.2, B.R.3**		Darne	1 × 7.7		Rear cockpit
	1919					
Fiat C.R.1	**C.R.1**	F		2 × 7.7	f	Fuselage
	1924	240				
Fiat C.R.20	**C.R.20, C.R.20bis**	F	Vickers	2 × 7.7	f	Optional fuselage sides
1927		541	Vickers	2 × 7.7	f	Fuselage
	CR.20 Idro	F	Vickers	2 × 7.7	f	Fuselage
	1928	17				
Fiat R.2	**R.2**	R	Revelli	1 × 6.5		Rear cockpit
	1918	129				
	Development of the S.I.A. 9B. Alternatively, a Lewis was fitted.					
Macchi L.1	**L.1**	R	Fiat	1 × 6.5		Bow
	1915					
Macchi L.3	**L.3**	RB	Fiat	1 × 6.5		Bow
	1916	220				
Macchi M.5	**M.5**	F	Vickers	1 × 7.7	f	Bow, some were equipped with
	1917	244				two guns
	M.5 Mod	F	Vickers	2 × 7.7	f	Bow
	1918	100				
Macchi M.7	**M.7**	F	Vickers	2 × 7.7	f	Bow
	1918	11				
	M.7ter	F	Vickers	2 × 7.7	f	Bow
	1923	100				
Macchi M.8	**M.8**	PB	Lewis	1 × 7.7		Bow
	1917	57				
Macchi M.9	**M.9**	PB	Lewis	1 × 7.7		Bow
	1918	30				

Macchi M.14	**M.14** 1919	F/T 10	Vickers	2 × 7.7	f	
Macchi M.18	**M.18** 1920	PB/T 100	Lewis	1 × 7.7		Bow
Macchi M.24	**M.24** 1924	F	Vickers	2 × 7.7	f	Bow
Macchi M.41	**M.41** 1927	F 43	Vickers	2 × 7.7	f	Bow
Macchi M.71	**M.71** 1930	F 12	Vickers	2 × 7.7	f	Bow
Piaggio P.6, P.6ter	**P.6ter** 1929	R 15		1 × 7.7		Rear cockpit
Piaggio P.10	**P.10** 1932	R		1 × 7.7		
Pomilio PC, PD, PE, PY	**PC, PD** 1917 **PE** 1918 *Built in Italy and the USA.*	R R 1,071	Revelli Revelli Revelli Lewis	1 × 6.5 1 × 6.5 1 × 6.5 1 × 7.7	f f	Rear cockpit Rear cockpit, one or two
Savoia-Marchetti S.55	**S.55** 1925	PB 200		2 × 7.7 2 × 7.7		Guns in stern of each hull Guns in bow of each hull
Savoia-Marchetti S.59	**S.59bis** 1927	PB 150	Lewis	1 × 7.7		
Savoia-Marchetti S.62	**S.62** 1926 **S.62bis** 1928 *S.62bis was offered with 20 mm Oerlikon L in bow mounting.* *Most of the production was sold to the USSR (24) or built there (29).*	PB PB	Lewis Lewis Lewis Lewis	2 × 7.7 2 × 7.7 2 × 7.7 2 × 7.7		Dorsal Bow Dorsal turret Bow
S.I.A. 7	**7B1, 7B2** 1917	R/B 570	Revelli Revelli	1 × 6.5 1 × 6.5	f	Rear cockpit
S.I.A. 9	**9B** 1918	B 62	Revelli	1 × 6.5		Rear cockpit
SIAI S.8	**S.8** 1917	PB 172	Revelli	2 × 6.5		Bow
SIAI S.67	**S.67** 1930	F 3	Vickers	2 × 7.7	f	Top of bow
JAPAN						
Aichi E3A	**E3A1**	R		1 × 7.7 1 × 7.7	f	Rear cockpit
Hiro G2H	**G2H1** 1935	B 8		1 × 7.7 2 × 7.7 1 × 7.7		Nose Dorsal, retractable turret Ventral, retractable turret

Hiro H1H	**H1H1, 2, 3**	PB		1 × 7.7		Dorsal
	1929	65		1 × 7.7		Bow
Hiro H2H	**H2H1**	PB		2 × 7.7		Two dorsal gunners
	1930	17		2 × 7.7		Bow
Hiro H4H	**H4H1, 2**	PB		1 × 7.7		Bow
	1932	47		1 × 7.7		Dorsal
Kawanishi H3K	**H3K1, 2**	PB		2 × 7.7		Tail
	1930	5		4 × 7.7		Two dorsal gunners
				2 × 7.7		Bow
	Japanese version of Short S.15.					
Kawasaki KDA 2	**Type 88-I**	R/B		1 × 7.7	f	
	1928	710		1 × 7.7		Rear cockpit, one or two
	Type 88-II	B		1 × 7.7	f	
	1929	407	Type 89	1 × 7.7		Rear cockpit, one or two
Kawasaki KDA 5	**Type 92-I, -II**	F		2 × 7.7	f	
	1932	380				
Mitsubishi 2MR	**2MR**	R		2 × 7.7		
	1922	159		2 × 7.7		
Mitsubishi B1M	**B1M1**	TB		2 × 7.7		Dorsal
	1923					
	B1M2, 3	TB		2 × 7.7		Dorsal
	1931			2 × 7.7	f	
Mitsubishi B2M	**B2M**	TB		1 × 7.7	f	Port fuselage
	1932	204		1 × 7.7		Rear cockpit
Mitsubishi Type 10	**Type 10**	F	Vickers	2 × 7.7	f	
	1923					
Nakajima A1N	**A1N**	F	Vickers	2 × 7.7	f	
	1929	150				
	Japanese version of the Gloster Gambet.					
Nakajima A2N	**A2N1, 2, 3**	F	Vickers	2 × 7.7	f	
	1932	100				
Nakajima E2N	**E2N1**	R		1 × 7.7		Dorsal
	1927	77				
Nakajima Type 91 Fighter	**Type 91**	F		2 × 7.7	f	
	1931	442				
Yokosho E5Y	**E5Y1**	R		2 ×	f	
	1931			1 ×		Ventral
				1 ×		Dorsal
Yokosho B3Y	**B3Y1**	B		1 × 7.7	f	
	1933	130		1 × 7.7		Rear cockpit
Yokosho E1Y	**E1Y**	R		2 × 7.7		Dorsal
	1923	320				

NETHERLANDS

Fokker C.IV	**C.IV**	O		1 ×	f	Engine cowling
	1923	159		2 ×		Rear cockpit
	Widely exported. Armament selection depended on the customer.					
Fokker C.V, VI	**C.Vb, c**	O		1 × 7.92	f	
	1924	34		2 × 7.92		Rear cockpit, one or two
	C.Vd	O/B/F		1 × 7.92	f	
	1924			2 × 7.92		Rear cockpit, one or two
	The C.Vd was also delivered in an escort fighter version with two fixed and one flexible gun.					
	C.Ve	B		1 × 7.92	f	
	1924			1 × 7.92		Rear cockpit
	Also built in Italy as the Meridionali Ro.1.					
	C.VI	O		1 × 7.92	f	
		33		2 × 7.92		Rear cockpit
	Different engine, otherwise equivalent to C.Vd.					
Fokker C.VIII	**C.VIIIW**	R		1 ×	f	Engine cowling
	1930	9		2 ×		Rear cockpit
Fokker C.IX	**C.IX**	R/T		1 ×	f	
	1932	6		1 ×		Dorsal
				1 ×		Ventral
Fokker C.X	**C.X**	F/R/O	FN-Browning	1 × 7.9	f	One or two fixed
	1937	69				synchronised guns
			Lewis	1 ×		Rear cockpit
	The 29 Finnish aircraft had 7.7 mm Browning guns and a 7.62 mm L-33/34 in the rear cockpit.					
Fokker C.XI	**C.XI-W**	R	FN-Browning	1 × 7.92	f	
	1938	14	FN-Browning	1 × 7.92		Rear cockpit
Fokker D.X	**D.X**	F	FN-Browning	2 × 7.92	f	
	1923	12				
	Ten built for Spain, one for Finland.					
Fokker D.XI, PW-7	**D.XI**	F	LMG 08/15	2 × 7.92	f	Synchronised
	1924	180				
	Three delivered to the USAAS as PW-7s, the rest to the USSR, Romania and Switzerland.					
Fokker D.XIII	**D.XIII**	F	LMG 08/15	2 × 7.92	f	Engine cowling
	1925	50				
	The D.XIII was ordered by the Germans for use at their secret training centre at Lipetsk in the USSR. In 1933 the 30 surviving aircraft were handed over to the USSR.					
Fokker D.XVI	**D.XVI**	F	FN-Brow. M.36	2 × 7.92	f	Engine cowling
		19				
Fokker D.XVII	**D.XVII**		FN-Brow. M.36	2 × 7.92	f	
	1932	10				
Fokker F.VI, PW-5	**PW-5**	F	Browning .30	2 × 7.62	f	
	1922	12				
	Alternatively, one .50 and one .30. Built for the USAAC.					
NVI FK.31	**FK.31**	F		×	f	One or two guns
	1925	18		1 ×		Rear cockpit

NORWAY

| Høver M.F.9 | **M.F.9** | F | Colt | 1 × 7.62 | f | |
| | 1926 | 10 | | | | |

POLAND

PWS 10	**PWS 10**	F	Vickers	2 × 7.7	f	
	1931	80				
Plage and Laskiewicz/	**R-VIII**	TB		1 × 7.7	f	Starboard side of fuselage
Lublin R-VIII	1928	5		2 × 7.7		Dorsal
				1 × 7.7		Ventral (optional)
Plage and Laskiewicz/	**R-X**	O		1 × 7.7		Rear cockpit
Lublin R-X	1929	7				
Plage and Laskiewicz/	**R-XIII**	O	Vickers	1 × 7.7		
Lublin R-XIII	1932	273				

ROMANIA

| IAR 14 | **14** | F/T | Vickers | 2 × 7.7 | f | |
| | 1934 | 20 | | | | |

SWEDEN

Svenska Aero J 6	**J 6, J 6A, J 6B**	F		2 × 8	f	Top fuselage decking
Jaktfalk	1930	18				
Thulin K	**K**	F				
	1917	17				

Delivered unarmed, but in Dutch service several were fitted with machine guns. A few were tested with 20 mm Madsen cannon.

SWITZERLAND

Häfeli DH-1	**DH-1**	O	MG-94	1 × 7.5		Rear cockpit
	1916	6				
Häfeli DH-2	**DH-2**	O	MG-94	1 × 7.5		Rear cockpit
	1917					
Häfeli DH-3	**DH-3**	O		1 × 7.5	f	
	1917	110	MG-11	1 × 7.5		Rear cockpit
Häfeli DH-5	**DH-5**	R		2 × 7.5	f	
	1922	82	Flieger-Dpplpst.	2 × 7.65		Rear cockpit
	DH-5A	O	Fl.Mg 29	2 × 7.5		Rear cockpit

UNITED KINGDOM

AD Scout	**Scout**	F	Davis 2 pdr	1 × 40	f	Underside of nacelle
	1915 Prototype	4				
ADC 1	**1**	F	Vickers	2 × 7.7	600 f	Synchronised
	1924	8				
Airco D.H.1	**D.H.1**	F	Lewis	1 × 7.7		Nose
	1915	170				

| Airco D.H.2 | **D.H.2** | F | Lewis | 1 × 7.7 | | Nose |
| | 1915 | 400 | | | | |

Although this was a single-seater, the nose gun was flexible. In service it was often fixed, and later a spring clamp was adopted.

| Airco D.H.4 | **D.H.4** | B | Vickers | 1 × 7.7 | 600 f | Engine cowling |
| | 1917 | 1,149 | Lewis | 1 × 7.7 | 582 | Rear cockpit, one or two guns fitted |

In RNAS service two fixed guns were fitted. A few D.H.4s flew with upward-firing COW guns or Davis 2 pdr recoilless guns.

| | **D.H.4** | B | Marlin | 2 × 7.62 | f | Engine cowling |
| | | 3,327 | Lewis | 1 × 7.7 | | Rear cockpit, one or two guns fitted |

Aircraft built in the USA.

| Airco D.H.5 | **D.H.5** | F | Vickers | 1 × 7.7 | 750 f | Top of engine cowling, offset to port |
| | 1915 | 590 | | | | |

| Armstrong Whitworth Atlas | **Atlas Mk I** | O/T | Vickers Mk II | 1 × 7.7 | 600 f | |
| | 1927 | 440 | Lewis Mk III | 1 × 7.7 | 470 | Rear cockpit |

| Armstrong Whitworth F.K.3 | **F.K.3** | R | Lewis | 1 × 7.7 | | Rear cockpit |
| | 1915 | 500 | | 1 × 7.7 | | |

| Armstrong Whitworth F.K.8 | **F.K.8** | R | Vickers | 1 × 7.7 | f | Cowling |
| | 1917 | 1,650 | Lewis | 1 × 7.7 | | Rear cockpit |

| Armstrong Whitworth Scimitar | **Scimitar** | F | Vickers Class E | 2 × 7.7 | 600 f | |
| | 1936 | 6 | | | | |

| Armstrong Whitworth Siskin | **Siskin Mk III, IIIA** | F | Vickers Mk II | 2 × 7.7 | 600 f | Top fuselage decking |
| | 1924 | 412 | | | | |

| Armstrong Whitworth Wolf | **Wolf** | R/T | Vickers | 1 × 7.7 | f | Port side of cowling |
| | | | Lewis | 2 × 7.7 | | Rear cockpit |

Avro 504	**504C, 504D**	F	Lewis	1 × 7.7	f	Fixed firing 45 degrees upwards
	1915	116				
	504K (modified)	F	Lewis	1 × 7.7	f	Single gun on Foster mounting on upper wing
	1918					

Trainer, modified for fighter operations.

Avro Aldershot	**Aldershot Mk III**	B	Vickers	1 × 7.7	f	Port side of fuselage
	1924	15	Lewis	1 × 7.7		Rear cockpit
			Lewis	1 × 7.7		Ventral

| Avro Bison | **Bison** | O | Lewis | 1 × 7.7 | | Rear cockpit |
| | 1925 | 47 | | | | |

| Beardmore WB.III | **WB.III** | F | Lewis | 1 × 7.7 | f | |
| | 1917 | 55 | | | | |

| Blackburn Blackburn | **Blackburn** | TB/R | Vickers | 1 × 7.7 | f | |
| | 1923 | | Lewis | 1 × 7.7 | | Rear cockpit |

Blackburn Iris	**Iris Mk I**	PB	Lewis	1 × 7.7		Bow
			Lewis	1 × 7.7		Dorsal
			Lewis	2 × 7.7		Beam hatches, optional

	Iris Mk II, V	PB	Lewis	1 × 7.7		Tail
	1926	4	Lewis	1 × 7.7		Dorsal
			Lewis	1 × 7.7		Nose
Blackburn Kangaroo	**Kangaroo**	B	Lewis	1 × 7.7		Nose
	1918		Lewis	1 × 7.7		Dorsal
Blackburn Lincock	**Lincock Mk III**	F	Vickers	2 × 7.7	f	Fuselage
	1930 Service Test	5				
Blackburn Perth	**Perth**	PB	Lewis	1 × 7.7		Tail
	1934	4	Lewis	1 × 7.7		Dorsal
			Lewis	1 × 7.7		Nose

There was provision for a 37 mm COW gun in the bow position on a Vickers-Westland mounting.

Blackburn Ripon	**Ripon Mk II, IIA,**	TB	Vickers	1 × 7.7	f	
	IIC, IIF		Lewis	1 × 7.7		Rear cockpit
	1929	123				

Finnish aircraft later had L-33 guns installed.

Blackburn Velos	**Velos**	TB	Lewis	1 × 7.7		Rear cockpit, one or two
	1925					

Built for export. Flown as a single-seater when armed with a torpedo.

Boulton Paul Bittern	**Bittern**	F	Lewis	2 × 7.7		Fitted to the sides of the fuselage,
	1924 Prototype	1				with elevation from 0 to 45 degrees
	Bittern	F	Vickers	2 × 7.7	f	Sides of front fuselage
	1924 Prototype	1				
Boulton Paul	**Sidestrand**	B	Lewis	1 × 7.7		Ventral
Sidestrand	**Mk I, II, III**		Lewis	1 × 7.7		Dorsal
	1928	18	Lewis	1 × 7.7		Nose
Bristol Bagshot	**Bagshot**	NF	COW	1 × 37		Dorsal gunner
	1927 Prototype	1	COW	1 × 37		Gunner in nose
			Lewis	1 × 7.7		Dorsal gunner with Scarff ring
Bristol Bulldog	**Bulldog Mk II, IIA**	F	Vickers Mk II	2 × 7.7	f	Sides of the fuselage
	1930	360				
	Bulldog Mk II	F		2 ×	f	Sides of the fuselage
	1930	24				
	For Latvia and Estonia.					
	Bulldog Mk IVA	F	Vickers Mk II	2 × 7.7	f	Sides of the fuselage
	1935	17				
	For Finland.					
	105D	F	Madsen	2 × 7.62	f	Sides of the fuselage
		4				
	For Denmark.					
Bristol F.2 Fighter	**F.2A, F.2B**	F	Vickers	1 × 7.7	f	Engine cowling
	1917	4,797	Lewis	1 × 7.7		Rear cockpit, one or two fitted
Bristol M.1	**M.1B**	F	Vickers	1 × 7.7	f	Port wing root
	1917	4				
	M.1C	F	Vickers	1 × 7.7	f	On top of engine cowling
	1917	125				

Bristol Scout	**Scout D**	F	Lewis	1×7.7		f	On top of upper wing
	1915	80					
	Most Scouts were (officially) unarmed, but various experimental or improvised armament was common. A Lewis on top of the upper wing was most widespread. A few had a synchronised Vickers.						
de Havilland D.H.9	**D.H.9, 9A**	B	Vickers	1×7.7	750	f	
	1918	4,085	Lewis Mk III	1×7.7	582		Rear cockpit
de Havilland D.H.10 Amiens	**D.H.10**	B	Lewis	1×7.7	582		Dorsal position. Two could be fitted instead of one
	1918	220	Lewis	1×7.7	582		Nose position. Two could be fitted instead of one
de Havilland D.H.77	**D.H.77**	F	Vickers	2×7.7		f	Sides of the fuselage
	1929 Prototype	1					
Fairey III	**IIIA**	O	Lewis	1×7.7			Rear cockpit
	1917	52					
	IIIB	O	Lewis	1×7.7			Rear cockpit
	1917	24					
	IIIC	O	Vickers	1×7.7		f	
	1919		Lewis	1×7.7			Rear cockpit
	IIID	O	Lewis	1×7.7			Rear cockpit
	1920	207					
	IIIF	R	Vickers	1×7.7	600	f	Port side of fuselage
	1926	352	Lewis	1×7.7	582		Rear cockpit
Fairey Campania	**Campania**	O	Lewis	1×7.7			Rear cockpit
	1917	60					
Fairey Firefly	**Firefly Mk IIM**	FR	FN-Browning	2×7.7		f	Sides of fuselage
Fairey Fawn	**Fawn Mk II, III**	B	Vickers	1×7.7		f	
	1924	68	Lewis	1×7.7			Rear cockpit, one or two
Fairey Flycatcher	**Flycatcher**	F	Vickers	2×7.7		f	Sides of the fuselage
	1923	206					
Fairey Fox	**Fox Mk I, IA**	B	Vickers Class E	1×7.7		f	Port side of fuselage
	1925	28	Lewis	1×7.7			Rear cockpit, Fairey High Speed mount
	Fox Mk II, IIM	B	Vickers	1×7.7	300	f	Port side of fuselage
	1933		Lewis	1×7.7	582		Rear cockpit, Fairey HS mount
	Fox Mk III, IV	B		2×7.7	300	f	Sides of fuselage
	1933		Lewis	1×7.7	582		Rear cockpit, Fairey HS mount
	Fox Mk IVC	F/R	FN-Browning	2×7.6		f	Sides of the fuselage
	1935	50	Lewis	1×7.6			Rear cockpit; later an FN-Browning
	Fox Mk VII, VIII	F	FN-Browning	2×7.6		f	Sides of the fuselage
	1935	14	FN-Browning	4×7.6		f	Upper wing
	Only the Mk I saw service in the RAF; other models were built mainly in and for Belgium.						
Fairey Gordon	**Gordon**	B/T	Vickers Mk II	1×7.7	600	f	Port side of fuselage
	1930	163	Lewis Mk III	1×7.7	582		Rear cockpit
Fairey Hamble Baby	**Hamble Baby**	ASW	Lewis	1×7.7		f	
	1917	174					

Fairey Seal	**Seal**	O	Vickers Mk II	1 × 7.7	600 f	
	1933	90	Lewis Mk III	1 × 7.7		Rear cockpit
Felixstowe F.2	**F.2A**	PB	Lewis	1 × 7.7		Dorsal, one or two
	1917		Lewis	2 × 7.7		Beam positions
			Lewis	1 × 7.7		Nose, one or two
Felixstowe F.3	**F.3**	PB	Lewis	2 × 7.7		Beam positions
	1917		Lewis	1 × 7.7		Dorsal, one or two guns
			Lewis	1 × 7.7		Bow, one or two guns
Felixestowe F.5	**F.5**	PB	Lewis	3 × 7.7		Dorsal gunners
	1918		Lewis	1 × 7.7		Bow
				2 × 7.7		Beam positions
Gloster Gamecock	**Gamecock Mk I**	F	Vickers	2 × 7.7	600 f	Sides of the fuselage
	1925	82				
Gloster Gauntlet	**Gauntlet Mk I**	F	Vickers Mk V	2 × 7.7	600 f	Fuselage
	1934	228				
Gloster Grebe	**Grebe Mk II**	F	Vickers Class E	2 × 7.7	600 f	Sides of the fuselage
	1923	112				
Gloster Nighthawk	**Nighthawk**	F	Vickers	2 × 7.7	f	
	1922	4				
Gloster Nightjar	**Nightjar**	F	Vickers	2 × 7.7	f	
	1922	22				
Gloster Sparrowhawk	**Sparrowhawk**	F	Vickers	2 × 7.7	f	Fuselage top decking
	1921	40				
	Ten more were delivered as unarmed trainers.					
Handley Page Heyford	**Heyford Mk I, II, III**	B	Lewis	1 × 7.7		Ventral dustbin turret
	1930	124	Lewis	1 × 7.7		Dorsal
			Lewis	1 × 7.7		Nose
Handley Page Hinaidi	**Hinaidi Mk I, II**	B	Lewis	1 × 7.7	582	Ventral
	1929	52	Lewis	1 × 7.7	582	Dorsal
			Lewis	1 × 7.7	582	Nose
Handley Page Hyderabad	**Hyderabad**	B	Lewis	1 × 7.7	582	Ventral
	1926	38	Lewis	1 × 7.7	582	Dorsal
			Lewis	1 × 7.7	582	Nose
Handley Page O/100	**O/100**	B	Lewis	1 × 7.7		Nose
	1916		Lewis	2 × 7.7		Dorsal, two pillar mounts
				1 × 7.7		Ventral
	Some O/100 or O/400 fitted with 6 pdr Davis gun.					
Handley Page O/400	**O/400**	B	Lewis	1 × 7.7		Ventral
	1916		Lewis	2 × 7.7		Dorsal, two pillar mounts, sometimes one gun on rocking pillar
			Lewis	1 × 7.7		Nose, one or two guns

Handley Page V/1500	**V/1500**	B	Lewis	1 × 7.7		Tail
	1918	32	Lewis	1 × 7.7		Ventral gunner
			Lewis	1 × 7.7		Dorsal gunner
			Lewis	1 × 7.7		Nose
	In each position two guns could also be fitted.					
Hawker Audax	**Audax Mk I**	O	Vickers	1 × 7.7	500 f	
	1932		Lewis	1 × 7.7	776	Rear cockpit
Hawker Danecock	**Danecock**	F	Madsen	2 × 7.7	720 f	Sides of the fuselage
	1925	15				
	Built for Denmark.					
Hawker Hart	**Hart**	B	Vickers Mk II	1 × 7.7	500 f	Left side of cockpit
	1929	265	Lewis Mk III	1 × 7.7	776	Rear cockpit
Hawker Hartbees	**Hartbees**	O	Vickers	2 × 7.7	f	
		69	Lewis	1 × 7.7		Rear cockpit
Hawker Horsley	**Horsley Mk I, II**	B	Vickers	1 × 7.7	600 f	
	1927	112	Lewis	1 × 7.7	582	Rear cockpit
Hawker Nimrod	**Nimrod Mk I, II**	F	Vickers	2 × 7.7	600 f	
	1931	81				
Hawker Osprey	**Osprey**	F	Vickers Mk II	1 × 7.7	500 f	
	1932	110	Lewis Mk III	1 × 7.7	776	Rear cockpit
Hawker Woodcock	**Woodcock II**	F	Vickers	2 × 7.7	750 f	Sides of fuselage
	1925	63				
Martinsyde Buzzard	**Buzzard F.3**	F	Vickers	2 × 7.7	f	
	1918					
	Buzzard F.4	F	Vickers	2 × 7.7	f	
	1918					
	Buzzard F.4A	F	Vickers	2 × 7.7	f	
	1921		Lewis	1 × 7.7		Rear cockpit
	Total production about 370.					
Martinsyde G.100	**G.100**	F/B	Lewis	1 × 7.7	f	On top of upper
			Lewis	1 × 7.7		wing. Later added, dorsal
	G.102	F/B	Lewis	1 × 7.7	f	One or two on
	1916					top of upper wing
			Lewis	1 × 7.7		Later added, dorsal
	Total production about 270.					
Parnall Plover	**Plover**	F	Vickers	2 × 7.7	f	
	1923	13				
Pemberton-Billing P.B.25	**P.B.25**	F		1 × 7.7	f	
	1915 Service Test	20				
Pemberton-Billing P.B.29	**P.B.29**	F		1 × 7.7		Gunner in nacelle between
	1915 Experimental	1				the upper wings
Royal Aircraft Factory B.E.2	**B.E.2c**	F	Lewis	1 × 7.7		Various mountings
	1914	1,216				
	B.E.2d	F	Lewis	1 × 7.7		Front cockpit
	1916	1,320				

Royal Aircraft Factory B.E.12	**B.E.12** 1916	O/B	Lewis	1 × 7.7	f	Upward-firing mount to clear propeller
	Early aircraft. Some had propellers with deflectors and forward-firing guns.						
	B.E.12, 12a 1916	F	Vickers	1 × 7.7	f	Synchronised
	B.E.12b 1917	F 130	Lewis	1 × 7.7	f	On upper wing, one or two guns
Royal Aircraft Factory F.E.2	**F.E.2a** 1915	F 1,309	Lewis	1 × 7.7		Gunner in front cockpit
	F.E.2b	F	Lewis	1 × 7.7		Gunner in front cockpit
			Lewis	1 × 7.7		Firing rearwards
	F.E.2c 1916	F	Lewis	1 × 7.7		Gunner in aft cockpit
			Lewis	1 × 7.7		Nose
	F.E.2d 1916	F 300	Lewis	1 × 7.7		Firing rearwards
			Lewis	1 × 7.7		Gunner in front cockpit
			Lewis	1 × 7.7	f	Operated by pilot
	Some fitted with 1.59 in Crayford, others with Vickers 1 pdr Mk III.						
Royal Aircraft Factory F.E.8	**F.E.8** 1916	F 270	Lewis	1 × 7.7		Nose
Royal Aircraft Factory R.E.7	**R.E.7** 1916	B 250	Lewis	1 × 7.7		Front cockpit
			Lewis	1 × 7.7		Rear cockpit
Royal Aircraft Factory R.E.8	**R.E.8** 1916	R/B 4,077	Vickers	1 × 7.7	f	
			Lewis	2 × 7.7		Rear cockpit
	Early aircraft had a fixed Lewis and deflector plates on the propeller. One fitted with 2 pdr Davis.						
Royal Aircraft Factory S.E.5	**S.E.5, 5a** 1917	F 5,205	Lewis	1 × 7.7	f	Foster mount on upper wing
			Vickers	1 × 7.7	f	Top of engine cowling, offset to port
Saro Cloud	**Cloud** 1933	PB/T 16		2 × 7.7		
Saro Cutty Sark	**Cutty Sark** 1930	PB	Vickers	1 × 7.7		Bow
Saro Valkyrie	**Valkyrie** 1927	PB	Lewis	1 × 7.7		Bow
			Lewis	2 × 7.7		Two dorsal positions
Short 166	**166** 1914	TB 26	Lewis	1 × 7.7		Rear cockpit
Short 184	**184** 1915	TB 900	Lewis	1 × 7.7		Rear cockpit
Short 310	**310** 1917	TB 127	Lewis	1 × 7.7		On upper wing
Short 827, 830	**827, 830** 1914	R/B 120				
	Some had a Lewis on the upper wing.						
Short Bomber	**Bomber** 1916	B 82	Lewis	1 × 7.7		On upper wing or in dorsal position

Short Rangoon	**Rangoon**	PB	Lewis	2 × 7.7		Two dorsal gunners
	1931	6	Lewis	1 × 7.7		Bow gunner
Short Singapore	**Singapore**	PB	Lewis	1 × 7.7		Bow
	1926		Lewis	2 × 7.7		Two dorsal positions
Short Singapore III	**Singapore III**	PB	Lewis	1 × 7.7		Bow
	1935	37	Lewis	1 × 7.7		Tail
			Lewis	1 × 7.7		Dorsal
Sopwith 1½-Strutter	**1½-Strutter**	F	Vickers	1 × 7.7	300 f	Engine cowling,
	1916	6,000				not on shipboard version
			Lewis	1 × 7.7	485	Rear cockpit
	Of this production about 5,400 were built in France. Some had a Lewis added on the upper wing.					
Sopwith Baby	**Baby**	F	Lewis	1 × 7.7	f	Fixed synchronised gun on nose
	1917					
	Total production 286. Some had two Lewis guns on the upper wing instead.					
Sopwith Camel	**F.1 Camel**	F	Vickers	2 × 7.7	250 f	On top of engine cowling
	1917	5,290				
	Aircraft modified as night-fighters had two Lewis guns on the upper wing instead.					
	2F.1	F		1 × 7.7	194 f	On upper wing
	1917	200		1 × 7.7	250 f	On top of engine cowling, port side
Sopwith Dolphin	**5F1 Dolphin**	F	Lewis	2 × 7.7	f	Upper wing, one
	1918	1,532				or two guns fitted, firing upwards
			Vickers	2 × 7.7	f	Engine cowling
Sopwith Dragon	**Dragon**	F	Vickers	2 × 7.7	f	On top of
	1919 Service Test	200				fuselage decking
	Extremely unreliable engine, never issued to a service unit.					
Sopwith Gun Bus	**Gun Bus**	F	Lewis	1 × 7.7		Front cockpit
	1914					
Sopwith Pup	**Pup**	F	Vickers	1 × 7.7	f	On top of engine cowling
	1916	1,770				
	RNAS aircraft carried a Lewis gun on a tripod in front of the cockpit.					
Sopwith Salamander	**T.F.2 Salamander**	A	Vickers	2 × 7.7	1,000 f	Top of fuselage
	1918 Service Test	419				
	Armoured ground-attack fighter, never issued to a service unit.					
Sopwith Schneider	**Schneider**	F		1 × 7.7	f	Angled upwards,
	1915	136				firing through gap in upper wing
	Some had propellers with deflectors and forward-firing guns.					
Sopwith Snipe	**7F1 Snipe**	F	Vickers	2 × 7.7	f	On top of engine cowling
	1918	497				
	A few had a Lewis on the upper wing.					
Sopwith S.P.Gn	**S.P.Gn**	O		1 × 7.7		Front cockpit
	1914	6				
Sopwith Triplane	**Triplane**	F	Vickers	1 × 7.7	500 f	Engine cowling
	1917	140				
	A few had two guns.					

Supermarine Scapa	**Scapa**	PB	Lewis	1 × 7.7	582	Bow
	1935	14	Lewis	2 × 7.7	582	Two dorsal positions
Supermarine Southampton	**Southampton** **Mk I, II**	PB	Lewis	1 × 7.7	582	Bow
			Lewis	2 × 7.7	582	Two dorsal positions
	1925	68				
Vickers 121	**121**	F	Vickers	2 × 7.7	f	
	1926	26				
Vickers 143 Bolivian Scout	**143**	F	Vickers	2 × 7.7	f	Fuselage sides
	1930	6				
Vickers 161	**161**	F	COW	1 × 37	50 f	Right side of the
	1931 Prototype	1				cockpit, angled up 45 degrees
	Built to the F.29/27 COW gun Fighter specification.					
Vickers EFB.1 Destroyer	**EFB.1**	F	Maxim	1 × 7.7		Nose
	1913 Prototype	1				
Vickers EFB.2	**EFB.2**	F	Vickers	1 × 7.7		Nose, ball and
	1913 Prototype	1				socket mount
Vickers EFB.3	**EFB.3**	F	Vickers	1 × 7.7		Nose
	1914 Service Test	6				
Vickers F.B.5	**F.B.5**	F	Lewis	1 × 7.7		Nose, Vickers
	1914	119				on early aircraft
Vickers F.B.7	**F.B.7**	F	Vickers 1 pdr	1 × 37		Nose
	1915 Prototype	2				
Vickers F.B.9	**F.B.9**	F		1 × 7.7		Nose
	1916	120				
Vickers F.B.14	**F.B.14D**	FR	Vickers	1 × 7.7	f	
	1916		Lewis	1 × 7.7		Rear cockpit
Vickers F.B.19	**F.B.19**	F	Vickers	1 × 7.7	f	Port side of fuselage
	1916	62				
Vickers Vimy	**Vimy**	B	Lewis Mk III	1 × 7.7	582	Ventral
	1918	240	Lewis Mk III	1 × 7.7	582	Dorsal gunner. One or two guns fitted, in peacetime usually omitted
			Lewis Mk III	1 × 7.7	388	Nose, one or two guns
Vickers Virginia	**Virginia**	B	Lewis Mk III	1 × 7.7	485	Ventral
	Mk II, IV, V, VI, VII		Lewis Mk III	1 × 7.7	485	Dorsal gunner
	1924		Lewis Mk III	1 × 7.7	485	Nose gunner
	Virginia Mk IX, X	B	Lewis Mk III	2 × 7.7	485	Tail gunner
	1927		Lewis Mk III	1 × 7.7	485	Nose gunner
	Total production was 126. Many older aircraft were converted to new standards, some repeatedly.					
Westland F.29/27	**F.29/27**	F	COW	1 × 37	f	
	1930 Prototype					
Westland Wallace	**Wallace Mk I, II**	B	Vickers Mk II	1 × 7.7	600 f	Left side of fuselage
	1933	172	Lewis Mk III	1 × 7.7	582	Rear cockpit
Westland Wapiti	**Wapiti Mk I, II**	B	Vickers Mk II	1 × 7.7	600 f	
		25	Lewis Mk III	1 × 7.7	582	Rear cockpit

Westland Westbury	**Westbury**	F		COW	1 × 37		f	Aft fuselage, firing upwards
	1926 Prototype	2		Lewis	1 × 7.7			Ventral
				Lewis	1 × 7.7			Dorsal
				COW	1 × 37			Nose
Wight A.D.1	**A.D.1**	A		12 pdr	1 × 76		f	
	1916 Prototype				2 × 7.7			
	Multi-role naval attack aircraft. One variation had a 12 pdr gun.							

USA

Aeromarine PG-1	**PG-1**	F/A			1 × 12.7		f	
	1922 Prototype	2		Baldwin	1 × 37		f	Firing through propeller hub
Berliner-Joyce P-16, PB-1	**P-16**	F			2 × 7.62		f	Cowling
	1932	25			1 × 7.62			Rear cockpit
Boeing F2B	**F2B-1**	F		Browning .30	1 × 7.62		f	Engine cowling
	1928	34		Browning .50	1 × 12.7		f	Engine cowling
	Alternatively, two 7.62 mm guns.							
Boeing F3B	**F3B-1**	F		Browning .30	1 × 7.62		f	Cowling
	1928	74		Browning .50	1 × 12.7		f	Cowling
	Alternatively, two 7.62 mm guns.							
Boeing GA-2	**GA-2**	A			1 × 37		f	
					2 × 7.62			
				Browning .50	5 × 12.7			
Boeing P-12, F4B	**F4B-1, -2**	F		Browning .30	2 × 7.62		f	Fuselage
	1929	73						
	F4B-3, -4	F		Browning .30	1 × 7.62	600	f	Engine cowling
	1931	113		Browning .50	1 × 12.7	200	f	Engine cowling
	Alternatively, two 7.62 mm guns.							
	P-12B	F		Browning .30	2 × 7.62	600	f	Fuselage
	1930	90						
	P-12C	F		Browning .30	2 × 7.62	600	f	Fuselage
	1931	96						
	P-12D	F		Browning .30	2 × 7.62	600	f	Fuselage
	1931	35						
	P-12E	F		Browning .30	2 × 7.62	600	f	Fuselage
	1931	110						
	P-12F	F		Browning .30	2 × 7.62	600	f	Fuselage
	1932	25						
Boeing PW-9, FB	**FB-1, -2, -3, -4, -5**	F		Browning .30	2 × 7.62		f	Engine cowling
	1925	37						
	This was a version of the PW-9 for the US Navy.							
	PW-9, -9A, -9D	F		Browning .30	2 × 7.62		f	Engine cowling
	1925	111						
Consolidated O-17	**O-17**	O		Browning .30	1 × 7.62			Rear cockpit
	1928	29						
Consolidated P2Y	**P2Y-1, -2, -3**	PB		Browning .30	1 × 7.62			Bow
	1932	46		Browning .30	2 × 7.62			Two dorsal hatches

Curtiss A-3 Falcon	**A-3A, B**	A	Browning .30	2 × 7.62	f	Wings
	1927	154	Browning .30	2 × 7.62	f	Engine cowling
			Lewis	2 × 7.62		Rear cockpit
Curtiss B-2 Condor	**B-2**	B	Lewis	4 × 7.62		Gunners seated
	1929	12				in aft ends of both engine nacelles
			Lewis	2 × 7.62		Gunner in nose
Curtiss BF2C,	**BF2C-1**	F/SB	Browning .30	2 × 7.62	f	
Hawk III, Hawk IV	1934	27				
	Hawk III, Hawk IV	F	Browning .30	2 × 7.62	f	Fuselage
	1935	138				
	The BF2C-1 was originally known as the F11C-3, but the designation was changed before the aircraft were delivered.					
Curtiss CS	**CS-1, -2**	TB		1 × 7.62		Dorsal gunner
	1925	8				
Curtiss F6C Hawk	**F6C-1, -2, -3, -4**	F	Browning .30	2 × 7.62	f	Cowling
	1925	75				
	The F6C-1, -2 and -3 were Navy equivalents of the P-1. The F6C-4 had a radial engine.					
Curtiss F7C Seahawk	**F7C-1**	F	Browning .30	2 × 7.62	f	Fuselage
	1927	17				
Curtiss F8C	**F8C-1, -3**	FB		2 × 7.62	f	
	1928	27		1 × 7.62		Rear cockpit
	F8C-4, -5	F/SB		2 × 7.62	f	
	1930	79		1 × 7.62		Rear cockpit
	The F4C-4 dual-role fighter and dive-bomber was also known as the O2C-1.					
Curtiss F9C	**F9C-2**	F	Browning .30	2 × 7.62 600	f	Fuselage
Sparrowhawk	1932	6				
Curtiss F11C	**F11C-2**	F	Browning .30	2 × 7.62 600	f	
Goshawk	1933	28				
	Redesignated BFC-2.					
Curtiss H.4	**H.4**	PB	Lewis	1 × 7.7		Bow, one or two guns
'Small America'	1914	62	Lewis	1 × 7.7		Dorsal, one or two guns
	Built for export to Britain					
Curtiss H.12	**H.12**	PB	Lewis	1 × 7.7		Dorsal, one or two guns
'Large America'	1916	91	Lewis	1 × 7.7		Bow, one or two guns
Curtiss H.16	**H.16**	PB	Lewis	2 × 7.62		Bow
	1918	345	Lewis	2 × 7.62		Waist
			Lewis	1 × 7.62		Cockpit, one or two guns
Curtiss Hawk II	**Hawk II**	F		2 × 7.62	f	
	1932	129				
	Built for export. Two 7.62 mm guns were the standard armament fit.					
Curtiss HS	**HS**	PB		1 × 7.62		Bow
	1918					
	The HS-1 did not carry gun armament					
Curtiss NC	**NC-4**	PB		2 ×		Flexible guns
	1918	10				

Curtiss O-1 Falcon	**O-1, O-1B, O-1E**	O	Browning .30	2 × 7.62	f	
	1924	102	Lewis	2 × 7.62		
Curtiss O-39	**O-39**	O	Browning .30	1 × 7.62 300	f	Engine cowling
			Browning .30	1 × 7.62 600		Rear cockpit
Curtiss P-1 Hawk	**P-1A, B, C**	F	Browning .30	2 × 7.62	f	Engine cowling
	1925	101				
	Alternatively one .30 in and one .50 in gun.					
	P-1D, E, F	F	Browning .30	1 × 7.62	f	Engine cowling
	1929	63				
	These aircraft were converted from AT-4 and AT-5 advanced trainers.					
Curtiss P-3 Hawk	**P-3A**	F	Browning .30	2 × 7.62	f	Fuselage
	1928	5				
Curtiss P-5 Superhawk	**P-5**	F	Browning .30	2 × 7.62	f	Fuselage
	1928	5				
Curtiss P-6 Hawk	**P-6, P-6A, P-6D**	F	Browning .30	2 × 7.62	f	
	1929	29				
	P-6E	F	Browning .30	2 × 7.62 600	f	Engine cowling
	1931	45				
	P-6S	F				
	1939	3				
	For Cuba.					
	XP-6H	F	Browning .30	2 × 7.62	f	Lower wings
	1932 Prototype	1	Browning .30	2 × 7.62	f	Upper wings
			Browning .30	2 × 7.62	f	Fuselage
Curtiss PW-8	**PW-8**	F		2 × 7.62	f	Engine cowling
	1923	25				
Curtiss-Orenco D	**D**	F		2 × 7.62	f	Engine cowling
	1921	50				
Douglas DT	**DT-2**	TB	Browning .30	2 × 7.62		
	1922	92				
Douglas O-2	**O-2**	O	Browning .30	2 × 7.62	f	
	1925		Browning .30	1 × 7.62		Rear cockpit
	Numerous versions, some (such as the O-2B) unarmed trainers.					
Douglas O-25	**O-25**	O		1 × 7.62		Rear cockpit, one or two
	1930	49				
	The O-25B and O-25C did not carry armament					
Douglas O-38	**O-38**	O	Browning .30	1 × 7.62	f	
	1931	156	Browning .30	1 × 7.62		Rear cockpit
	The O-38F model was unarmed.					
Engineering Division GA-1	**GA-1**	A	Baldwin	1 × 37		
	Service Test	10	Lewis	8 × 7.7		
Engineering Division XB-1A	**XB-1A**	A	Browning	2 × 7.62	f	Synchronised
	1920	44	Lewis	2 × 7.7		Rear cockpit
	This was an improved version of the Bristol F.2B Fighter.					

General Aviation O-27	**O-27**	O	Browning .30	1 × 7.62		Nose
	1932 Service Test	6	Browning .30	1 × 7.62		Dorsal
Great Lakes BG	**BG-1**	SB	Browning .30	1 × 7.62	f	
	1934	60	Browning .30	1 × 7.62		Rear cockpit
Grumman F2F	**F2F-1**	F	Browning .30	2 × 7.62	f	Engine cowling
	1935	54				
Grumman F3F	**F3F-1, -2, -3**	F	Browning .30	2 × 7.62	f	Engine cowling
	1936	162				
Grumman FF Goblin	**FF-1**	F	Browning .30	2 × 7.62	f	Engine cowling
SF	1933	27	Browning .30	1 × 7.62		Rear cockpit
	FF-2	F/T	Browning .30	1 × 7.62	f	Engine cowling
	1936	22	Browning .30	1 × 7.62		Rear cockpit
	Converted from SF-1.					
	SF-1	O/F	Browning .30	1 × 7.62	f	Engine cowling
	1933	33	Browning .30	1 × 7.62		Rear cockpit
Keystone B-3	**B-3A**	B	Browning .30	1 × 7.62		Ventral
	1930	36	Browning .30	1 × 7.62		Dorsal
			Browning .30	1 × 7.62		Nose
Keystone B-4	**B-4A, Y1B-4**	B	Browning .30	1 × 7.62		Ventral
	1931	30	Browning .30	1 × 7.62		Dorsal
			Browning .30	1 × 7.62		Nose
Keystone B-5	**B-5A**	B	Browning .30	1 × 7.62		Ventral
	1930	27	Browning .30	1 × 7.62		Dorsal gunner
			Browning .30	1 × 7.62		Nose
Keystone B-6 Panther	**B-6A, Y1B-6**	B	Browning .30	1 × 7.62		Ventral
	1931	45	Browning .30	1 × 7.62		Dorsal
			Browning .30	1 × 7.62		Nose
Hall PH	**PH-1**	PB	Browning .30	1 × 7.62		Bow
	1932	9	Browning .30	1 × 7.62		Dorsal
	The PH-2 and PH-3 were delivered without armament, but after Pearl Harbor the PH-3s were reportedly equipped with four Lewis guns.					
Huff-Daland/	**LB-1**	B		2 × 7.62		Nose
Keystone LB-1	1927 Service Test	10		2 × 7.62		Dorsal
				1 × 7.62		Ventral
Huff-Daland/	**LB-5**	B		2 × 7.62		Nose
Keystone LB-5	1927	10		2 × 7.62		Dorsal
				1 × 7.62		Ventral
Keystone LB-6	**LB-6**	B		2 × 7.62		Nose
	1929	17		2 × 7.62		Dorsal
				1 × 7.62		Ventral
Keystone LB-7	**LB-7**	B		2 × 7.62		Nose
	1929	18		2 × 7.62		Dorsal
				1 × 7.62		Ventral

LWF G-2	**G-2**	F/R/B		4 × 7.62		f	Fuselage	
	1918 Prototype	2		1 × 7.62			Ventral	
				2 × 7.62			Dorsal	
Loening M-8	**M-8**	F/O	Vickers	2 × 7.62		f	Upper nose, present only on	
	1918	56					fighter versions	
			Lewis	2 × 7.62			Rear cockpit	
Martin BM	**BM-1, BM-2**	SB		1 × 7.62		f	Right side of fuselage	
	1931			1 × 7.62			Rear cockpit	
Martin MB	**MB-1, GMB**	B	Lewis	2 × 7.62			Nose	
	1918	10	Lewis	2 × 7.62			Dorsal	
			Lewis	1 × 7.62			Ventral	
	MB-2, NBS-1	B	Lewis	2 × 7.62			Nose	
	1920	130	Lewis	2 × 7.62			Dorsal	
			Lewis	1 × 7.62			Ventral	
Martin P3M	**P3M-1, -2**	PB		2 × 7.62			Gunner in aft fuselage	
	1929	9		2 × 7.62			Gunner in bow	
Martin T3M	**T3M-1, T3M-2**	TB		1 × 7.62			Rear cockpit	
	1926	24						
Martin T4M,	**T4M-1**	TB		1 × 7.62			Rear cockpit	
Great Lakes TG		102						
Naval Aircraft Factory PN	**PN**	PB		1 × 7.62			Gunner in nose	
				1 × 7.62			Gunner in aft fuselage	
Naval Aircraft Factory TF	**TF**	F	Lewis	× 7.62		f	Stern turret	
	1920	4	Lewis	× 7.62		f	Bow turret	
	Three guns in total.							
Naval Aircraft Factory TS	**TS-1**	F	Browning .30	1 × 7.62		f		
	1922	39						
Packard-Lepere	**LUSAC-11**	F	Marlin	2 × 7.62		f	Engine cowling	
LUSAC-11	1918 Cancelled	30	Lewis	1 × 7.62			Rear cockpit	
Stinson model O	**O**	T/A		2 ×		f		
	1933	13		1 ×			Rear cockpit	
	Built for export.							
Thomas-Morse M.B.3	**MB-3**	F	Marlin	2 × 7.62		f	Engine cowling	
	1920	50						
	MB-3A	F	Browning .30	1 × 7.62		f	Engine cowling	
	1920	200	Browning .50	1 × 12.7		f	Engine cowling	
Thomas-Morse O-19	**O-19**	O	Browning .30	1 × 7.62	300	f	Engine cowling	
	1928	180	Browning .30	1 × 7.62	500		Rear cockpit	
Thomas-Morse S-4	**S-4C**	T	Marlin	1 × 7.62		f	Optional	
	1917	498						
Vought FU	**FU-1**	F	Browning .30	2 × 7.62		f	Engine cowling	
	1926	20						
	Some later converted to FU-2 trainers.							

Vought O2U Corsair	**O2U**	O	Browning .30	2 × 7.62	f	Top wing centre section
	1926	260	Lewis	2 × 7.62		Rear cockpit
Vought O3U Corsair	**O3U-1, -2**	O	Browning .30	1 × 7.62	f	Top wing centre section
	1930		Browning .30	2 × 7.62		Rear cockpit, one or two guns
Vought SU Corsair	**SU-2, SU-4**	O	Browning .30	1 × 7.62	f	Unsynchronised fixed gun, centre wing section
	1930		Browning .30	1 × 7.62		Rear cockpit, one or two guns
Vought UO	**UO-3**	F	Browning .30	2 × 7.62	f	Engine cowling
	1922	20				
The UO-1 and UO-2 did not carry guns.						
Vought V-80	**V-80**	F	Browning .30	2 × 7.62	f	Engine cowling
	1935	5	Browning .30	2 × 7.62	f	Upper wing centre section
	Three sold to Peru, one to Argentina.					
Vought VE-7	**VE-7G**	F	Vickers	1 × 7.62	f	
		65	Lewis	1 × 7.62		Rear cockpit
	VE-7SF	F	Vickers	1 × 7.7	f	
	1921	64				
	Alternatively, one Browning .30.					

USSR/Russia

Anatra Anade	**Anade**	O		1 × 7.7		machine gun in rear cockpit
	1916	170				
Anatra Anasal	**Anasal**	R	Vickers	1 × 7.7	f	Synchronised
	1916	70		1 × 7.7		Rear cockpit
Grigorovich I-2	**I-2bis**	F	PV-1	2 × 7.62	f	Sides of fuselage
	1925	211				
Grigorovich M-5	**M-5**	PB		1 × 7.62		Rear cockpit, optional
	1915	300				
Grigorovich M-9	**M-9**	F	Vickers	1 × 7.7		Bow
	1917	500				
	Flying-boat fighter, a pusher biplane. Also fitted were the 7.5 mm Hotchkiss, the 20 mm Oerlikon, or the 37 mm Puteaux.					
Grigorovich TSh-2	**TSh-2**	A	PV-1	8 × 7.62	f	Four guns in boxes under each lower wing
	1931	10	DA	2 × 7.62		Rear cockpit
Khioni VKh Anasalya	**VKh**	B		×		Gunner in nacelle on upper wing
	1917 Cancelled			×		Two gunners in aft fuselage
	Production ordered, but halted by the Russian Revolution.					
Lebed XII	**XII**	F				
	1915	214				
	One or two machine guns could be installed.					
Polikarpov I-1	**I-1M-5**	F	PV	2 × 7.62	f	
	1924 Service Test	33				

Polikarpov I-3	**I-3** 1928	F 399	PV-1	2 × 7.62		f	
Polikarpov I-5	**I-5** 1930	F 803	PV-1	4 × 7.62	1,000	f	
	Four guns, or two guns and bombs. The first few built had only two guns with 600 rpg.						
Polikarpov I-15	**I-15** 1934	F 384	PV-1 PV-1	2 × 7.62 2 × 7.62	1,000 500	f f	Added to sides of fuselage during production run
	I-15 1938	F	BS	2 × 12.7		f	
Polikarpov I-152	**I-152** 1938	F	BS	2 × 12.7		f	
	I-152 1938	F	PV-1	4 × 7.62	650	f	
	PV-1 guns were later often replaced by ShKAS. 2,408 built.						
Polikarpov I-153	**I-153** 1939	F	ShKAS	4 × 7.62		f	
	I-153BS 1939	F	BS	4 × 12.7		f	
	I-153P 1939	F	ShVAK	2 × 20		f	
	The cannon-armed version saw only limited production. *Total production 3,437.*						
Polikarpov R-1	**R-1** 1920	O 2,447	PV-1 DA	1 × 7.62 1 × 7.62	200 500	f	Rear cockpit, one or two guns fitted
	This was a refined copy of the de Havilland D.H.9.						
Polikarpov R-5	**R-5** 1930	O 4,914	PV-1 DA	1 × 7.62 1 × 7.62		f	Rear cockpit, one or two fitted
	MR-5 111	R	PV-1 DA	1 × 7.62 1 × 7.62		f	Rear cockpit, one or two fitted
	Floatplane version of the R-5.						
	R-5Sh 1931	A	PV-1	8 × 7.62		f	Packs under lower wing
	Later the guns were replaced by ShKAS.						
	R-5SSS	R	ShKAS	2 × 7.62		f	Some aircraft, one ShKAS and one PV-1
			DA	1 × 7.62			Rear cockpit, one or two fitted
Polikarpov R-Z	**R-Z** 1935	O 1,031	PV-1 ShKAS	1 × 7.62 1 × 7.62		f	Rear cockpit, one or two fitted
	Redesign of the R-5SSS.						
RBVZ *Ilya Muromets*	*Ilya Muromets* 1914	B 80					
	Up to six rifle-calibre machine guns of various types: Maxim, Lewis, Madsen, Browning …						
RBVZ S-XII	**S-XIIbis** 1914	O 10					
	Originally built as single-seaters, some were converted to two-seat aircraft with a Madsen gun for the observer.						

RBVZ S-XVI	**S-XVIser**	F	Colt	1 ×		f	Synchronised
	1916	15					
	Some also had a second gun on the upper wing.						
Tupolev I-4	**I-4**	F	PV-1	2 × 7.62	f		Top of fuselage
	1928	347					
	One I-4 was used in 1931 to evaluate the 76 mm DRP and APK recoilless cannon.						
Tupolev R-3	**R-3**	O	Vickers	1 × 7.62		f	Or PV-1.
	1927	110	DA	2 × 7.62			Tur-4 ring mount in rear cockpit

Appendix 2

AMMUNITION DATA TABLE

Many of the more common cartridges were available in a wide range of different loadings. Those included here are the most typical. Muzzle velocities will have varied to some extent in guns with different barrel lengths.

KEY: AP = armour-piercing; I = incendiary; HE = high-explosive; T = tracer. National abbreviations used are international motoring codes except: SU = Soviet Union/Russia, A-H = Austria-Hungary

METRIC CALIBRE	PROJECTILE TYPE/ WEIGHT (G)	MUZZLE VELOCITY (M/S)	MUZZLE ENERGY (JOULE)	NAME/GUNS CHAMBERED IN/COUNTRY OF ORIGIN
6.5 × 52	10.5	700	2,570	Mannlicher Carcano for Fiat M1914 (I)
6.5 × 54	10.3	680	2,380	Greek Mannlicher for Schwarzlose M12 (A)
7.5 × 54	9.1	790	2,840	Darne M1929 (F)
7.5 × 55	11.3	780	3,440	MG 94, MG 11, Furrer Fl. Mg 29 (CH)
7.62 × 54R	9.65	870	3,650	Soviet/Russian RCMGs (SU)
7.62 × 63	9.7	823	3,280	.30-06: American RCMGs (USA)
7.65 × 22	6.0	380	430	Furrer Flieger-Doppelpistole 1919 (CH)
7.65 × 53	11.3	750	3,180	Belgian Mauser round for FN-Browning (B)
7.7 × 56R	11.3 HE/11.0 I/9.5	744 670 762	3,130 2,470 2,760	.303 in: all British (and some Italian and Japanese) MGs (UK). HE = RTS Mk II I = Buckingham Mk III
7.92 × 57	10.0 AP/11.5	880 765	3,872 3,360	Mauser round used in all German (and many other) MGs (D). AP = S.m.K
8 × 50R Lebel	12.8	750	3,600	Hotchkiss M1909 (F)
8 × 50R Mann.	15.8	620	3,040	Mannlicher round for Schwarzlose (A-II)
9 × 19	7.9	320	400	Glisenti pistol round for Villar-Perosa (I)
11 × 59R	I/17.5	610	3,260	Vickers 'Balloon gun' (F, USA)
11.35 × 62	20	850	7,200	Madsen M1927 (DK)

12.7 × 99	52	722	13,550	.50 in Browning 1923 ball (USA)
20 × 70RB	AP/130	490	15,600	Becker aircraft, early Oerlikon F (D/CH)
20 × 100RB	HE/127	670–700	28,500–31,000	Oerlikon L (CH)
20 × 110RB	HE/127	830	43,750	Oerlikon S (CH)
25 × 87	HE/200	440	19,400	Fiat/Revelli Modello 1917 (I)
37 × 69R	HE/450	365	30,000	Vickers 1 pdr Mk III/V (UK)
37 × 94R	HE/555	367	37,400	Hotchkiss M1885 (F)
37 × 190	HE/680	580–610	114–126,000	1½ pdr COW gun (UK)
37 × 201R	APHE/500 I/720	830 600	172,000 130,000	Hotchkiss M1902 (F)
40 × 79R	HE/540 AP/540	240 300	15,500 24,300	Vickers-Crayford 1.59 in (UK)
40 × 378R	HE/900	330	49,000	Davis 2 pdr recoilless (USA)
57 × 390R	HE/2,700	300	121,000	Davis 6 pdr recoilless (USA)
76 × 513R	HE/5,400	300	243,000	Davis 12 pdr recoilless (USA)

Appendix 3

GUN DATA TABLE

KEY TO TYPE: 1–2 = no. of barrels; R = recoil-operated; LR = long-recoil; G = gas-operated; M = manually loaded; B = blowback; rB = retarded-blowback; apiB = advanced primer ignition blowback

NB: the overall and barrel lengths are shown in col. 4. For some weapons the gun length varied depending on whether a butt-stock or a spade grip was fitted. Quoted barrel lengths also vary between sources, depending on whether or not the chamber was included in the measurement.

NAME	METRIC CALIBRE	GUN (KG)	LENGTH/ BARREL (CM)	TYPE	CARTRIDGE FEED	RATE OF FIRE (RPM)
AUSTRIA-HUNGARY						
Schwarzlose M12	6.5 × 54 Mann.	13.2	107/53	1rB	belt	350–420
Schwarz. M07/12	8 × 50R Mann.	19.3	107/53	1rB	belt	400–570
Schwarz. M16A	8 × 50R Mann.	13.2	107/53	1rB	belt	600–880
CZECHOSLOVAKIA						
CZ vz.30	7.92 × 57	10.4–11.95	102/72	1R	belt or pan-100	900–1,000
DENMARK						
Madsen (Rexer)	6.5–7.92mm	9	114/48	1R	box-25/40	420–650
Madsen M1927	6.5–7.92mm	9–9.2	100–110/48–59	1R	belt	1,000–1,200
Madsen M1927	11.35 × 62	10.5	128–135/75	1R	belt	900–1,050
FRANCE						
Hotchkiss Aviation	8 × 50R Lebel	12.2	89/60	1G	strip 24, belt 100	600–700
Darne M1918	7.7 × 56R	8.4	94/61	1G	belt	800
Darne M1929	7.5 × 54	8.4	94/61	1G	belt	1,100–1,200
Lewis Gun	7.7 × 56R	7.7–11.5	108–128/61	1G	pan 47/97	550–700
Vickers Balloon Gun	11 × 59R	12.9	115/63	1R	belt	600
Hotchkiss M1885	37 × 94R	47	?/76	1M	single	–
Hotchkiss M1902	37 × 201R	147	?/148	1M	single	–
GERMANY						
LMG 08 (Spandau)	7.92 × 57	16	110/72	1R	belt	450
LMG 08/15 (Spandau)	7.92 × 57	13	110/72	1R	belt	450

MG 14 Parabellum	7.92 × 57	9.5	122/70	1R	belt	600–700
MG 15nA Bergmann	7.92 × 57	9.8	112/71	1R	belt	800
2 cm Becker	20 × 70RB	30	137/80	1apiB	box-15	300
ITALY						
Fiat M1914 (Revelli)	6.5 × 52	17	119/65	1rB	box-50	450–500
7.7 mm Scotti M1928	7.7 × 56R	10	107/54	1G+B	mag-20	500
7.7 mm Fiat M1928	7.7 × 56R	10.9	?/?	1R	belt	800
Villar Perosa	9 × 19	6.5	60/31	2rB	box-25 × 2	2,400
Fiat M1917 (Revelli)	25 × 87	45	133/67	1LR	box-8	150
RUSSIA/SOVIET UNION						
Maxim M1910	7.62 × 54R	17.6	110/59	1R	belt	300–600
Lewis	7.62 × 54R	11.5	128/61	1G	pan-47	600
PV-1	7.62 × 54R	14.5	105/?	1R	belt	750
DA	7.62 × 54R	8.4	101/60	1G	pan-63	600
SWITZERLAND						
MG 94 (Maxim)	7.5 × 55	16	107/72	1R	belt	500
MG 11 (Maxim)	7.5 × 55	15	125/72	1R	belt	500
Furrer Fl.Mg.29	7.5 × 55	8.5–9.5	90–110/60–70	1R	belt	1,100–1,300
Doppelpistole 1919	7.65 × 22	9.5	75/27	2R	box-50 × 2	2,200
Oerlikon F	20 × 70RB	30	135/80	1apiB	box-15	450
Oerlikon L (SEMAG)	20 × 100RB	43	182/120	1apiB	drum-15	350
Oerlikon S	20 × 110RB	62	212/140	1apiB	box-15	280
UNITED KINGDOM						
Lewis Mk I	7.7 × 56R	11.5	128/67	1G	pan-47	550
Lewis Mk III	7.7 × 56R	7.7	108/61	1G	pan-97	700
Vickers Mk I	7.7 × 56R	12.9	115/63	1R	belt	550–850
Vickers Mk II	7.7 × 56R	10	115/63	1R	belt	750
Vickers Class E	7.7 × 56R	12	120/72	1R	belt	900
Vickers Class F	7.7 × 56R	11.8	125/61	1R	pan-97	650
Vickers 1 pdr Mk III/V	37 × 69R	62	143/81	1LR	belt	?
1½ pdr COW gun	37 × 190	95	234/152	1LR	clip-5	100–120
Vickers-Crayford 1.59 in	40 × 79R	21	126/93	1M	single	–

USA

Colt-Browning 1914	7.62 × 63	15.9	108/56–71	1G	belt	480
Lewis	7.62 × 63	7.7	108/61	1G	pan-97	700
Marlin M1917/18	7.62 × 63	10	90–102/59–71	1G	belt	640
Browning M1918	7.62 × 63	10–11	100/61	1R	belt	1,000
Browning M1921	12.7 × 99	?	141/91	1R	belt	500
Davis 2 pdr	40 × 378R	24	213/94*	1M	single	–
Davis 6 pdr	57 × 390R	76	305/137*	1M	single	–
Davis 12 pdr	76 × 535R	109	305/137*	1M	single	–

* = length of rifling only (i.e. not including the chamber). With the long cartridge cases used in the Davis guns, measurements with or without the chamber varied considerably.

Appendix 4

GUN DRAWINGS

The drawings on the following pages represent the principal types of aircraft gun in service between 1914 and 1933 for which measurements and appropriate illustrations could be obtained. They have all, as far as possible, been drawn to the same scale to enable comparisons to be made, but must not be regarded as accurate scale drawings, as some were made from photographs, and in others there is some uncertainty about whether the listed measurements include grips, flash hiders, etc. It must be remembered that this was an experimental period for aircraft guns, and they could vary in appearance due to changes (some made by manufacturers, some in the field) which particularly affected the barrel casings. An instance of the variations is provided by the 25mm FIAT (Revelli). The drawing in this appendix was made from an official sectioned drawing and a photograph; a much shorter casing, with more of the barrel visible, is shown on page 99.

Particular thanks are due to Harry Woodman for permission to copy drawings used in his book, *Early Aircraft Armament*.

APPROXIMATELY ONE METRE

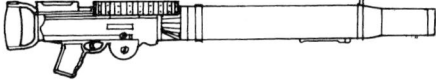

LEWIS MK I (UK) with 47-round magazine, radiator casing and spade grips ◀

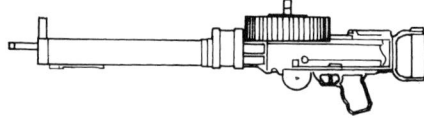

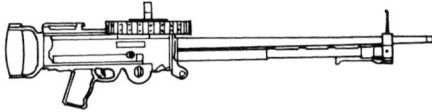

LEWIS MK II (UK) with 97-round magazine ▶

LEWIS MK I (UK) stripped 'RNAS Pattern', with radiator completely removed and 47-round magazine ◀

VICKERS MK I* (UK) of 1916, with air-cooling louvres in jacket, and loading handle ▶

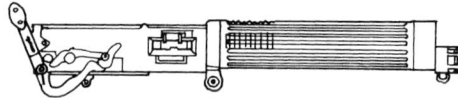

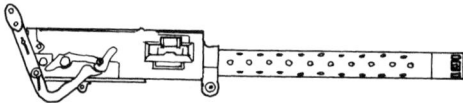

◀ VICKERS MK II (UK)

MAXIM LMG 08 (D) ▶

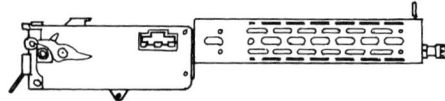

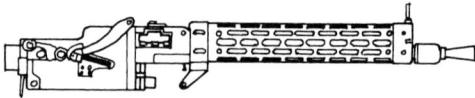

◀ MAXIM LMG 08/15 (D) with improved muzzle booster and cut-away breech case

PARABELLUM MG 14 (D) later models had a slimmer barrel casing ▶

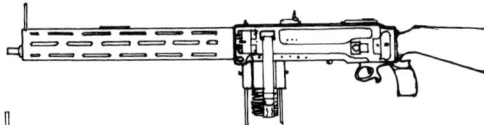

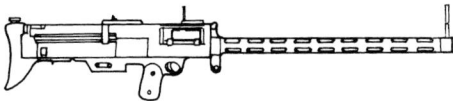

◀ BERGMANN MG 15nA (D)

SCHWARZLOSE M07/12 (A-H) with jacket drained and slotted ▶

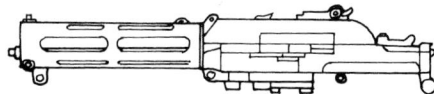

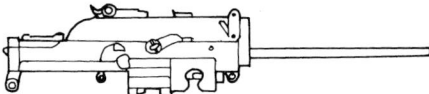

◀ SCHWARZLOSE M16 (A-H) of 1916, without jacket

APPROXIMATELY ONE METRE

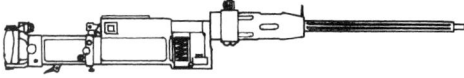

FIAT REVELLI M1914 (I) with water jacket removed and grooved barrel to aid cooling ◄

◄ HOTCHKISS M1909 AVIATION (F) ►

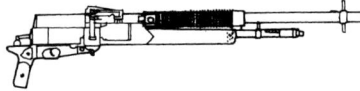

COLT-BROWNING MODEL 1914 (USA) ◄

MARLIN MODEL 1918 (USA) ►

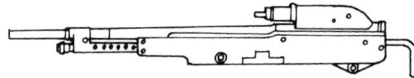

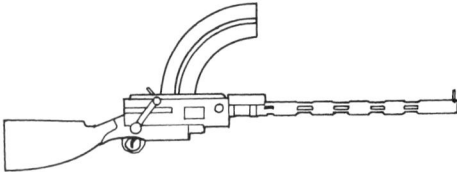

MADSEN M1902 (DK) with curved box magazine for rimmed cartridges (7.62 x 54R Russian) ◄

MAXIM M1910 (SU) ►

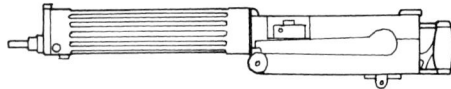

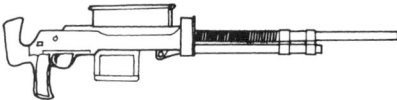

DEGTYAREV DA (SU) ◄

PV-1 (SU) *Pulemyot Vozdushnyi* = aircraft machine gun ►

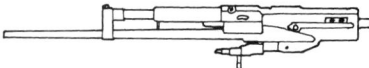

DARNE M1929 (F) ◄

FL.MG.29 (CH) long barrel, without muzzle booster ►

FL.MG.29 (CH) short barrel with full-length sleeve and muzzle booster ◄

GUN DRAWINGS

APPROXIMATELY ONE METRE

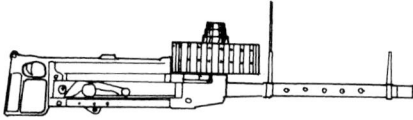

VICKERS CLASS F (UK) export model for flexible mounting, with 97-round Lewis pan magazine

MADSEN M1927 (DK) ▶

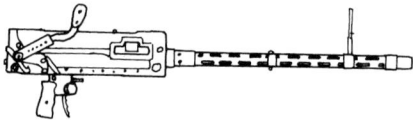

CZ vz.30 (CZ) improved Vickers design

BROWNING MODEL 1922 (USA) in 7.62 x 63 calibre ▶

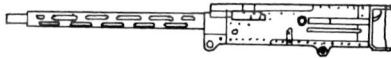

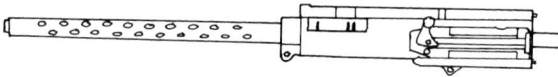

BROWNING M2 (USA) in 12.7 x 99 calibre

BECKER 2cm (D) with 15-round box magazine ▶

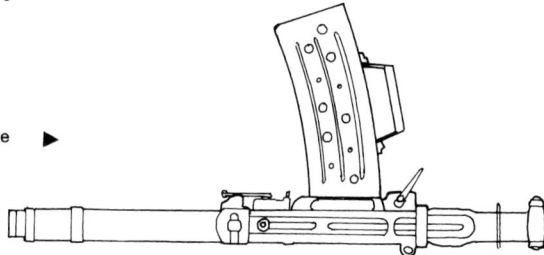

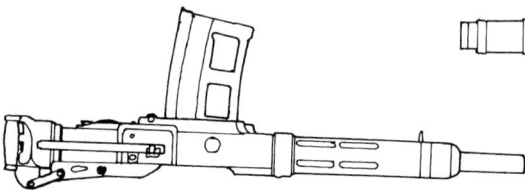

FIAT REVELLI 25mm M1917 (I)
with 8-round box magazine.

VICKERS 1 pdR MK III (UK) ▶

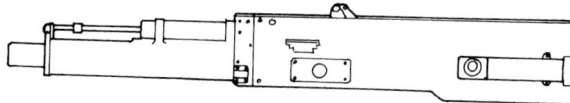

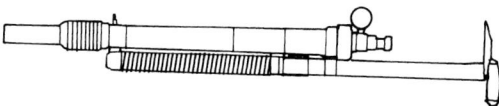

VICKERS CRAYFORD 1.59 INCH (UK)

6 pdr DAVIS GUN (USA) ▼

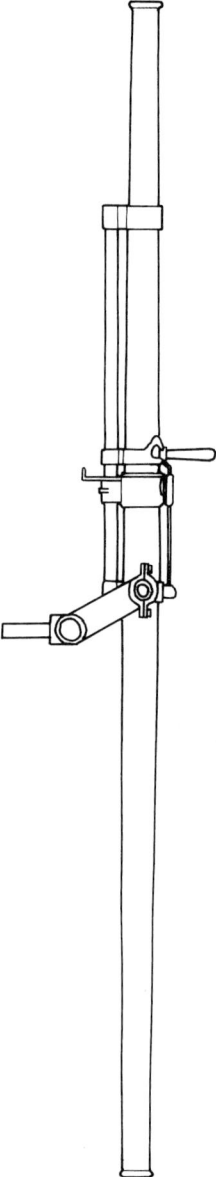

1½ pdr C.O.W. GUN (UK)
loaded with 5-round clip ▼

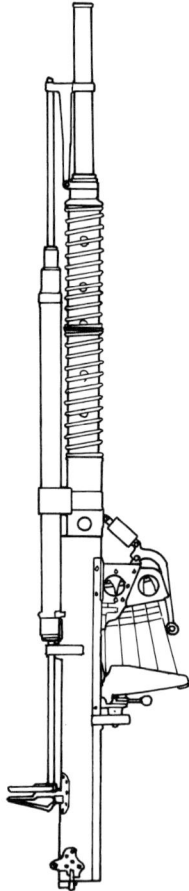

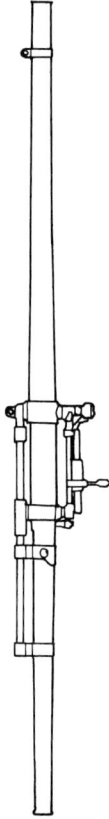

OERLIKON L (SEMAG) (CH) in 20 x 100RB,
with 15-round drum magazine ▼

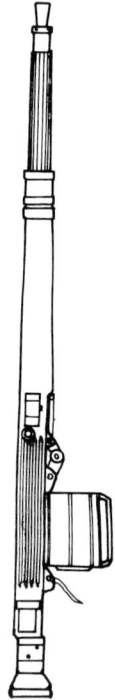

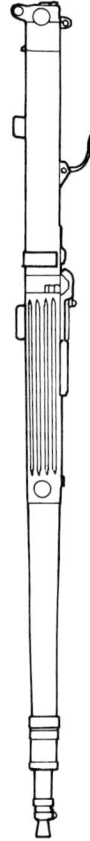

APPROXIMATELY ONE METRE

▲ 2 pdr DAVIS GUN (USA)

▲ OERLIKON S (CH) in 20x110RB

Glossary

AA	anti-aircraft
AEF	American Expeditionary Force
AFV	armoured fighting vehicle
air-cooled	a weapon which achieves barrel cooling by exchange direct with the atmosphere
ammunition	collective name for cartridges (or equivalent)
AP	armour-piercing: a projectile designed to penetrate armour, or a cartridge loaded with such a projectile
APC(BC)	armour-piercing, capped, (ballistic capped): an AP shot with a softer cap to aid penetration of face-hardened armour (and a streamlined cap to reduce air resistance)
APHE	armour-piercing high-explosive
API	armour-piercing incendiary: a dual-purpose projectile
API blowback	advanced primer ignition blowback: a type of automatic mechanism in which the cartridge is ignited before it is completely chambered
Armée de l'Air	French air force
ASW	anti-submarine warfare
AT	anti-tank
automatic	a weapon which continues to fire and reload automatically for as long as the trigger or firing button is pressed
B	added to a cartridge designation to identify a belted case (e.g. 20 × 105B)
ball (round)	a small-arms projectile or bullet, i.e. not AP, I, HE, or T
ballistics	the science concerning the passage of a projectile from the instant of firing to the end of its flight
ballistic cap	a streamlined (steel or light alloy) nose cone used to improve the ballistic coefficient of a blunt projectile

ballistic coefficient	a factor which measures the aerodynamic drag of a projectile and therefore the rate at which it loses velocity: the higher the number, the lower the drag
barrel	the tube connected to (or integral with) the chamber, down which the projectile is accelerated
barrel extension	the part of the barrel which extends behind the chamber, usually to accommodate a locking mechanism
base fuze	a detonating fuze fitted to the base of an HE shell
belt	(1) a raised strip around a cartridge case, in front of the extractor groove (2) a strip of fabric or (more usually) metal, into which cartridges are fitted to facilitate feeding them into a weapon. Metal belts may be disintegrating, non-disintegrating or a continuous loop
belted case	a cartridge case with a raised section in front of the extractor groove to aid location in the chamber
belt feed	the use of a belt to supply ammunition to a gun mechanism
belt link	a piece of metal which constitutes a part of a belt of ammunition
blimp	unofficial term for a non-rigid airship
blowback	a type of automatic weapon mechanism which utilises the force of the cartridge case being blown backwards out of the chamber
bolt	a part of the operating system, containing the firing mechanism, which slides in line with the barrel, pushing a cartridge into the chamber and holding it there during firing
bore	the inside of the barrel
bottle-necked cartridge	a cartridge with a case whose diameter decreases sharply to the neck, creating a shoulder

box magazine a type of magazine in which the cartridges are stacked on top of each other (they may be single or double stacked)

breech the opening at the rear of the chamber which allows cartridges to be loaded and fired cases extracted

breech-block alternative term for bolt, normally used when its operating movement involves pivoting, or sliding vertically or horizontally

breech face the part of the barrel surrounding the breech

bullet a small-arms projectile

calibre (1) the diameter of a projectile, or of the inside of a barrel
(2) designation of the cartridge a weapon is designed for

calibre length the barrel length divided by the calibre, usually prefixed with 'L'; e.g. a 40 mm L/70 indicates a barrel (40 mm $\times$ 70 =) 280 cm long

canister see case shot

cannelure a groove around a small-arms bullet for receiving a crimp

cannon (modern) a large-calibre, fast-firing automatic weapon, generally taken to be between 20 mm and around 57 mm calibre; also used in World War I to describe manually loaded guns of 37 mm+

cartridge a unit or round of ammunition, normally comprising the cartridge case, projectile, propellant and primer

cartridge case the part of the cartridge which contains the propellant and holds the projectile and primer firmly in place

case shot a thin-walled projectile containing several balls which separate on leaving the muzzle to give shotgun effect

CC Constantinesco-Colley hydrosonic synchronising gear

chamber the space at the rear of the barrel in which the cartridge is positioned and supported during firing

chemical fuze a contact fuze on an HE shell which operates by percussion

c.g. centre of gravity

clip a piece of metal which holds together several cartridges (normally by the case heads) for feeding into a weapon; or several cartridges held together by a clip

closed bolt an automatic weapon designed to commence the firing cycle with the cartridge already loaded into the chamber (see open bolt)

column type of flexible mounting, using a vertical column (see pillar and pintle)

contact fuze a fuze which is initiated by impact with the target

cook-off the unwanted ignition of a cartridge by heat in a gun chamber

cordite a type of propellant

cowling mounting an automatic weapon mounted in the cowling of a propeller-driven fighter and synchronised to fire through the propeller disk

crimp a depression in the neck of a cartridge case, intended to hold the projectile firmly in place prior to firing

deflection the angle between the position of a crossing target (usually an aircraft) and the required aiming point, which will be ahead of it

detonation the explosion of an HE projectile

dirigible airship with a rigid structural frame, e.g. Zeppelin

disintegrating-link a type of ammunition belt consisting of metal links, which fall apart as each cartridge is chambered

driving band a strip of soft metal or plastic around a projectile, which is intended to be gripped by the rifling in order to induce spin

dorsal the location of a defensive gun position on top of the fuselage, usually between the wings and the tail

drum magazine a type of circular magazine in which the cartridges are held parallel to each other (sometimes used to describe a pan magazine); see helical drum and pan magazine.

ejection the act of throwing an extracted cartridge case clear of the gun

elevation the movement of a gun in its mounting through a vertical arc

engine-driven gun a type of gun in which the operating cycle is directly driven by the engine

erosion wear on the inside of a barrel caused by hot propellant gases and friction generated by projectiles

external ballistics the science of projectile flight from the muzzle of a gun

externally powered a gun mechanism which requires an external source of power to operate; this is usually electric but may be hydraulic or manual, or in aircraft, powered by the

	engine, engine gas or the slipstream
extraction	the act of pulling a fired cartridge case from the chamber
extractor claw	a hook, attached to the bolt, which fits into the extractor groove in order to pull the cartridge out of the chamber
extractor groove	a groove around the head of a cartridge case, into which the extractor claw fits
FAA	(British) Fleet Air Arm (1924 onwards)
feed	the method of delivering ammunition to the gun
firing cycle	the sequence of loading, firing, extracting, ejecting and reloading
firing pin	a spring-loaded steel pin which strikes a primer to cause ignition
flak (*FlaK*)	*Fliegerabwehrkanone* (German) AA artillery; also sometimes given as *Flugabwehrkanone* or *Flugzeugabwehrkanone*
flat trajectory	the flight of a projectile which involves minimum drop due to gravity; associated with high velocity
flexible mounting	a simple, unpowered gun mounting in which the gun can be moved in traverse and elevation by the gunner's hands
fluted chamber	longitudinal grooves in the chamber to permit gun gas to seep back around the cartridge case to prevent it from sticking
flying-boat	a seaplane with a flotation hull that is an integral part of the fuselage
fuze	a device for initiating the detonation of an HE shell
gas-operated	a type of gun mechanism using gas tapped from the barrel to drive the firing cycle
gas-unlocked blowback	a type of gun mechanism using gas tapped from the barrel to unlock the breech-block, the remainder of the firing cycle being blowback
Gast	a type of twin-barrel automatic gun mechanism
Gatling	an early type of manually powered rotary gun; sometimes used to refer to any rotary weapon
grain	measure of weight used in UK and USA for propellant charges and (in smaller calibres) projectiles. 1 gram = 15.432 grains
gravity feed	the use of gravity to supply ammunition to the gun mechanism
grooves	the larger interior diameter of a rifled barrel; between the lands (q.v.)
gun gas	gas generated by ignition of the propellant

	in a cartridge
hang fire	a delay in the ignition of a cartridge after the primer has been struck
HE	high-explosive: the normal filling of cannon shells
headspace	the accurate location of a cartridge in the chamber ready for ignition
headstamp	information about the cartridge, stamped into the head
heavy machine gun	a machine gun with a calibre significantly larger than a military rifle cartridge but smaller than a cannon; in effect, 12.7–15 mm
helical drum	a type of circular magazine in which the cartridges point towards the centre and are arranged in a spiral
HMG	heavy machine gun
HV	high-velocity
hybrid	a mechanism which uses more than one operating principle
ignition	the igniting of propellant by a primer
IJA	Imperial Japanese Army
IJN	Imperial Japanese Navy
interceptor	a fighter aircraft specialised for the interception and destruction of bombers
internal ballistics	the science of the passage of a projectile down a gun barrel
inverted vee-engine	a vee-engine with a crankcase and crank shaft located above the cylinder banks
lands	the smaller interior diameter of a rifled barrel; between the grooves (q.v.)
linear action	a gun mechanism in which the elements reciprocate in line with the gun barrel
link	an element of an ammunition belt
linkless feed	a method of supplying ammunition to a gun in which the cartridges are not linked together
LMG	light machine gun
lock time	the period of time between pressing the trigger or gun button and the first shot being fired
long-recoil	a type of gun operating mechanism, in which the barrel and bolt recoil together for the full length of the action
Luftwaffe	German air force
LV	low-velocity
machine gun	an automatic weapon of less than 20 mm calibre
magazine	a container which holds ammunition ready

manually operated a gun in which the firing cycle is operated by a manual crank or lever

MG machine gun (German: *Maschinengewehr*)

moteur-canon (French) motor cannon: an aircraft cannon designed for mounting between the cylinder banks of a vee-engine, firing through a hollow propeller hub.

mounting the method of supporting a gun ready for firing

muzzle the end of the barrel from which the projectile emerges

muzzle blast the violent escape of gun gas from the muzzle as a projectile leaves the barrel

muzzle booster a device fitted to the muzzle to use some of the muzzle blast to increase recoil, to assist the action of recoil-operated guns

muzzle brake a device fitted to the muzzle which deflects part of the muzzle blast to the side or rear in order to reduce recoil

muzzle energy a calculation of the energy of a projectile as it leaves the muzzle; a function of projectile velocity and weight

muzzle velocity the speed of a projectile as it leaves the muzzle

neck the part of a cartridge case which holds the projectile

necked-down a cartridge case which has its neck reduced in diameter to accept a smaller-calibre projectile than the case was designed for

necked-up (or necked-out) a cartridge case which has its neck increased in diameter to accept a larger-calibre projectile than the case was designed for

obturation the sealing of a gun breech to prevent the escape of gun gas on firing (in automatic weapons, normally achieved by the cartridge case); also forward obturation achieved by the driving bands

open bolt an automatic weapon designed to commence the firing cycle without a cartridge loaded into the chamber (see closed bolt)

ounce (oz) UK and USA measure of weight; 1 ounce = 28.35 grams

PaK *Panzerabwehrkanone* (German): anti-tank gun

pan magazine a type of circular magazine in which the cartridges point inwards towards the centre

parasol monoplane an aircraft with a single wing that is raised above the fuselage by struts or a pylon.

Patrone (German): cartridge

pdr pounder: used to describe the size of a cannon by the weight of the shell fired; also written as *pr*

penetration the ability of an AP shot to penetrate armour

percussion ignition a method of igniting cartridges by striking a percussion primer with a firing pin

pillar mounting a type of flexible mounting in which the gun is mounted at the top of a vertical rod (see column and pintle)

pintle mounting a type of flexible mounting in which the gun is mounted at the top of a vertical rod (see column and pillar)

pdr see pounder

pom-pom unofficial name for a slow-firing automatic weapon, usually of 37 or 40 mm calibre

pounder (usually abbreviated to pr or pdr) a description of the size of a gun using the approximate weight of the projectile it fires

primer a percussion cap fitted into the head of a cartridge case, used to ignite the propellant

primer pocket the part of a cartridge case into which the primer fits

projectile any bullet, shot or shell fired from a gun

propellant the chemical which burns rapidly to generate gas which accelerates the projectile up the gun barrel

propeller disk the area swept by the blades of an aircraft propeller

propeller hub or boss the central part of an aircraft propeller, which may be made hollow to allow an engine-mounted gun to fire through it

R rimmed cartridge case (when it occurs at the end of a cartridge designation, as in 20 × 99R)

radial engine an engine in which the cylinders are arranged radially, with the crankshaft in the centre

rate of fire (RoF) frequency with which individual shots are fired in an automatic weapon, usually measured in rpm

rebated rim a cartridge case with a rim of smaller diameter than the case body

RAF (British) Royal Air Force (since 1918); also Royal Aircraft Factory (World War I)

RB rebated rim (case description, added to the end of a cartridge designation, also given as RR)

RCMG   rifle calibre machine gun, typically of 6.5–8 mm calibre

receiver   the body of the gun, to which the barrel and operating mechanism are attached

recoil-operated   a gun mechanism operated by the recoiling gun barrel

RFC   (British) Royal Flying Corps (1912–18)

rifling   the spiral grooving within a gun barrel which grips the projectile and spins it in order to ensure its stability

rimless (case)   a cartridge case in which the rim is the same diameter as the case body, separated from it by an extractor groove

rimmed (case)   a cartridge case with a rim which has a larger diameter than the case body

ring mounting   a type of flexible mounting in which the cockpit is surrounded by a circular track around which the gun mounting can rotate

RN   (British) Royal Navy

RNAS   (British) Royal Naval Air Service (1914–18)

rotary engine   a type of radial engine in which the crankshaft is stationary and the crankcase and cylinders rotate with the propeller

rotary gun   a multi-barrel gun with several parallel barrels rotating around a common axis, each barrel being loaded and fired in turn

round (of ammunition)   a single cartridge (or equivalent)

RP   rocket projectile

rpg   rounds per gun

rpm   rounds per minute: the usual measure of rate of fire; also revolutions per minute, when describing engines or propellers

RR   rebated rim (also given as RB)

saddle drum   a type of drum magazine in which the cartridges are held in two small connected drums on either side of the action, from each of which rounds are fed in turn

SAP(HE)   semi-armour-piercing (high-explosive)

Scarff mounting   a type of British ring mounting

SD   self-destruct: an HE projectile which is designed to detonate a few seconds after firing

SDR   sectional density ratio; the ratio between calibre and projectile weight: together with the projectile shape this determines the ballistic coefficient

seaplane   an aircraft equipped with floats and/or a flotation hull that allow it to land on and take off from water

semi-automatic   a gun which automatically fires, ejects and reloads each time the trigger is pulled: also used to describe artillery in which the fired case is automatically ejected but a new round is manually loaded

semi-rimmed (case)   a cartridge case which has a rim only slightly larger in diameter than the case body, separated from it by an extractor groove: also known as semi-rimless

sesquiplane   a variation on the biplane in which one wing (usually the lower one) is much smaller than the other

shell   a projectile which is hollow in order to contain HE or other contents

short-recoil   a type of recoil-operated gun mechanism, in which the barrel and bolt recoil together for a short distance before the bolt is unlocked

shot   any solid armour-piercing projectile (i.e. contains no HE)

shoulder   the part of a cartridge case where the diameter decreases sharply from the case body to the neck

shrapnel   a type of anti-personnel artillery ammunition which consists of a shell containing metal balls in the forward part and a small bursting charge at the rear, detonated by a time fuze to explode just before reaching the target: named after its nineteenth-century inventor (nowadays loosely used to describe shell fragments)

sights   the devices used to aim a gun

sponson   a small wing-like extension to the fuselage of an aircraft, intended either for weapons carriage or, in the case of flying-boats, to stabilise them in the water

SR   semi-rimmed (or semi-rimless): a type of cartridge case

straight-cased cartridge   a cartridge case with little or no taper between the head and the neck; which therefore has no shoulder

stressed skin   a construction in which the skin of the aircraft is a load-bearing structure

striking angle   the angle at which an AP projectile strikes armour plate: two different conventions have applied; in one, a strike perpendicular to the plate is called 0°, in NATO it is called 90°

strip   a number of cartridges linked rigidly together for ease of loading

synchronised   a gun mounting fitted to a fighter in which the gun is designed to fire through the

T tracer (when attached to a projectile designation)

taboo zone restriction on the freedom of movement of a flexible gun mounting to prevent firing at own aircraft

t/c thickness/ the ratio between the depth of a wing
chord ratio profile and the distance between its leading and trailing edge

terminal the science concerning the performance of
ballistics projectiles on striking the target

time fuze a fuze fitted to an HE shell which detonates it a predetermined time after firing

time of flight the time taken for a projectile to reach its target

TP target practice; a type of projectile or cartridge used for training

tracer a chemical compound in the base of a projectile which burns slowly, giving a visible indication of its trajectory

trajectory the curve traced by a projectile in flight

traverse the movement of a gun in its mounting through a horizontal arc

USAAC United States Army Air Corps (1926–47)
USAAS United States Army Air Service (1918–26)
USMC United States Marine Corps
USN United States Navy

vee-engine a piston engine in which the cylinders are arranged in two banks, set at an angle to each other, driving a common crankshaft

ventral the location of a defensive gun position, underneath the fuselage

water-cooled a weapon which achieves barrel cooling by means of a water jacket

CONVERSION FACTORS

The following approximate conversion factors convert metric to imperial measure:

To convert millimetres to inches   divide by 25.4
To convert centimetres to inches   divide by 2.54
To convert metres to feet   multiply by 3.28
To convert metres to yards   multiply by 1.1
To convert kilometres to miles   divide by 1.609
To convert grams to grains   multiply by 15.432
To convert grams to ounces   divide by 28.35
To convert kilograms to pounds   multiply by 2.2

Bibliography

The following publications, covering current and historical equipment, were consulted in the preparation of this book. This information has been supplemented by various manufacturers' published data.

BOOKS

Allsop, D.F. *Cannons*, Brassey's, 1995

Allward, Maurice *F-86 Sabre*

Anderson, D.A. *North American F-100 Super Sabre*, Osprey, 1987

Anderton, D.A. and Watanabe, R. *Aggressors Volume 3: Interceptor vs Heavy Bomber*, Airlife, 1991

Angelucci, E. and Matricardi, P. *World Aircraft: Origins – World War 1*, Mondadori, Milan, 1975

Anon. *Oerlikon Pocket Book*, Oerlikon-Bührle AG, Zurich, 1981

Anon. *Small-Caliber Ammunition Identification Guide*, 2 volumes, US Army, 1977–8

Ashworth, C. *RAF Bomber Command 1936–1968*, Patrick Stephens Ltd, 1995

Beamont, R. *Tempest Over Europe*, Airlife, 1994

Belyakov, R.A. and Marmain, J. *MiG – Fifty Years of Secret Aircraft Design*, United States Naval Institute, 1994

Bernád, D. *Henschel Hs 129 in Action*, Squadron/Signal Publications, 2001

Birch, D. *Rolls-Royce Armaments*, Roll-Royce Heritage Trust, 2000

Bishop, E. *Mosquito – The Wooden Wonder*, Max Parish & Co. Ltd, 1959

Bodie, W.M. *Republic's P-47 Thunderbolt*, Widewing Publications, USA, 1994

Bowman, M.W. *De Havilland Mosquito*, Crowood Press Ltd, 1997

Bowyer, C. *Beaufighter at War*, Ian Allan Ltd, 1976

Bowyer, C. *Sunderland at War*, Ian Allan Ltd, 1976

Bowyer, M.J.F. *Interceptor Fighters for the Royal Air Force 1935–45*, Patrick Stephen's Ltd, 1984

Braun, M. *Handbuch der Flugzeug Bordwaffenmunition*, 1977

Bridgman, L. (ed) *Jane's All the World's Aircraft 1945 Collectors' Edition*, HarperCollins, 1994

Brookes, A. *Handley Page Victor*, Ian Allan Ltd, 1988

Brown, D. *Carrier Fighters 1939–1945*, Macdonald and Jane's, 1975

Brown, Capt. E.M. *Testing for Combat*, Airlife, 1994

Brown, Capt. E.M. *Wings of the Luftwaffe*, Pilot Press Ltd, 1977

Brown, G.I. *The Big Bang, A History of Explosives*, Sutton Publishing, 1998

Bruchiss, L. *Aircraft Armament*, Aerosphere, New York, 1945

Bueschel, R.M. *Nakajima Ki-84a/b Hayate*, Schiffer, USA, 1997

Bürli, A. *Flugzeug-bewaffnung: Die Schusswaffen der Schweizerischen Militärflugzeug*, Verlag Stocker-Schmid, Dietikon-Zürich, 1994

Butowski, P. and Miller, J. *OKB MiG – A History of the Design Bureau and its Aircraft*, Midland Counties Publications, 1991

Buttler, Tony *British Secret Projects – Jet Fighters since 1950*, Midland, 2000

Casey, L.S. and Batchelor, J. *The Illustrated History of Seaplanes & Flying-boats*, Hamlyn, 1980

Chant, C. *World Encyclopaedia of Modern Air Weapons*, Patrick Stephens, 1988

Chinn, G.M. *The machine gun, 5 volumes*, Vols I-IV, Bureau of Ordnance, Department of the Navy, USA, 1951–55; Vol V RAMP Inc., 1987

Clarke, R. Wallace *British Aircraft Armament*, 2 volumes, Patrick Stephens Ltd, 1993 and 1994

Cole, C. and Cheesman, E.F., *The Air Defence of Britain 1914–1918*, Putnam, 1984.

Collier, B. *Japanese Aircraft of World War II*, Sidgwick and Jackson, 1979

Cooksley, P. *German Bombers of World War 1 in Action*, Squadron/Signal Publications, USA, 2000

Cross, R. *The Bombers*, Bantam Press, 1987

Cuny, J. *Latécoère – Les avions et hydravions*, Docavia Vol. 34, Editions Larivière, France, 1992

Danel, R. and Cuny, J. *L'Aviation Française de bombarde-*

ment et de renseignment (1918–1940), Docavia Vol. 12, Editions Larivière, France

Davis, D.M. *Historical Development Summary of Automatic Cannon Calibre Ammunition: 20–30 Millimeter*, Air Force Armament Laboratory, USA, 1984

Davis, L. *Gunships: A Pictorial History of Spooky*, Squadron/Signal Publications, USA, 1982

Dean, F.H. *America's Hundred-Thousand – US Production Fighters of World War Two*, Schiffer, 1997

Deichmann, P. *Spearhead for Blitzkrieg: Luftwaffe Operations in Support of the Army, 1939–45*, Greenhill Books, 1996

de Seversky, A. *Air Power: Key to Survival*, USA, 1950

Donald, D. (ed) *The Encyclopedia of World Aircraft*, Orbis, 1997

Dorr, R.F. *McDonnell F-101 Voodoo*, Osprey, 1987

Douhet, G. *The Command of the Air*, Translated by Dino Ferrari, originally published in 1921

Dressel, J. and Griehl, G. *Heinkel He 219 Uhu*, Schiffer, USA, 1995

Dunning, C. *Courage Alone – The Italian Air Force 1940–1943*, Hikoki Publications, 1998

Filley, B., Greer, D., Manley, P. and Sewell, J. *Junkers Ju 88 in Action Part 2*, Squadron/Signal Publications, 1991

Fozard, J.W. (ed) *Sydney Camm and the Hurricane. Perspectives on the Master Fighter Designer and his Finest Achievement*, Smithsonian, 1991

Francillon, R.J. *Japanese Aircraft of the Pacific War*, Putnam, 1979

Freeman, R.A. *Combat Profile: Mustang:The P-51 Merlin Mustang in World War 2*, Ian Allan Ltd, 1989

Freeman, R.A. and Osborne, D. *The B-17 Flying Fortress Story*, Arms and Armour, 1998

Friedman, N. *Desert Victory; the War for Kuwait*. Naval Institute Press, USA, 1991

Goldsmith, D.L. *The Devil's Paintbrush: Sir Hiram Maxim's Gun*, Collector Grade Publications, Ontario, 1993

Goldsmith, D.L. *The Grand Old Lady of No Man's Land: The Vickers Machinegun*, Collector Grade Publications, Ontario, 1994

Golley, J. *The Day of the Typhoon*, Patrick Stephens, 1986

Gooderson, I. *Air Power at the Battlefront: Allied Close Air Support in Europe 1939–45*, Frank Cass, 1998

Gordon, Y. and Khazanov, D. (with Medved, A.) *Soviet Combat Aircraft of the Second World War*, 2 volumes, Midland Publishing Limited, 1998 and 1999

Gordon, Y. and Sweetman, B. *Soviet X-Planes – Experimental and Prototype Aircraft, 1931 to 1989*, Motorbooks International, 1992

Goulding, J. *Interceptor*, Ian Allan Ltd, 1986

Green, C.M., Thomson, H.C. and Roots, P.C. *United States Army in World War II. The Technical Services. The Ordnance Department: Planning Munitions for War*, Dept of the Army, Washington, 1955

Green, W. *War Planes of the Second World War*, 10 volumes, Macdonald & Co., 1960–8

Green, W. and Swanborough, G. *Japanese Army Fighters (Part 1, Part 2)*, MacDonald and Jane's, 1976

Green, W. and Swanborough, G. *US Navy and Marine Corps Fighters*, MacDonald and Jane's, 1976

Grey, C.G. *Jane's All The World's Aircraft 1938*, Sampson Low, 1938

Griehl, M. and Dressel, J. *German Anti-Tank Aircraft*, Schiffer, 1993

Griehl, M. and Dressel, J. *Focke-Wulf Fw 190/Ta 152*, Motorbuch Verlag Stuttgart, 1997

Griehl, M. and Dressel, J. *Heinkel He 177, 274, 277*, Airlife, 1998

Grosz, P.M., Haddow, G, and Schiemer, P. *Austro-Hungarian Army Aircraft of World War One*, Flying Machines Press, 1993

Gunston, B. (ed) *Chronicle of Aviation*, Chronicle Communications Ltd, 1992

Gunston, B. *Faster Than Sound – The Story of Supersonic Flight*, Patrick Stephens Ltd, 1992

Gunston, B. *Japanese & Italian Aircraft*, Leisure Books, 1985

Gunston, B. *The Illustrated Encyclopedia of the World's Rockets & Missiles*, Salamander, 1979

Gunston, B. *The Osprey Encyclopedia of Russian Aircraft 1875–1995*, Osprey Aerospace, 1995

Gunston, W. *Encyclopedia of Aircraft Armament*, Salamander Books, 1987

Gunston, W. *Night Fighters: a Development and Combat History*, Patrick Stephens, 1976

Gunston, W. and Gordon, Y. *Yakovlev Aircraft Since 1924*, Putnam, 1997

Guttman, J. *Fighting Firsts. Fighter Aircraft Combat Debuts from 1914–1944*, Cassell, 2000

Hackley, F.W., Woodin, W.H. and Scranton, E.L. *History of Modern US Military Small Arms Ammunition, Volumes I and II*, The Macmillan Company, New York, 1967, and The Gun Room Press, USA, 1978

Haddow, G.W. and Grosz, P.M. *The German Giants: the German R-Planes 1914–1918*, Putnam, 1988

Hahn, F. *Deutsche Geheimwaffen 1939–45*, Erich Hoffman Verlag, Heidenheim, 1963

Hallion, R.P. *Strike from the Sky: The History of Battlefield Air Attack, 1911–1945*, Airlife, 1989

Hardy, M.J. *Sea, Sky and Stars – An Illustrated History of Grumman Aircraft*, Arms and Armour, 1987.

Harmann, D. *Focke-Wulf Ta 152 – The Story of the Luftwaffe's Late-War, High-Altitude Fighter*, Schiffer, 1999

Hartcup, G. *The War of Invention: Scientific Developments, 1914–18*, Brassey's, 1988

Hickman, I. *Operation Pinball: The USAAF's Secret Aerial Gunnery Program in WWII*, Motorbooks International, 1990

Hitchcock, T.H. *Messerschmitt 'O-Nine' Gallery*, Monogram Aviation, 1973

Hobart, F.W.A. *Pictorial History of the machine gun*, Ian Allan Ltd, 1971

Hoffschmidt, E.J. *German Aircraft Guns and Cannons*, WE Inc., Greenwich, USA

Hogg, I.V. *Jane's Directory of Military Small Arms Ammunition*, Jane's Publishing Company, 1985

Hogg, I.V. (introduction) *The American Arsenal: the World War II Official Standard Ordnance Catalogue*, Greenhill Books, 1996

Hogg, I.V. *The Cartridge Guide*, Arms and Armour Press, 1982

Holley, Capt. I.B. Jr *Development of Aircraft Gun Turrets in the AAF 1917–1944*, AAF Historical Office, Headquarters Army Air Forces, 1944

Howson, G. *Arms for Spain*, John Murray, 1998

Huon, J. *Military Rifle and machine gun Cartridges*, Arms and Armour Press, 1986

Isby, D.C. *Jane's Fighter Combat in the Jet Age*, HarperCollins, 1997

Jackson, R. *Hawker Tempest and Sea Fury*, Blandford, 1989

James, L. *The Rise and Fall of the British Empire*, St Martin's Press, 1994

Jarrett, P. (ed) *Aircraft of the Second World War: The Development of the Warplane 1939–45*, Putnam, 1997

Keith, C.H. *I Hold My Aim*, Tinling & Co., 1946

Kennett, L. *The First Air War 1914–1918*, The Free Press, New York, 1991

Kent, D.W. *German 7.9 mm Military Ammunition 1888–1945*, Privately published, USA

King, H.F. *Armament of British Aircraft 1909–39*, Putnam, 1971

Kosin, R. *The German Fighter since 1915*, Putnam, 1988

Labbett, P. *British Small Arms Ammunition 1864–1938*, Privately published, 1993

Labbett, P. *Military Small Arms Ammunition*, Presidio Press, USA, 1980

Labbett, P. and Mead, P. *.303 inch*, Privately published, 1988

Lande, D.A. *Messerschmitt 109*, MBI, 2000

Lawson, E. and J. *The First Air Campaign: August 1914 – November 1918*, Combined Books, Pennsylvania, 1996

Leaman, Paul *Fokker Aircraft of World War One*, The Crowood Press, 2001

Lenselink, J. and de Hek, W.D. *Notes on Small and Medium Calibre Military Cartridges*, Delfia Press, Rijswijk, 1986

Lenselink, J. and de Hek, W.D. *Military Cartridges Part 1, 3.5 × 45 > 20 × 138B*, Privately published, Netherlands, 1995

Levinson, J. *Alpha Strike Vietnam: The Navy's Air War, 1964 to 1973*, Presidio Press, USA, 1989

Lewis, C. *Farewell to Wings*, Temple Press, 1964

Lindsay, R. *Lightning*, Ian Allan Ltd, 1989

Lippert, J. *Deutsche Bordwaffen Munition Bis 1945*, Privately published, München, 1989

Lovell, Sir B. *Echoes of War – The Story of H2S Radar*, Adam Hilger, 1991

Mackay, R. *Messerschmitt Bf 110*, The Crowood Press Ltd, 2000

Mason, F.K. *The British Fighter since 1912*, Putnam, 1992

Mason, F.K. *The British Bomber since 1914*, Putnam, 1994

Mason, F.K. *The Hawker Hurricane*, Aston, 1987

Mason, R. (ed) *War in the Third Dimension: Essays in Contemporary Air Power*, Brassey's, 1986

Mason, T. *British Flight Testing. Martlesham Heath, 1920–1939*, Putnam, 1993

Mason, T. *The Secret Years. Flight Testing at Boscombe Down 1939–45*, Hikoki, 1998

Matthews, B. *Cobra! Bell Aircraft Corporation 1934–1946*, Schiffer Publishing Ltd

McDowell, E.R. *B-25 Mitchell in Action*, Squadron/Signal Publications, USA, 1978

McMichael, S. *Stumbling Bear; Soviet Military Performance in Afghanistan*, Brassey's, 1991

Meekcoms, K.J. and Morgan, E.B. *The British Aircraft Specifications File*, Air-Britain, 1994

Merrick, K. *German Aircraft Interiors 1939–45. Vol. 1 – Day Fighters*, Monogram Aviation Publications, Massachusetts, 1996

Mikesh, R.C. *Broken Wings of the Samurai*, Airlife, 1993

Mikesh, R.C. *Japanese Aircraft Code Names & Designations*, Schiffer, 1993

Mikesh, R. and Abe, S. *Japanese Aircraft 1910–1941*, Putnam, 1990

Mikesh, R.C. *Zero – Combat & Development History of Japan's Legendary Mitsubishi A6M Zero Fighter*, Motorbooks International, 1994

Mikesh, R.C. and Tagaya, O. *Moonlight Interceptor*, Smithsonian Press, 1985

Miller, J. *Lockheed Martin's Skunk Works*, Midland Publishing Ltd, 1995

Moyes, P.J.R. *Lockheed F-104 Starfighter*, Aerodata International, 1984

Moyes, P.J.R. *McDonnell Douglas F-4 Phantom II*, Aerodata International, 1980

Moyes, P.J.R. *North American F-100A Super Sabre*, Aerodata International, 1982

Musgrave, D.D. *German Machineguns*, Greenhill Books, 1992

Nemecek, V. *The History of Soviet Aircraft*, Williams Collins, 1986

O'Neill, B.D. *Half a Wing, Three Engines and a Prayer*, McGraw-Hill, 1999

Ovcacik, M. and Susa, K. *Westland Whirlwind*, Mark 1 Ltd, Prague, 2002

Pape, G.R. and Campbell, J.M. *Northrop Flying Wings – A History of Jack Northrop's Visionary Aircraft*, Schiffer, 1995

Paris, M. *Winged Warfare: The Literature and Theory of Aerial Warfare in Britain 1859–1917*, Manchester University Press, 1992

Peebles, C. *The Moby Dick Project – Reconnaissance Balloons over Russia*, Smithonsian Institution, 1991

Pegg, M. *Hs 129 Panzerjäger*, Classic Publications, 1996

Polmar, N. and Kennedy, F. *Military Helicopters of the World*, Arms and Armour Press, 1981

Postan, M., Hay, D. and Scott, J. *Design and Development of Weapons*, HMSO, 1964

Prados, J. *Combined Fleet Decoded*, Random House, 1995

Price, A. *Combat Development in World War Two: Fighter Aircraft*, Arms and Armour Press, 1989

Price, A. *Focke-Wulf Fw 190 in Combat*, Sutton Publishing, 1998

Price, A. *The Bomber in World War II*, McDonald and Jane's, 1976

Price, A. *The Spitfire Story – Revised Second Edition*, Arms and Armour Press, 1995

Radinger, W. and Schick, W. *Secret Messerschmitt Projects*, Schiffer, 1996

Reed, A. and Beamont, R. *Typhoon and Tempest at War*, Ian Allan Ltd, 1974

Richardson, D. *Republic F-105 Thunderchief*, Salamander Books, 1992

Richardson, D. *The History of the Revolver Cannon*, Oerlikon-Contraves, Zurich, 1994

Roberston, B. *Beaufort Special*, Ian Allan Ltd, 1976

Robertson, B. *Halifax Special*, Ian Allan Ltd, 1990

Robinson, A. *Night Fighter – A Concise History of Nightfighting Since 1914*, Ian Allan Ltd, 1988

Rudel, H-U. *Stuka Pilot*, Euphorion Books, Dublin, 1952

Sárhidai, G., Punka, G. and Kozlik, V. *Hungarian Eagles. The Hungarian Air Forces 1920–1945*, Hikoki, 1996

Schick, W. and Meyer, I. *Luftwaffe Secret Projects – Fighters 1939–1945*, Midland, 1997

Schliephake, H. *Die Bordwaffen der Luftwaffe von der Anfängen bis zur Gegenwart*, Motorbuch Verlag, Stuttgart, 1977

Scutts, J. *Messerschmitt Bf 109 – The Operational Record*, Airlife, 1996

Shores, C. *Ground Attack Aircraft of World War II*, Macdonald and Jane's, 1977

Sinnott, C. *The Royal Air Force and Aircraft Design 1923–1939*, Frank Cass, 2001

Smith, J.R., Creek, E.J. and Hitchcock, T.H. *Dornier Do 335 Arrow*, Monogram Aviation Publications, 1983

Smith, P. C*lose Air Support: an Illustrated History, 1914 to the Present*, Orion Books, New York, 1990

Smith, P. *Dive Bomber!*, Moorland Publishing, UK, and Naval Institute Press, USA, 1982

Smith, P. *Dive bombers in action*, Blandford Press, 1988

Stapfer, H-H. *Il-2 Stormovik in Action*, Squadron/Signal Publications, USA, 1995

Stoff, J. *The Thunder Factory*, Motorbooks International, 1990

Tanner, J. (ed) *British Aircraft Guns of World War Two*, Arms and Armour Press, 1979

Tanner, J. (ed) *Fighting in the Air: The Official Combat Technique Instructions for British Fighter Pilots, 1916–1945*, Arms and Armour Press, 1978

Tapper, O. *Armstrong Whitworth Aircraft since 1913*, Putnam, 1973

Taylor, J.W.R. (ed) *Jane's All the World's Aircraft 1978–79*, Jane's Yearbooks, 1978

Taylor, J.W.R. (ed) *Jane's All the World's Aircraft 1986–87*, Jane's Yearbooks, 1986

Taylor, J.W.R. (ed) *Jane's All the World's Aircraft 1989–90*, Jane's Defence Data, 1989

Taylor, M.J.H. *The Aerospace Chronology*, Tri-Service Press, 1989

Thetford, O. *British Naval Aircraft since 1912*, Putnam, 1982

Treadwell, T.C. *The Ironworks – Grumman's Fighting Aeroplanes*, Airlife, 1990

Vanags-Baginskis, A. and Watanabe, R. *Aggressors Volume 1: Tank Buster vs Combat Vehicle*, Airlife, 1990

van der Klaauw, B. *Water- en transportvliegtuigen wereldoorlog II*, De Alk

ver Elst, A. *Icarus in oorlog en vrede* (2. 1941–1953), De Goudvink, 1972

Wachsmuth, W. *B-36 Peacemaker*, Squadron/Signal Publications, 1997

Wadman, D., Bradley, J. and Ketley, B. *Aufklärer – Luftwaffe Reconnaissance Aircraft & Units 1935–1945*, Hikoki Publications, 1997

Wallace, G.F. *Guns of the Royal Air Force 1939–1945*, William Kimber & Co., 1972

Watson, B. et al. *Military Lessons of the Gulf War*, Presidio Press, USA, 1991

Wegg, J. *General Dynamics Aircraft and their Predecessors*, Putnam, 1990

Weston-Burt, D. *Tank-Busters*, in Bowyer, C. *Hurricane at War*, Ian Allan, 1974

Whitney, D.D. *Vee's For Victory! The Story of the Allison*

V-1710 Aircraft Engine 1929–1948, Schiffer Publishing Ltd, 1998

Williams, A.G. *Rapid Fire: The Development of Automatic Cannon, Heavy machine guns and their Ammunition for Armies, Navies and Air Forces*, Airlife, 2000

Wilson, S. *F-86 Sabre – MiG-15 'Fagot' – Hawker Hunter – The Story of Three of the Classic Jet Fighters of the 1950s*, Aerospace Publications, 1995

Wilson, S. *Vulcan, Boeing B-47 & B-52 – The Story of Three Classic Bombers of the Cold War*, Aerospace Publications, 1997

Winter, W. *War Planes of All Nations*, USA, 1943

Wragg, D. *Carrier Combat*, Budding Books, USA, 1997

Woodman, H. *Early Aircraft Armament*, Arms and Armour Press, 1989

Zijun, D. (ed) *China Today: Aviation Industry*, Chinese Social Science Press, 1989

JOURNAL AND MAGAZINE ARTICLES

Alegi, G. translated by Gaudet, G. 'L'Aile Brisée: L'aviation italienne dans la Deuxième Guerre mondiale', *Le Fana de l'Aviation Hors Série No. 13*

Aloni, S. translated by Méal, X. 'Des "Mystère" contre des MiG', *Le Fana de l'Aviation* (October and November 1995)

Aloni, S. translated by Méal, X. 'Du «Sambad» à «Sa'ar» – L'histoire de Dassault «Super Mystère» B.2 dans la force aérienne israélienne', *Le Fana de l'Aviation* (November 1997)

Aloni, S. translated by Méal, X. 'L'épopée du «Mirage» III en Israel', *Le Fana de l'Aviation* (September 1998 to February 1999)

Aloni, S. translated by Bénichou, M. 'Les deux guerres des Dassault "Ouragan"', *Le Fana de l'Aviation* (No. 298 of August 1994)

Aloni, S. translated by Méal, X. 'Les «Vautour» en Israël', *Le Fana de l'Aviation* (July, August and September 1997)

Aloni, S. 'In a class of its own – The Sud Vautour in Israeli Service', *Air Enthusiast* (July/August 1997, November/December 1997, March/April 1998)

Ashworth, C. 'The 'Shack' . . . Forty Years On – and Serving Still', *Air International* (May 1989)

Baeza, B. 'La logique d'un effondrement – Les avions de combat Japonais de la Deuxième Guerre Mondiale', *Le Fana de l'Aviation Hors Série No. 3*

Barnes, S. 'Helicopter Gunnery: Options and Tactics', *Military Technology* (8/94)

Bedford, A. 'Early American Carrier Jets – Evolving operations with the US Fleet', *Air Enthusiast* (May/June, July/August and September/October 1999)

Benichou, M. and Bousquet G. 'Blériot 127 – Quelque chose troubla la fête', *Le Fana de l'Aviation* (December 2002)

Boniface, P. 'Boeing's Lone Ranger', *Aeroplane* (January 1997)

Boulay, P. 'Comment L'Hélicoptère de Combat est né en France', *Le Fana de l'Aviation* (February and March 1996)

Bowyer, M. 'Boulton Paul's Defiant... and the turret fighter saga', *Air International* (July 1991)

Broden, D. 'Revolutionising Combat Capability', *Global Defence Review*, 1999

Buttler, T. 'Draken – A Swedish Masterpiece', *Air International* (March/April 2000)

Buttler, T. 'Vickers' Last Fighter – The Type 432 "Tin Mossie"', *Air Enthusiast* (January/February 1997)

Dorr, R.F. and Burgess, R.R. 'Ferreting Mercators', *Air International* (October 1993)

Dorr, R.F. and Mills, R.J. 'Rockwell's COIN Machine', *Air International* (June 1992)

Eckelmeyer, E.H. Jr. 'The story of the self-sealing fuel tank', *United States Naval Proceedings* (Vol. 72 No. 2, February 1946)

Eliot, J. 'Assessing the Market for Combat Helicopters', *Military Technology* (6/97)

Francillon, R.J. 'From Torpedo and Scout Bombers to Attack Aircraft', *Air International* (August, September and October 1995)

Fricker, J. 'Switzerland's P-16: Father of the Learjet', *Air International* (March 1991)

Fricker, J. 'The Falklands . . . Air Claims and Losses Analysed', *Air International* (5/83)

Frommer, H. 'Status and Trends in Automatic Cannons', *Military Technology* (3/85)

Gaillard, P. 'Les Chasseurs oubliés de Semyon Alexeïev', *Le Fana de l'Aviation* (February 1998)

Gaillard, P. and Ricco, P. 'Les trois premiers chasseurs embarqués à réaction francais', *Le Fana de l'Aviation* (April 1995)

Green, H. 'Coronado Connection', *Aeroplane* (March 1996)

Grosz, P.M. 'The 2 cm Becker Aircraft Cannon – Development and Use', *Over the Front* (Vol. 7 No. 2, Summer 1992)

Gryazev, V. and Zelenko, V. 'Russia's Modern Aircraft Gun Armament', *Military Parade* (July–August 1997)

Hall, T. 'Cutaway Kings – Frank Munger', *Aeroplane* (April 1999)

Hoehn, J-P. 'La Guerre Électronique des Douglas B-66 Destroyer', *Le Fana de l'Aviation* (March 1996)

Hoehn, J-P. 'Le Lockheed F-94, ou . . . l'inconvenient d'être le premier', *Le Fana de l'Aviation* (May 1994)

Hooton, T. 'Nocturnal Navigator', *Aeroplane* (June and July 1996)

Jackson, P. 'Lament for the Lightning', *Air International* (June 1988)

Joly, P. 'La naissance du tir axial des avions de chasse', *Pégase* (June 1988)

Kennedy, A. and Ridley, J.A. 'Troublesome Turret', *Flypast* (September 1992)

Klaussner, S.H. 'Dornier 24 – Queen of the Flying-boats', *Flypast* (September 1995)

Labbett, P. 'Cannon Ammunition 15 mm to 35 mm, 1945–1990', *Guns Review* (two parts; November and December 1990)

Labbett, P. 'Russian 20 mm ShVAK Aircraft Ammunition', *Guns Review* (June 1993)

Labbett, P. 'Russian 23 × 115 mm Aircraft Ammunition', *Guns Review* (July 1993)

Labbett, P. 'Russian 23 × 152 mm Cannon Ammunition', *Guns Review* (August 1993)

Labbett, P. 'Russian 30 mm and 37 mm Cannon Ammunition', *Guns Review* (September 1993)

Labbett, P. '30 mm Hispano Suiza Type 825 Ammunition', *Guns Review* (June 1989)

Lake, J. 'Classics Compared – Javelin and Tornado F.3', *Air International* (February 2001)

Lake, J. 'Classics Compared – Sea Hawk and Sea Harrier', *Air International* (December 1999)

London, P. 'Attacker', *Aeroplane* (January 1996)

London, P. 'From Seagull to "Shagbat" – The Life and Times of the Supermarine Walrus', *Air Enthusiast* (March/April and July August 1998)

Nesbit, R. 'The Tsetse and the U-boat', *Aeroplane* (May and June 1991)

Nordeen, L. and Barnes, S. 'Armed Scout and Attack Helicopters in the Gulf Conflict', *Military Technology* (8/91)

Nordeen, L. and Barnes, S. 'Helicopter Air-to-Air Combat', *Military Technology* (2/93)

Pitchers, M. 'Stirling Work', *Aeroplane* (April 1995)

Price, A. 'Arado's Blitz', *Air International* (November 1996)

Price, A. 'Gap That Bridge', *Air International* (December 1997)

Price, A. and Ethel, J. translated by Bénichou, M. 'Bachem "Natter" – La folie furieuse', *Le Fana de l'Aviation* (August 1997)

Price, A. and Ethell, J. translated by Bénichou, M. 'L'Arado Ar 234, photographe insaissable, bombardier anodin', *Le Fana de l'Aviation* (April 1997)

Price, A. and Ethel, J. translated by Bénichou, M. 'Le Heinkel He 162, Une réussite fulgurante', *Le Fana de l'Aviation* (June 1997)

Price, A. and Ethel, J. translated by Bénichou, M. 'Le Lockheed P-80 – Meilleur pour le moral que pour la guerre', *Le Fana de l'Aviation* (July 1997)

Price, A. and Ethel, J. translated by Bénichou, M. 'Messerschmitt Me 163 – Un avion trop loin . . .', *Le Fana de l'Aviation* (February 1997)

Price, A. and Ethel, J. translated by Bénichou, M. 'Messerschmitt Me 262 – Derrière le mythe, le calvaire de la réalité', *Le Fana de l'Aviation* (October, November and December 1996)

Razoux, P. 'Suez or la tentation de tout aérien', *Le Fana de l'Aviation* (March, April and May 2001)

Redemann, H. 'Mädchen für alles – Das Bordflugzeug der Kriegsmarine', *Flug Revue Edition Klassiker der Luftfahrt 2.*

Reynolds, S. 'Evolution of Fighter vs Helicopter Air Combat', *Air International* (February 2001)

Scutts, J. 'Tractable Turtle: The Lockheed Neptune Story', *Air International* (January and February 1995)

Scutts, J. 'Vought Kingfisher', *Air International* (January 1996)

Spick, M. 'Starfighter – The Early Years', *Air Enthusiast* (No. 46 of June–August 1992)

Spick, M. 'The Iron Tigers', *Air International* (June 1991)

Strandli, K.R. 'Multipurpose Ammunition', *Military Technology* (9/91)

Terraine, J. 'World War 1 and the Royal Air Force', *The Proceedings of the Royal Air Force Historical Society* (Issue 12, 1994)

Thompson, W. 'Fighter Combat over Korea Part 1: First Kills', *Wings of Fame* (Vol. 1)

Underwood, J. 'Tachikawa Album', *Aeroplane* (May 1999)

Whitford, R. 'Fundamentals of Fighter Design: Armament and Tactics', *Air International* (1 and 3/98)

Williams, R. 'Meteor Nightfighters', *Aeroplane* (April, May, June and July 1995)

Wixey, K. 'Flugboots from Hamburg', *Air Enthusiast* (July/August 1999)

Wixey, K. 'Incidental Combattant – Focke-Wulf's Fw 200 Condor', *Air Enthusiast* (November–December 1996 and January–February 1997)

Wixey, K. 'Javelin – Gloster's Innovative Delta', *Air International* (December 1995)

Wixey, K. 'Seagull', *Flypast* (August 1994)

Wixey, K. 'Triple One Lineage', *Air Enthusiast* (July/August 1998)

Zhirnikh, G. 'The Development of Soviet Aircraft Armament', *Aviatsiya I Kosmonavtika* (8/1967)

Various contributors: Many items in *The Cartridge Researcher*, the Official Bulletin of the European Cartridge Research Association.

Unattributed:
'A cat for dogfighting – Northrop's Tougher Tiger', *Air Enthusiast* (October 1972)

'Last of a Genus . . . The Heinkel 115', *Air International* (February 1987)

'Mr Mac's First Phantom – The Story of the McDonnell FH-1', *Air International* (November 1987)

'Vickers Warwick – The Good-Samaritan Bomber', *Air International* (March and April 1988)

OTHER PUBLICATIONS

Anon. *Ammunition for Aircraft Guns,* Dept of the Army TM 9-1901-1, Dept of the Air Force TO 11A-1-39 (USA, 1957)

Anon. *Japanese Explosive Ordnance*, Dept of the Army TM 9-1985-4, Dept of the Air Force TO 39B-1A-11 (USA, 1953)

Bruderlin, E.B. and Nelson, R.S. *Research, Development and Production of Small Arms and Aircraft Armament of the Japanese Army*, Ordnance Technical Intelligence Report Number 19, 1946 (reprinted in USA, 1971)

Elks, K. *Japanese Ammunition 1880–1945*

Labbett, P. and Brown, F.A. *12.7 mm × 108 and 14.5 mm × 114 Ammunition (Communist)*

Labbett, P. and Brown, F.A. *British Air Service Ammunition, Special Loadings .45 in to .707 in 1914–1918*

Labbett, P. and Brown, F.A. *British-Made .5 inch and 13 mm machine gun Ammunition, not for British Service*

Labbett, P. and Brown, F.A. *British 30 mm & 30/20 mm Ammunition*

Labbett, P. and Brown, F.A. *German 2 cm Cannon Ammunition 1935–1945*

Labbett, P. and Mead P.J.F. *British 20 mm Hispano Ammunition*

Legendre, J-F. *Soviet Union machine gun Belt Links* (1998)

Legendre, J-F. *Atelier de Fabrication de Mulhouse: CEAM-AME 1947–1967: Munitions de Moyen Calibre* (1998)

Newport, W.H.A. *Evolution of American Fighter Aircraft Armament 1910–1964 – Barrelled Weapons from the 1903 Springfield Rifle to the M61A1 Vulcan Cannon*, UMI Dissertation Services, 1998

UNPUBLISHED DOCUMENTS

(Mainly held in the Ministry of Defence Pattern Room or the Public Record Office)

Ackers, T. *General Survey of Main Problems Connected with Installation, Functioning and Accuracy of Aircraft Gun Armament During the War*, Technical Note Arm. 383, A&AEE Monograph No. 4.08, Royal Aircraft Establishment, 1947

Anon. *Comparative Efficiency of Calibre .30 and .50 Aircraft Guns (1928–1931)*, PRO AIR 2/347

Anon. *Air Attack on Land Targets (Armour)*, Air Ministry OR Report 1944 (PRO AIR 37/1236)

Anon. *Me 410 A-1/U4 Flugzeug-Handbuch*, (1944)

Anon. *Development of German Fighter Armament*, Air Ministry (UK) 1944

Anon. *German Aircraft Armament and Ammunition During the War of 1939–45*, A.D.I. (K) Report No. 11/1946

Anon. *Gun Ammunition in 37mm Calibre*, D. of A. (India) Japanese Ammunition Leaflets Section E, Leaflet E11 (1945)

Anon. *Handbook of Aircraft Armament C.B. 1161* (Official British publication, WW1)

Anon. *Japanese Air Weapons and Tactics*, The US Strategic Bombing Survey, 1947

Anon. *Japanese Ammunition,* Military Intelligence Division, War Department (USA)

Anon. *New Japanese Aircraft Types and Miscellaneous Armament Development*, Technical Air Intelligence Summary #14, DNI, 1944

Anon. *Preliminary Notes on the Ammunition for Vickers Class 'S' Mk I Gun* (Official British publication, status unclear)

Anon. *The Second World War 1939–1945 Royal Air Force Armament Volume II: Guns, Gunsights, Turrets, Ammunition and Pyrotechnics*, S.D. 737 Air Ministry (1954)

Anon. *Large Calibre Guns (1921)* PRO AIR 2/217

Anon. *AGA Motor MG (1921)* PRO AIR 2/217

Anon. *Tank und Flieger MG (1921)* PRO AIR 5/217

Anon. *Vickers 11mm Balloon Gun (1918)* PRO MUN 4/715

Anon. *Vickers 1.45" Gun (1916–17)* PRO MUN 4/2884

Anon. *Davis Gun Ammunition (1916)* PRO MUN 4/2886

Anon. *1½ pdr COW Gun (1917–18)* PRO MUN 4/2896

Bradstreet, T. *Checklist of German Disintegrating Links Used in Automatic and Semi-Automatic Weapons to 1945*, 1998

Bradstreet, T. *The Luftwaffe MG-FF,* 1998

Bradstreet, T. *Notes on Japanese Aircraft Guns and Cartridges Over 13.2 mm*, 1998

Bühler, Dipl. Ing. and Sörensen, Ing. *Table of German Armament Equipment (Approved and Experimental) Small Arms, Automatic Arms and Guns up to 55 mm Calibre*, Unterlüss Report 295/I, 1948

Bühler, Dipl. Ing. Burgmueller, Dr. and Sörensen, Ing. *Table of German Armament Equipment (Approved and Experimental) Ammunition up to 55 mm Calibre*, Unterlüss Report 295/II, 1948

Cabeen, C. *The Calibre Ninety Aircraft Gun*, Lafayette College, Easton, Pennsylvania

Mix, Dipl. Ing. (late Director of Aircraft Weapon Development, R.L.M.) *Development of Aircraft*

Weapons, Munitions and Installations – A comprehensive review of the German position at the end of the War, Unterlüss Report 376 T, 1948

Various: *Reich Ministry of Armaments and War Production: Interrogation of Speer, Saur, Mommen and Bosch*, Combined Intelligence Objectives Sub-committee, G-8 Division, SHAEF, May/June 1945

NB: The 'Unterlüss Reports' (named after a Rheinmetall establishment) were written immediately after the end of the Second World War following interrogation of German technical staff by the British. They provide detailed information about the state of German armament developments at the end of the war. Copies are kept at the Pattern Room.

WEBSITES

At the time of writing, the following websites contained useful information about aircraft guns or air combat:

http://home.att.net/~jbaugher/
Baugher, J. 'American Military Aircraft'

www.bharat-rakshak.com/IAF/index.html
Chattopadhyay, Rupak and Mohan, PVS Jagan 'The Indian Air Force Site'

www.acig.org
Chick, C., Kyzer, J. and Cooper, T. Comprehensive lists of aircraft successes in combat

www.csd.uwo.ca/~pettypi/elevon/baugher_other/lavi.html
Deurenberg, R. 'Israel Aircraft Industries (IAI) Lavi'

www.canit.se/~griffon/aviation/text/sv_akan.html
Fredriksson, U. 'Automatic cannon used by the Swedish Air Force'

www.uboat.net/allies/aircraft/hudson.htm
Garner, F. and Gustin, E. 'Lockheed Hudson Patrol Bomber'

http://users.skynet.be/Emmanuel.Gustin/fgun/fgun-in.html
Gustin, E. Website on fighter guns

www.ixpress.com/ag1caf/usplanes/
Hanson, D. 'American Aircraft of World War II'

http://uboat.net/
Helgason, G. 'Uboat.net – The U-boat war 1939–1945'

www.panzerlehr.de/
Huber, T. Modern and historical German military equipment

www.rt66.com/~korteng/SmallArms/history.htm
Kortegaard, B. 'The Korean War'

www.achtungpanzer.com/gen9.htm
Parada G. Brief history of Hans-Ulrich Rudel

www.ctrl-c.liu.se/misc/ram
Savine, A. Russian Aviation Museum site containing details of Soviet weapons

www.lam.lt/~lam
Štukas, S. 'Lithuanian Aviation Museum'

www.stirling.box.nl/home.htm
van Gelderen, P. 'Stirling Bomber'

www.quarry.nildram.co.uk
Williams, A.G. Website about military guns and ammunition

Unattributed:

www.wpafb.af.mil/museum/history/korea/korea.htm
'Korean War History Gallery' of the USAF Museum

www.fas.org/index.html
Federation of American Scientists; information about current USAF equipment

www.p2vneptune.org
'P2V Neptune.org'

http://british.forces.com/aircraft/aircraft.html
'The aircraft of the RAF'

Index